The Power Of Team

Three Ordinary People and Their Run to Greatness

by
Peter Wortham

Bloomington, IN authorHOUSE™ Milton Keynes, UK

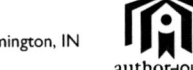

AuthorHouse™
1663 Liberty Drive, Suite 200
Bloomington, IN 47403
www.authorhouse.com
Phone: 1-800-839-8640

AuthorHouse™ *UK Ltd.*
500 Avebury Boulevard
Central Milton Keynes, MK9 2BE
www.authorhouse.co.uk
Phone: 08001974150

© 2007 Peter Wortham. All rights reserved.

No part of this book may be reproduced, stored in a retrieval system, or transmitted by any means without the written permission of the author.

First published by AuthorHouse 4/17/2007

ISBN: 978-1-4343-0558-9 (sc)
ISBN: 978-1-4343-0557-2 (hc)

Printed in the United States of America
Bloomington, Indiana

This book is printed on acid-free paper.

Team Illinois Credits and Honorable Mentions

Cover Photo: Special Thanks to Lester Lim for the great shot of the "Yellow Train".

Thanks to Mary Gadams and RacingThePlanet for race statistics and background information on Nancy, Joel and Dave. Be sure to check out http://www.racingtheplanet.com for upcoming race information, competitor biographies and wearable gear. Thanks also to photographers Michael A. Shoaf and Cathy Cole for all their background photographs; they tell an amazing story of the 4 Deserts series.

Thanks also to the East Bank Club for their never ending support and sponsorship of Team Illinois. Check out their amazing facility at: http://www.eastbankclub.com/

Team Illinois would like to thank the following sponsors for helping them realize their goal of conquering the four great deserts:

> The East Bank Club
> Dave Carlins and Magellan Development
> Conference Center Concepts
> Running Away
> McHugh Construction
> 1st Funding Mortgage
> GoLite
> CW-X
> Patagonia
> The Facktor Family
> The Mervis Family
> The Holt Family
> The Burrows Family
> The Kuhnau Family
> Kevin Covey

Joe Perry
Dawn Birch
GDI Solutions
First Step Fitness

Team Illinois would also like to thank "Running Away" in Chicago for early and generous sponsorship. Check them out at http://www.runningawaymultisport.com/

Big thanks to Greg Domantay, coach and friend to Team Illinois. Check out Greg's running store in Chicago, "Run Chicago" http://www.runchicago.com

Dedication and Author Credits

I would like to recognize the new friends and business teams that I've met both here in the U.S. and in Europe these past 20 years. Your partnership, collaborative spirit and "never say die" approach to problem solving proved to be a great inspiration to me when writing this book. Best of luck to you all wherever you may be.

Big thanks and hugs to my enduringly patient wife **Shirley** and my infinitely supportive friend **Mona**, for being my perpetual editors. Thanks to John Baraldi as well for his edit work. You have all kept me on the straight and narrow pronoun path, and that's a good thing.

A special thanks to **Peter Stacholy** for his ideas and for helping to expand the target audience for the book.

Finally, thanks to Dave for your friendship and for splitting the tab with me at Bruno's after discovering that the water, bread basket, and antipasti dish automatically brought to the table were in fact, not free. Meeting in New York was fortuitous, and the dinner excursions since then have been pretty interesting. I'm not sure how we top the Reindeer Steaks in Reykjavik, but it's worth a try. I wish the best of luck to you, Nancy and Joel on all your future endeavors.

Contents

PREFACE	XV
CHAPTER 1 - BLAME IT ON THE BURRITO	1
CHAPTER 2 - PREPARING FOR HELL	7
CHAPTER 3 - THE ATACAMA CROSSING	17
CHAPTER 4 - ATACAMA IN RETROSPECT	53
CHAPTER 5 - THE GOBI MARCH	61
CHAPTER 6 - THE LEARNING RACE	109
CHAPTER 7 - SAHARA	115
CHAPTER 8 - CELEBRATION AND TRAGEDY	155
CHAPTER 9 – ANTARCTICA	171
CHAPTER 10 - ENDING THE JOURNEY	221
CHAPTER 11 - IN NANCY'S WORDS	227
CHAPTER 12 - IN JOEL'S WORDS	237
CHAPTER 13 - IN DAVE'S WORDS	245
CHAPTER 14 - THE POWER OF "YOU"	253
EPILOGUE	275

Preface

Our first meeting was held at Dave's Chicago Brownstone in March of 2006, a full month after their return from Antarctica. The three members of "Team Illinois" sat quietly and expressionless at first, but then changed body language as soon as another memory rushed back from wherever it had been locked away. Nancy and Joel reclined deep into Dave's leather couch, and Nancy had casually thrown her legs across Joel's, giving her husband the opportunity to massage a sore calf from an earlier training run. Dave was pulling descriptions from memory as soon as a word or a phrase triggered the specific mental imagery.

The boys had started to tease Nancy about her constant "puking" during previous races as if it were as natural and insignificant as wiping your nose. "Puke and move on." Nancy replied while Joel and Dave smiled and nodded. Joel looked toward me with a smirk. "Nancy threw up a lot, at every one of the races".

I was struck instantly by the way they communicated with each other, poked fun, and challenged what the other was saying during our first conversation. They had become a team with a common goal during the first 150 mile race in Chile. The challenge, the training, the "project" that had brought them all together would push them literally to their physical and mental limits. They relied on each other, they encouraged each other, they carried each other. The young adventurous couple and the lanky stranger born and raised in Iowa had indeed become a close knit family in the span of two years, but more interestingly had stayed together as that "family" now that the four desert races were complete. Nancy

Fudacz-Burrows, Joel Burrows and Dave Kuhnau might as well be brothers and a strong-willed sister.

"What about those awesome yellow jerseys from Gobi?" Dave went on about one stretch of open salt flats during the race in China on a typical 120 degree day. While Dave began the description about fabric's ability to absorb sweat and still stay flexible, I had to remind myself that Team Illinois was actually running through the desert with backpacks, 30 pound backpacks.

Joel interrupted as brothers sometimes do. "Other teams were commenting on how great the color looked and how they should have considered yellow themselves. We weren't about to tell them how horribly dysfunctional the jerseys actually were."

Dave continued, "Apparently the jersey fabric we chose didn't handle sweat or salt build up that well. Over time, the salt would dry and the fabric would turn into a stiff sheet of sandpaper. At one point I had to stop because the shirt under my shoulder-straps was rubbing me raw. Joel took a look at the skin on my back and made only one comment, hamburger."

"And that was when we pulled out the duct tape." Joel said.

"Duct tape?" I asked.

"It's sort of like emergency skin replacement."

Nancy broke in. "Duct tape and dental floss. You can fix just about anything with duct tape and dental floss."

"Duct tape?" I asked again. Apparently I had a lot to learn.

Before further explanation was provided we were onto another story as each of them became excited about the memory of one race or one particular stage. Most often it was a fond remembrance of a challenge met, an obstacle overcome, and the sense of achievement they all shared together as a team. Sometimes it was to tease a teammate. "And we almost lost our first race at Atacama because Dave let his shoe catch on fire."

Trying to understand at first just how much of a personal victory the RacingThePlanet challenges were to them, I found that I might never completely understand what it would be like to punish a human body to the extent they had punished theirs. The feeling of pure mental and physical exhaustion, offset by the sense of accomplishment and fulfillment at the completion of a major race, would be difficult for an outsider to comprehend.

The RacingThePlanet series of desert challenges were indeed unique from other forms of endurance races. It wasn't just a marathon; it was the equivalent of four full marathons in four days plus one brutal stage at 50 miles. 50 miles of running, hiking and climbing on unforgiving ground in 100+ degree heat with survival gear on your back. Each competitor carried their own food, water, clothing and medical supplies through the hottest, driest and windiest places on earth.

It had been 30 days since their return to the United States, and Team Illinois was speaking fondly of the last race in Antarctica which ended February 1, 2006. As Nancy and Joel spoke about events from the last race, friendships made with other competitors and memories of the four continents they had conquered, I sensed a sadness come over them.

The last 24 months had affected the members of Team Illinois in an elemental way. The physical and mental preparation for each race and the emotional toll the last two years had taken on them could have been overwhelming. Personal and professional sacrifices were consciously made to keep the team together during that period, while other family tragedies had hit them just as hard. Most people or more specifically most individuals would have cracked under the pressure, but Team Illinois was unique. Nancy, Joel and Dave had a bond beyond the simple definition of "team". There were many factors that led to their success. There were many things Team Illinois did right. There are many lessons to be gleaned from their collective experience.

Though this story will talk about the physical preparation and the personal sacrifice made for a series of the world's most challenging endurance races, the lessons to be learned don't really have anything to do with distance running. This story is about first setting small goals, then exceeding them. It is about building chemistry among the people you live or work most closely with. It is about never giving up when faced with adversity. It is about achieving things most people would have never imagined possible.

For these three recently introduced Chicagoans, the concept of "TEAM" carries a little bit more meaning than the definition typically tossed around in business conference rooms. Longer term achievements weren't made without short term failures or costs. There was much for Nancy, Joel and Dave to learn about themselves and each other before they truly became a "team".

It was clear that the difficulty of the journey for Nancy, Joel and Dave was also the glue that had bound them all together into the tightly knit group sitting in Dave's home. Their story is about more than just running a race in the desert. It is a story about learning to embrace the challenge, never giving up on a goal, and the importance of building the true definition of "team". This isn't just their success story. It can be yours as well.

Chapter 1 - Blame it on the Burrito

Before any description can begin for an event like a race across 150 miles of burning sand in one of the world's most abrasive desert climates, we should probably discuss how anyone in their right mind would think this was a good idea. The story of Team Illinois and their entry into exactly this type of event actually starts in the small bathroom of a Metro-Chicago home. Thirty-seven year old Nancy Fudacz-Burrows had been suffering through an all-night intestinal battle induced by her choice of late night snack food and she found herself with some rare magazine reading time the following morning.

Leafing through the pages of the December 2003 issue of Runner's World, Nancy ran across an article about a unique endurance race in the Gobi Desert. She had gotten used to, or more accurately stated bored by nationally available endurance races in previous years. Her experience with marathons and Ironman Triathlons were still challenging, but Nancy had in fact been looking for something new. Most people would ask "why" at this point in the story, but it has everything to do with wanting to maintain your personal competitive edge and pushing yourself towards goals you previously thought were impossible.

Many of us have that same drive, but it's focused on a different area of study or activity. For some people, the concept of drive is in wanting to excel at a particular skill or sport. For others it might be educational or artistic excellence. For Joel and Nancy who were veterans of the marathon circuit, a primal hunger existed for anything new and physically demanding. Nancy dog-eared the corner of the article and then went looking for her husband and long time running partner, Joel.

Joel and Nancy had been running endurance races together for years. Marathons and triathlons were becoming common to the couple who made fitness and personal training a career as well as a hobby. It wasn't a situation where they were regularly winning every competition, but they were improving on their own personal record times with each race. For the young couple, the thrill of achieving the "high" associated with accomplishing a near-impossible goal was fading.

Nancy described her first marathon experience by lifting her eyes towards the ceiling, smiling and remembering both the exhaustion and the elation of accomplishing that first milestone. After her goal was reached, excitement was created to a lesser degree by extending their travel to include more exotic race destinations. Even when winning a particular race, Nancy admitted that the sense of accomplishment and the feeling of satisfaction was never the same as completing the challenge for the first time. Both Joel and Nancy agreed that it was the completion of their first marathon or their first triathlon that provided the greatest sense of fulfillment.

Joel and Nancy had both run marathons in just over three hours which is a very respectable elapsed time for a non-professional marathoner. When Nancy noticed the competitor stage times from the "Gobi March" article in Runner's World, she performed the quick math and found that the average pace for the race leaders came in just over nine minutes per mile. Knowing she and Joel could easily maintain a pace less than 7.5 minutes per mile, she declared, "We have to do this. We'll smoke these guys."

The Power Of Team

After a little more research into the RacingThePlanet desert format, it became clear that the Gobi March and the upcoming Atacama Crossing races would be different from a flat terrain marathon. Some of the competitors were international icons and had been featured in newspapers, magazines and television specials. Along with the already race-proven competition, there were other factors to consider. Serious applicants needed to be prepared for the little things that made a RacingThePlanet challenge unique.

Each race was self supported. This is endurance racing lingo for "You're going to carry everything you need for survival on your back." All the clothing, food, and medical supplies you need for seven days in the desert needs to be in your backpack. Oh, and it better be comfortable and lightweight too because you're going to be running near marathon distance every day. Let's also not forget that the Atacama Desert chills down to near freezing temperatures at night then blasts up over 110 degrees Fahrenheit during the day.

This is about the point in the story where most people begin to shake their head in disbelief. "No such race exists" they would say. Comments made while discussing this topic as a possible book project included: "The people who do that must be insane. Don't people die out in the desert?"

An average sports enthusiast would never consider such a challenge because the training required to even complete the race takes a massive personal time commitment. For some elite international racers, it is their job or at least a commitment they can afford through sponsorship. For amateur racers like Joel and Nancy, it was an opportunity to see how far the human mind and body could be pushed. Nancy and Joel were clearly looking for a new challenge and the Atacama Desert seemed like the place to find it.

Joel and Nancy of course, had real responsibilities outside the world of competitive running. Both were employed at one of the country's largest fitness and training facilities, The East Bank Club in Chicago. They taught classes, organized training curriculums for members and in some cases acted as personal coaches and trainers for athletes in the Chicago area. Nancy was responsible for running all fitness programs for the East Bank Club, and Joel was a personal trainer and fitness coach. Nancy and Joel's own personal training for the "Atacama Crossing" would have to be conducted in their limited spare time.

Work commitments would place them at a disadvantage to those who could train full time for the desert challenge. It became clear that they might not be able to compete with the best individual competitors in the world their first time out, but a team might have a better chance to post a decent finish time. All Nancy needed now was another victim to join Joel and her for the Atacama Crossing race scheduled for July, 2004.

"But who's dumb enough?" Joel tried to think of somebody they might know at the East Bank Club who was strong enough of a runner and crazy enough to actually think that this might be fun. They were ultimately led to someone they knew from a local Chicago running club, Dave Kuhnau.

Dave had been running for a few years before meeting Joel and Nancy and had progressed up to marathons and triathlon competitions by the summer of 2003. He had met both Joel and Nancy on a couple of recreational runs along the shoreline of Lake Michigan and other locally sponsored races by an organizing group known as "Run Chicago". It had been a casual relationship but Nancy and Joel knew that Dave had posted decent times in his previous marathon events.

Nancy and Joel had also signed up for Ironman USA in Lake Placid, New York that same year. They were initially unaware that Dave would be at the same event, and it turned out to be the first sign that they all might share the same love for competition. Everyone ran as individual competitors in that triathlon, but it was good to see someone on the course that you knew, especially when the conditions are as bad as they were that year in Lake Placid. The 2003 Lake Placid race had later gained international fame for some of the worst weather conditions in Ironman history. Non stop rain coupled with extremely high winds pounded all competitors, though Dave, Joel and Nancy all finished well among the field. The young couple from Chicago, almost didn't make the starting line.

Earlier that day while trying to get out of the hotel parking lot and make it to the race staging area, construction workers at the hotel were directing traffic back through the hotel main lobby entrance and a low hanging awning. Nancy's new Jeep would have cleared it just fine, but the two specialty bikes on top of the Jeep (more than $2,500 each), were mangled. Jumping back to the present day, sitting in Dave's Brownstone and listening to their story, Nancy had started to describe the incident when Joel interrupted her. "Let's tell the whole story. YOUR bike needed a piece of electrical tape to hold a cable on, MY bike was trashed."

"But they were able to get it working… right?" Nancy referred to understanding race officials in Lake Placid who helped repair Joel's bike. You could tell from that little conversation that Joel was still looking to shift a little blame towards his darling wife, but Nancy was having none of it. "I drove where the hotel people told me to go. End of story."

The mutual experience of gutting it out under the extreme weather conditions in Lake Placid brought Dave a little closer to the husband and wife duo, although he swam and cycled and ran separated from them on the course. Still, they had each suffered through the same race and it became a bonding experience.

After the horrible weather experience in New York, Nancy had asked Dave about doing another triathlon down in Florida. An annual event in November, the Ironman Florida competition would at least provide a better opportunity for decent weather. "Warmer than Chicago in November" that is. Plans were made and the three of them met in Panama City, Florida. Not necessarily competing together, they all had a great day. Each of them set personal record times for a triathlon competition.

It was the accomplishment of completing the Lake Placid race and their great collective experience in Florida that convinced Nancy to call on Dave as their Atacama Crossing partner. Nancy approached Dave in the lobby of the East Bank Club after a long workout in January and simply asked what Dave was "planning to do this year". She had offered up the suggestion for a "race in the desert" and Dave blindly agreed. "Sounds cool, sign me up" was his only response. Dave would find out a week later that his verbal agreement really meant 150 miles with a backpack.

A phone call was placed the following week to Mary Gadams, the organizer at RacingThePlanet, and "Team Illinois" was born. Once the official paperwork was signed, Team Illinois began a half year journey to prepare for the type of endurance racing they might encounter in the desert of Chile. The training alone would be a challenge, but Team Illinois also needed to figure out what to carry in their backpacks. "Backpacks?" Dave asked. "Headlamps? Duct tape? Are you sure?"

Somewhere in the recruiting process, Nancy eventually explained to Dave how she found out about the whole RacingThePlanet desert series. Some of the details slipped out about a rare trip for Mexican food the night before reading the article in Runner's World. Dave reacted as politely as he could, given the source of Nancy's inspiration but it was clear to all that if Team Illinois did fail miserably in Chile, they could simply "blame it on the burrito".

Chapter 2 - Preparing for Hell

After the decision was made to ask Dave to join the husband and wife duo in the race, the next step was to plan a collective training strategy for the event. Nancy had started research into the requirements and preparation for the Atacama Crossing, but the enormity of the training didn't start to sink in until she uncovered all the race details.

When Joel started planning with Nancy, they added up the individual weights of water bottles or hydration pouches, cold and hot weather gear, sleeping bag, survival equipment, emergency medical equipment, freeze dried food, energy bars plus the weight of the backpack itself. Though each racer would be able to replenish water supplies at scheduled race checkpoints, all seven days of food and survival gear would need to be carried in their packs. The combined daily weight of the pack when full of water, was 25 to 30 pounds.

Replacement water and a tent to sleep in were provided to each competitor at the end of a stage, and not much else. Though a medical staff remained at the ready and advance teams made sure the campsites were in place each evening, the competitors and teams were truly on their own.

Mandatory lists for equipment were received from the event website and each competitor was required to carry:

> 1 Backpack capable of carrying all gear and daily water
> 1 Sleeping bag
> 7 Day supply of food (approximately 7 pounds or 2000 calories per day)
> 1 Head lamp with batteries
> 1 Backup light source (penlight)
> 1 Compass with degree markings
> 20 Safety pins
> 1 Survival or folding knife
> 1 Whistle
> 1 Safety blanket
> 1 Baseball cap, or similar with brim
> 1 Pair sunglasses
> 1 Windproof jacket with insulation
> 1 Pair Nylon running tights (sun and wind protection)
> 1 Pair running shoes
> 1 Fleece cap
> 1 Pair insulated gloves
> 1 Blister Aid kit (Needle, second skin patches, lubricant, alcohol wipes, duct tape)
> 7 Days electrolytes supply, gel or other forms

Equipment packs would be inspected before the start of the race. Failure to produce any one of the required items would result in the competitor's disqualification. In addition to those required items, other necessary items would need to be packed for common sense reasons. A long sleeve tee-shirt to protect against the sun, sunscreen and lip protection, utensils to eat with and a watch that indicated mountain elevations were all recommended options.

The RacingThePlanet Challenge Format

Each desert race was a seven day, six stage foot race through the hottest, driest, windiest and coldest deserts on the face of the Earth. There were four desert races in the series, each separated by approximately six months time. The half-year break would be allowed between races to give competitors the chance to take care of the little annoyances like surgery, casts for broken bones, exhaustion, muscle loss, and second degree burns. The same time period could be used to train for the next event in the series, by running up to 80 miles per week with a weighted backpack and a couple of marathons and triathlons thrown in for kicks.

Each race was designed to cover 150 miles or more than 240 kilometers in seven consecutive days, across the harshest of running conditions. The six stages of the race broke down differently from race to race but the first four day-stages of the race fell in between a distance at 20 miles to marathon distance at 26.2 miles. The fifth stage crossed two consecutive days because the distance was set at 50 miles. If an individual or a team could cross the 50 mile distance in a single day, they would be rewarded with a day of rest, though many people would require both days to complete stage five. The final stage of the race (on day seven), would be a short sprint (10 miles or less) to the finish line.

The 4 Deserts series of endurance challenges by RacingThePlanet included:

The "Atacama Crossing" in the high altitudes of Chile's Atacama Desert.
The "Gobi March" across the heat and varying terrain of China's Gobi Desert.
The "Sahara Race" including the extreme 24 hour heat of the Sahara Desert in Egypt.
"The Last Desert" pushing the temperature extreme in the opposite direction on Antarctica.

Both individuals and teams of three could enter each desert competition where overall champion was crowned based on the fastest completion time for individual male, individual female, and team categories. Teams could be made up of any three registered competitors where most had entered as teams of three men.

Along with race champions in the three categories, age group champions were also crowned based on the fastest completion time for both male and female in each 10 year bracketed age group. Just completing the challenge at all, afforded the competitor a handsome medallion to remind them of the personal and physical sacrifice that had to be made just to complete the distance.

There would be rules and regulations to govern each race, and most centered around restrictions for accepting outside aid during the event. Stopping in a small town for lunch along the way was frowned upon even though the local food in every town smelled far better that the freeze dried alternative waiting for each competitor in their own backpacks.

Team rules were only slightly different from those imposed on individuals. The team structure meant that your group of three had to stick together for the entire race. All three members of the team had to be seen on the course together and no single team member could be out of sight of the other two. Each team must come into each checkpoint together; start each stage together and cross all stage finish lines together. Breaking up the team meant disqualification from the team competition, though each disqualified team member could still finish the race with an "individual" time if they chose to continue the challenge.

Aside from the basic required equipment for survival, the content of a competitors backpack was up to them. Sleeping bag or no sleeping bag, hiking poles or no hiking poles, extra clothing or not, the items inside the backpack also determined its total weight.

Additional Research

As the newly named "Team Illinois" researched the climate and desert conditions of Atacama, other concerns surfaced. Temperatures ranged from freezing at night to slightly less than oven-bake during the day. Ground conditions varied from firm soil to soft sand, salt flats to mountain ranges. They all began to wonder how they would be able to train effectively on the endless paved flats of the Chicago area. Accomplished marathoners and triathlon competitors all, Team Illinois could not duplicate the Atacama Crossing race conditions for training.

They all agreed that triathlon competitions were now out for training purposes. It was a safe bet that there wouldn't be a desert lake to swim in, and cycling would be pretty tough across the dune sands anyway. Training for the Atacama Desert would have to involve running and lots of it. The desert endurance race would traverse the distance of multiple marathons and they had to train for that specific scenario, with the enjoyment of carrying a weighted backpack.

Nancy had heard about 50 mile off-road race competitions before and one of them was held in June up in Kettle Moraine, Wisconsin. "The Ice Age 50. I've heard of that race before. It's only a couple of hours away. We should go for it."

The early sign-up for the 50 miler in June was still far away, and they needed to start running distance intervals as soon as they could. Due to their differing work schedules, Joel and Nancy would have to train separately from Dave during the week and see him at the East Bank Club or at scheduled Run Chicago track sessions during the weekend.

Joel started experimenting with methods to add dead weight to a backpack, including wrapping up iron bench weights in towels. Nancy and Joel started with shorter runs first using the makeshift dead weight packs, but the hard weights pounded their shoulders and spine as they ran.

Dave tried the same approach and experienced similar discomfort on his run. The 25 pounds of iron weight never formed to the contours of the pack or the runner's posture. Dave later came up with the idea of filling his pack with a case of Gatorade. After adding the full bottles, Dave's pack came in just over 22 pounds. When he strapped it on, the bottles did a better job forming to the pack and to his spine. As a side benefit he had something to drink along the way.

The bottled beverage approach would turn out to be a decent training aid over distance, because the weight in the pack decreased as Dave ran. Not that he immediately drew a parallel to the conditions he would encounter at Atacama, but much of their daily pack weight would be water. As they ran through the desert, the weight on their backs would reduce over the course of the race as they hydrated themselves.

From January through April, the newly formed team mixed up their training schedules between indoor track and outdoor lake front depending on the weather. Backpack weight would vary, running distances would vary but all three teammates were running between 40 and 60 miles per week. It was a difficult transition to run distance with the backpack, and everyone suffered through new aches, and minor injuries. Running comfort improved significantly with their collective change over to a backpack designed especially for endurance racing. Lightweight with reinforced materials, body contoured adventure racing packs by GoLite eased the pain over long distances.

The First Real Test

Nancy seemed to be the one who instigated things when it came to training or race participation. By virtue of working at one of the nations largest training facilities, she had access to race information from just about everywhere. Though the team had been running intermediate distances with their backpacks, nobody had attempted 26.2 miles.

The Chicago Lakeshore Marathon was scheduled for May 2004, and Nancy became cheerleader for Joel and Dave to get them to sign up. It wasn't much of a fight. All three knew they needed to gut-out a full marathon with the weight just to see if they could compete in Atacama. After all, there was still time to pull out of the race if they faltered at the lakeshore.

It turned out to be a decent day for running. It was a little cool early in the day, especially along the Lake Michigan shoreline, but distance runners were accustomed to these conditions. There were approximately 1000 competitors on the starting line that morning, but only three of them were wearing backpacks.

Joel and Dave had measured out pack weight until they were slightly below 30 pounds, and Nancy was running with about 25 pounds of dead weight in her pack. Team Illinois drew strange looks from everyone around them on the starting line but no questions were asked. The gun eventually sounded and the race was underway.

Elapsed Time: 04:11:55

Ten miles into the event, Nancy, Joel and Dave started to pass other competitors along the race route. Their pace was steady but it was clear they were running considerably slower than a typical three hour marathon finishing time. By mile 20, Team Illinois continued to pass other competitors, some of whom were walking in the final five or six miles to the finish line. Occasionally drawing snide comments from the road, they ignored the words of non-encouragement and kept pushing towards the finish. "What's the matter, not hard enough for you?", was a common response from the road when three people wearing 30 pound backpacks pass you in a marathon.

Team Illinois ran the complete race together as a group, encouraging each other, supporting each other, pushing each other to keep up the pace. They crossed the finish line a little over four hours after their start. A photographer captured the picture as they stepped across the chalk line, as Joel, Nancy and Dave held each other's hands in unity. The gesture of teamwork was never really planned, but it would become a familiar sight at every finish line they would cross in the races ahead.

They placed 495th out of 946 finishers. Given the number of entrants that did not finish the race, Team Illinois had beaten half the field with a backpack handicap. It was an impressive accomplishment for three Chicagoans just hoping to finish the race.

The Ice Age 50

The next big training challenge came in June at the 50 mile off road challenge in Wisconsin, just one month before flying out to Chile and the Atacama Crossing race. Joel and Nancy had registered for the race in time to be considered official competitors, but Dave seemed to be too busy to remember little details like registration forms or entry fees.

Feeling like he had let the team down, Dave had planned to run with his teammates, but unofficially from a race perspective. Race officials objected to him even participating in the event although Dave offered to pay the fee knowing he could not post an official finish time. The Ice Age 50 was held in a Wisconsin state park however, and Dave simply paid his state park fees and ran on the public roads along side Joel and Nancy.

The 50 mile run was brutal and the pace was significantly slower than they had posted for the Lakeshore Marathon. At Lakeshore, Team Illinois averaged about a nine and a half minute mile. The uphill and downhill terrain of the Ice Age 50 had slowed them considerably, but they agreed that their overall time might still be

The Power Of Team

reasonable. Again, research of the past desert races showed that the 50 mile stage was all about survival, not speed. It was more important to keep moving rather than worry about a running pace.

They walked when they needed to shut down the running pace, and picked up speed once they hit level terrain. Dave had planned to run along side Joel and Nancy for the duration of the race, but at one checkpoint a race volunteer called out "We have a bandit runner!", referring to Dave not wearing an official race jersey. Dave simply dropped back in the pack to avoid causing his new teammates any trouble and eventually made it to the end of the course, turning into the parking lot before crossing the finish line.

Somewhere towards the end of the race, Nancy finally noticed that Dave was no longer running with them and asked the simple question. "What the hell do you think happened to Dave?"

Joel responded, "Dave's dead, lucky bastard."

Tough questions about the heavy backpacks continued as they still passed other competitors along the 50 mile trail, Joel kept his comments to himself. Nancy and Joel finished 198 and 199 out of a finishing field of 247 competitors. They managed to cross 50 miles in 11 hours and 22 minutes. In the end, all three teammates knew that the 50 miles would be possible, even if it required a combination of running and hiking to get it done. No one was sure what the true conditions would be like in Atacama, but they were finally confident they could accomplish the worst stage of the 150 mile desert race.

The 50 mile run was devastating to their bodies the following week. Marathons were bad enough at over 26 miles and a human body always needed time to recuperate, but the 50 mile test in Wisconsin kicked everyone's butt. It wasn't just feet, calves and thighs that were in pain, but thanks to the weighted backpacks, neck, back and shoulders were just as impacted. If a body part wasn't injured, it was definitely sore. It would take time to repair injuries and strains, but Team Illinois would heal in time for their flight to South America.

The last three weeks of June were a blur for everyone on the team as they rushed to find, purchase and pack everything they needed for the race. All three of them over packed, bringing too many pairs of running shorts, or too much food or too much of something. They all made sure that the required equipment was on-board.

Weekly running activities also waned as they approached their July departure. Dave, Nancy and Joel were cutting their run distances to 40 miles per week, then eventually to 20 miles per week. It was the time to conserve energy and rest up for the rigors of the Atacama Desert.

Getting personal schedules straightened out was perhaps the least stressful activity of all. Dave's client at the time was supportive of his upcoming Chilean adventure, though nobody thought he would finish well. Once Dave described the conditions of the race, the daily run distances and the whole concept of that self-supporting backpack, they just hoped he would return home alive. The East Bank Club wasn't only verbally supportive of Joel and Nancy's endeavor, but they sponsored them financially as well. It was great for Nancy and Joel to find an employer that believed as much in them as they did in their own work at the EBC.

Charity fundraising was the last major event on their calendar as they helped stage a silent auction at a friend's local pub/restaurant. Hosted by "Cans" on Damen Avenue, the silent auction did well and the monies collected were distributed equally between the charities selected by Team Illinois.

Chapter 3 - The Atacama Crossing

The three lanky Americans arrived in Santiago, Chile after more than 12 hours in the air. Hopping yet another plane, they eventually made it safely to Calama, just on the perimeter of the Atacama Desert. It was a short bus ride into the only commercial district of that small desert town and the entire group of competitors were taken by surprise at the luxury afforded them at the Adobe style hotel sponsored by race organizers. This would however, be everyone's last real taste of civilization for the next seven days.

While Calama remained a busy town supported by one of the world's largest copper mines, open views to the barren tundra and lifeless mountain ranges were relatively close to the hotel and easy to find. The challengers would sleep in one last night of comfort before crossing hell's border, just a minute or two away.

Dave, Joel and Nancy took the opportunity in the hotel lobby to size up their competition. It is a natural instinct really, to view others around you as competitive threats or not. We do it in the workplace. We do it during any business or sporting challenge, even family reunion softball games. For those of us less physically competitive, it's still a matter of evaluating ourselves against others. Whether it's a comparison of height, weight, clothing brands, number of grandchildren, jewelry or the automobile we drive, we're all guilty of performing that personal evaluation.

Some of the competitors that Team Illinois saw in the lobby were easily recognizable by name or from facial features. A few of their desert competitors were famous within endurance and eco racing circles. Some were even recognizable from the pages of Runner's World magazine or other fitness publications. Still, there were some in the room who looked less physically fit, or ill prepared for perhaps one of the toughest physical and mental challenges on the face of the Earth. The three members of Team Illinois looked at each other while commenting, "We've done marathons, we've done triathlons, and we've proven our skill. We're going to rock this thing."

There was evidence to support their burgeoning confidence. They all had run marathons in about three hours, they all had posted exceptional times running marathons with a weighted backpack. Team Illinois had even endured the 50 mile race with the same backpack, up hills and down gullies. Nancy, Joel and Dave had trained well for the Atacama event.

Dave had decided to bring a small digital video camera to document the trip and the race. One of the first entries in their video journal was to document their strategy for each stage. It was a brief discussion about the pace they would start out with on day one, followed by a small change in their approach to day two. At some point during the lobby discussion and planning session, Nancy had determined that she and her male counterparts, needed a warm-up run the day before the first 25 mile stage. Not only would she punish her own team, but she managed to convince some others in the lobby that this somehow sounded like a good idea.

The veterans of endurance racing just smiled and politely declined by shaking their heads "no". This should have been a significant clue for Team Illinois, but there were very few takers for the extra-curricular training that following morning. The excitement of the race and the tension had built up so much that a run was viewed as the only way to drive off the building adrenaline. Taking action was always better than "doing nothing", and a number of the competitors in the lobby had agreed to the idea. There would be a "Nancy Sponsored" warm up run after all.

Apologies to the original author of the "old age and treachery" quote, but sometimes old age and experience can overcome youth and skill. While Team Illinois and the lobby followers were out the next morning on their warm up run, the experienced competitors were resting, stretching and double checking their survival gear. 150 scheduled miles in the searing desert heat would be quite enough for them, thank you. Never mind that the elevations are so high that oxygen becomes a scarce commodity, or that the human body takes time to get used to that environment. Keep reminding yourself that Team Illinois had youth and skill.

Later in the day, all competitors were called to pile into minibuses for their trek to the starting line and the first night's camp. It was only a matter of minutes before entering the desert and attempting off-road maneuvers typically reserved for 4 wheel drive vehicles. The sand was flying everywhere and so was the dirt that had accumulated inside the busses. No one knew the actual distance from the hotel to the starting line, but it was an uncomfortable trip that shook internal organs and the liquids stored in them. After the arduous three hour dune ride, flags and tents and sponsor banners could be seen in the distance.

Team Illinois surveyed the camp and claimed space in the back of one of the tents while teams were all assigned tent-mates. Each tent housed eight people or four per side. Teams of three had to take on an individual competitor to round out the sleeping arrangements.

That night before the start of the first stage, the race organizers prepared a group meal and began to offer race instructions and rules for the following morning. All competitors would need to be ready to go at 7:00 a.m. desert time. Individual competitors and teams stocked up on water for their backpack hydration systems and checked their gear one last time before retiring to bed.

Chile's Atacama Desert gets cold at night. Despite being a place that routinely supports triple digit temperatures during the day, it falls below freezing soon after the sun goes down. Dave woke early the following morning and felt something on his skin other than just the cold of the Atacama morning air. He could feel something cold and wet behind his head, leading down his back. Fully awake, Dave checked under his sleeping bag but found the source of the cold water coming from his survival pack. The vinyl bladder of his water storage system had sprung a leak, trickling water underneath him and across the floor of the tent.

One runner must have heard Dave's shuffling and woke to exclaim, "Hey man, the tent is wet". Another competitor who was also awake before sunrise replied, "It's probably just condensation." Dave smiled remembering that they were supposed to be in the driest place on earth. "Condensation? I don't think so.", but Dave never did confess. The unidentified runner on the other side of the tent followed with, "condensation doesn't make a puddle". He slapped at the floor and splashed Dave's gear. Dave and two other members of the tent who were slightly downhill from his backpack had to deal with wet gear for the rest of the morning.

Day One

At sunrise, all competitors were taken up to the top of a nearby mountain which placed them at a starting elevation of 13,000 feet. All were concentrating on the length of the journey rather than the start of the race, which meant that the concept of a starting line had lost it's glamour in favor of the finish line some 25 miles away. It was an anticlimactic start, given the magnitude of the journey.

This desert challenge was something few people would ever read about or see on television. Despite RacingThePlanet organizers' attempt to secure press coverage, the idea of this type of grueling event hadn't yet caught on with the world news or sports media. Eco-challenges and endurance racing were still relatively new concepts at the time. There would be an occasional feature in a specialty sports magazine, and some world television press coverage at the conclusion of an event like this, but the 150 mile Atacama Crossing race would begin with only local fanfare.

Descending from 13,000 feet at the race starting line to 9,000 feet of elevation, the runners should have appreciated the easy transition into the week long event. Air is still thin at 9,000 feet however, and many of the competitors who train in countries a little closer to sea level were struggling to breathe. The lack of oxygen at that altitude had drained the energy of the competitors just a couple of hours into the race. Nausea, cramps, and vomiting were the order of the day as most of the field fought to acclimate themselves to the thin air. Many of them continued to push themselves despite the sickness, in order to keep up with the race leaders. This mistake would impact their performance for the rest of the event.

Team Illinois had recognized the altitude sickness for what it was, and controlled their pace to prevent as much physiological damage as possible. They had fallen behind most of the experienced individual competitors and some of the team competitors as well, but they were still positioned in the middle of the pack.

Towards the end of the first day, events started to unfold that could have led to the early elimination of Team Illinois from the competition. It is amazing when you look back at a string of relatively disconnected events, and how they can sometimes lead to a potentially catastrophic situation. Near the end of the first stage, runners had to cross a dusty plain leading to a small river bed. As shoes and socks and legs began to accumulate dust from the desert floor, the stream provided the necessary moisture to turn that mixture into a pasty grit that would cake everything it touched. It was bad enough running in wet shoes, worse running in wet shoes that were now filled with mud. Shoes would need to be cleaned after each race stage.

Team Illinois crossed the finish line together, not really caring about where they had placed in relation to the competition, but were relieved to be done with the first stage. It was also a chance to get out of their dirt crusted shoes. Dave was a guy who liked to be as comfortable as possible when running. Living near the Lake Michigan shoreline of Chicago, he might have to deal with a little sweat and a little dehydration, but that was about it. At the end of a training run, Dave could simply peel off his socks, air out his shoes and jump into the shower.

Joel and Nancy would tease Dave by calling him "Lincoln Park Boy", a reference to the young professional, comfortable neighborhood where he lived. When Dave did travel, he would proclaim his preference for the little comforts normally received at nicer hotels and corporate apartments. "Hey, when I travel, I like to do it right", Dave would say. In the campsites of the Chilean Desert however, you slept in the dirty clothes you ran in, and you scraped the dirt off your own wet and mud-crusted shoes. Shower? Fresh clothes? Not today, but one can dream.

Dave had placed his wet shoes near the open pit fire that was the only source of heat in the campsite. The shoes were far enough away from the flame to not be of concern, and Dave returned to other activities near the tent of his teammates.

Both Joel and Nancy were assisting one of their new buddies Derek, who was struggling with a small case of altitude sickness. Derek had stopped just before the finish line, and Joel wandered back to find him at the last stream crossing. Joel grabbed his backpack and helped coax him to the day one milestone. Nancy and Joel helped get Derek back to his tent, helped make his dinner and checked on him later in the evening to make sure he was recovering. Sometimes it's not about winning at any cost. Good team members will always reach out to help someone else who is struggling, even when it's a competitor. Derek was a strong runner, and he would fight his way back on day two after allowing his body to adjust to the altitude.

Sometime that same hour, Chilean race volunteers had decided to stoke the fire and build up the coals in expectation of another cold evening. As they piled more wood on the fire, existing hot coals were pushed out further towards the perimeter of the fire pit and of course, Dave's running shoes. Dave heard someone yell, "Hey, something's burning!" Jumping out of the tent and turning back towards the fire pit, Dave saw the destruction. The entire back half of the heel and ankle supporting foam and tread were melted away. The entire underside of the shoe as well as the mesh wrapping the upper part of the shoe had burned away. The buzz around the camp was instantaneous, and everyone wanted to get a look at the damage.

"Dave's shoe is cooked. They will be forced to drop from the team competition for sure."

Joel heard the banter from inside the tent and came out to see who the unfortunate victim was. He saw Dave in the distance, holding a shoe and carrying the body language of someone just defeated in a boxing match. Joel asked as he approached, "How bad is it?" Before Dave could respond, Joel saw the damage and dropped his head.

RacingThePlanet race director Mary Gadams, immediately offered to head back to the hotel to retrieve Dave's pair of backup shoes. Nobody wanted to see a team drop from the race under those conditions. Based on the travel time back and forth to the hotel in Calama however, Dave would still have to compete the next morning with the equipment he had with him in camp. Mary would never make it back from the hotel in time.

Day Two

The early morning hours found many runners stretching or filling water bottles before wandering off to the starting line. Some of the more experienced desert challengers had made it a point to purge themselves of as much body weight as possible before the run began. One had suggested to Dave that forcing a bowel movement might make his run more comfortable in the heat of the day. That idea spread quickly and everyone was looking for a private place to do exactly that sort of business. The desert however, is a difficult place to find privacy.

Dave had wandered away from camp a short distance and found a rather thick bush to hide behind. The mental picture of that gives a whole new meaning to the term "cop a squat", but Dave did just that out in the middle of the Atacama Desert. At some point in the exercise, Dave heard some rustling coming from the other side of the bush. Before they wandered over into his private stall, he did what most of us have done at one point in our lives. He called out politely to let them know "someone's in here". The rustling continued without a response. "I'll be done in a minute", Dave had elevated his tone to make sure he was heard, but the movement on the other side of the bush continued. As soon as he finished his business, Dave pulled some branches aside to see an adult bull, complete with mature horns, staring him in the face. Thankfully, the bull wasn't interested in chasing Dave back to camp which in retrospect was probably a good thing. Dave wouldn't have made any friends by turning the Atacama campsite into the streets of Pamplona.

Before the start of the second stage, Joel took the lead on strategy to help the team's overall performance and also to take some of the weight off Nancy's shoulders. The term "weight" was both a figurative and a literal description in this case. Nancy's backpack was set up just like the men's. She carried the same required survival materials, the same food and electrolyte packages, and roughly the same amount of water. For all practical purposes,

Nancy had been competing in the male race category by posting race times competitive with all women and most men, all while carrying the same weight on her back. Joel redistributed some of the weight from Nancy's pack into his and Dave's. The boys from Team Illinois would be helping their teammate, and by default, the entire team.

After the start of the second stage, Dave faced the first real test for his half-melted shoe. There was an early four mile stretch of trail that forced the competitors through a narrow stream before the trail opened up onto the plains. Four miles of running through cold water is tough enough on any shoe, but especially tough on seams barely holding together. Dave wondered throughout the day, if it really was the adhesive properties of the tread glue, the stitching, or something else keeping the shoe from falling apart.

Two of the equipment changes made just before arrival in Chile were actually working out pretty well for the team. This was a good thing given that other necessary pieces of equipment like Dave's running shoe might fail before the end of the race. Both the **GoLite** backpacks and the **CW-X** Pro Shorts picked by Team Illinois were performing well in the hot and sweaty conditions during the day. Team Illinois would need their remaining equipment to perform just as well now that everything had been broken in on day one.

The course that day was laid out across streams and hills and open desert. The competitors in The Atacama Crossing routinely passed through dry plains with sparse vegetation, but found cattle wandering all along the trail. Team Illinois was actually dodging cows on one stretch of the trail near a small ranch. As they continued on, Nancy took the opportunity to look back towards Dave to see if the seams were still holding. They were holding up nicely, and so was Dave.

During that race stage, other competitors from the individual bracket passed by or ran alongside with Team Illinois, and asked how the shoe was holding up. Dave would muster a smile or give a "thumbs up" while hoping that the damaged shoe would actually make it through the day. Dave remembers thinking somewhere in the middle of the stage, "If the shoe can hold it together, so can I". Apparently inspiration can be found in simple forms.

Day two was also the stage where Team Illinois was befriended by a not-so-wild desert animal. As Team Illinois stopped to take in some water and a little food, a mutt that looked like he was part German Sheppard with ears that flopped over at the tips, had strolled out of the desert and took a seat near all three. Dave offered the medium sized and friendly dog a small piece of beef jerky and that was all that was needed to secure the friendship. "Attie", as he was then named, began to watch over Dave, Joel and Nancy as they continued their trek through the sand on day two. Staying a little behind, but keeping pace, Attie would follow Team Illinois through the desert to the finish line and the awaiting campsite.

Back at camp, Dave, Joel and Nancy returned to body-maintenance and equipment-repair while Attie wandered around camp, making new friends. In the main tent, RacingThePlanet had managed to set up a remote internet connection so that competitors could stay in touch with friends and family. Dave had wandered into the tent and made his connection to the sponsored message website. There he found an e-mail from a good friend, Ken Luurs, who decided to send some well wishes and to lighten the team's mood. Dave would read the mail a day late.

"There is nothing in the rules that says you can't take a dog with you, and studies show that an average sized dog can carry up to 12 pounds on his back. So, you either have to find a dog somewhere out there or I'm sending you one."

Dave was immediately taken aback by the symbolism of their encounter in the desert and also from the assistance that friends on the other side of the world wished they could offer. Completely by coincidence or divine providence perhaps, one medium sized, domesticated dog came from nowhere to support Team Illinois just when they needed support and inspiration the most. As they packed in to retire for the night, Attie took up residence near the warmth of the fire, watching over Nancy's team.

Day 3

Nancy's dry heaves began almost from the onset of stage three as the desert heat had started to rise in tandem with the sun. She had fallen twice the day before along the 25 mile second stage, once crossing the slippery rock bed of a desert stream. Her muscles were tightening and joint pain continued to plague her as she tried to block out the discomforts she had grown accustomed to during the last year of heavy training. Each mile of stage three was a small victory for Nancy, though her body continued to cry out to her, begging for the feet and legs to stop the futile pounding of the Atacama Desert sand.

Each progressive day in the 150 mile Atacama endurance challenge punished her body and challenged her will, but Nancy pressed on. On day three she wasn't sure where the motivation was coming from, be it a promise to her teammates to finish the race or commitments to charities or just pure competitive drive, but she continued to rock forward from heel to toe always forward.

Her teammates started to offload a little non-required material weight out of Nancy's survival backpack once again. Water and food rations were shifted to her husband Joel's pack and teammate Dave's pack. It helped a little, but the load continued to pull hard on Nancy's shoulders. Gravity became everyone's enemy in a distance race. Stage one and two of the Atacama Crossing, had already pushed the international competitive field through the equivalent of two marathons. Day three, (stage three) saw competitors start to drop from the race. Some of the best athletes and best trained endurance racers, triathlon competitors and marathoners had already fallen to the desert sands and mountain elevations of Chile.

Later in the day, Nancy's dry heaves turned into the wetter variety. Joel had a more attractive way of describing it. "She was constantly puking her guts out." At some point under extreme physical stress, the human body will attempt to reject just about everything. Nancy's body was starting to expel anything that it found irritating. Unfortunately that included the one thing needed for survival in the desert, water.

They had slowed to an alternating pattern of walking and running, reducing the pace to just 5 minutes of running in each 10 minute time block. Both Joel and Dave took turns carrying Nancy's backpack, encouraging her to keep up with them, though Nancy was the one who would not quit. They all began to doubt the preparation and training for this race, as if the multiple marathons, triathlon competitions and 50 mile endurance race weren't enough. Nothing had really prepared them for the endless dry heat and the difficulty of running in the soft sand and treachery of the salt flats.

Nancy knew she had to keep pushing. Her teammates had been seduced by her promise of a new challenge. She started the sales pitch as soon as she read about the upcoming series of desert endurance races sponsored by RacingThePlanet. "Racing in the desert in Chile. International competitors. We have to go!" It was Nancy who convinced them to sign up for the Atacama Crossing the following week.

Mary Gadams, the founder of RacingThePlanet, had come up with the name "Team Illinois". Nancy joked about other possible team names like "Team Chalupa Extreme" and "Hoosier Daddy", but Mary probably knew "Team Illinois" would be better for both sponsors and charities. Regardless of the origin of the team name, Nancy wondered again how she ever thought this race was a good idea.

The Power Of Team

She dwelled on the guilt over convincing her husband and new running partner to share in the pain. She kept moving forward a step at a time although her brain could not muster a single good reason to continue. Nancy willed herself somehow to keep on moving. She was determined to finish the race or collapse trying.

Team Illinois crossed the next race checkpoint at mid-day and Nancy, Dave and Joel were offered a bottle of water each as they passed the checkpoint tent near the desert trail. A miscommunication between race officials and the checkpoint volunteers found Nancy's team short three bottles of water. They found out later that each runner should have received two bottles of water, not one.

Dehydration became the enemy in the heat of the mid-day sun. The ultraviolet punishment above their heads wasn't nearly as bad as the radiant heat pushing upward from the desert floor. Dave and Joel continued to aid Nancy by carrying her pack, but Nancy slowly fell off the running and walking pace. Water disappeared as the heat pulled the hydration through the body's pores and back into the air. Eventually they reached the next checkpoint out of water, and dangerously dehydrated.

News of the water bottle incident spread quickly, and race officials corrected the problem by the next checkpoint. The damage however, had already been done. Joel and Dave consumed water easily and quickly, but Nancy struggled to take it in. Symptoms of a more severe medical problem were evident in Nancy and the medical team would not allow her to continue the race until her condition improved and she could pass water. As Nancy still lay on the medical cot, Dave and Joel stopped back in to see how she was recovering from the dehydration. Nancy looked up with as much determination as she could form on her face and asked, "We're going to finish this thing, right?" Dave leaned forward with a reassuring smile, slapped her hand in a "high five" and said. "Rock on."

Forty minutes of water consumption later, Nancy was able to force a trickle of urine from her body. Uncerimoniously squatting in the desert, she accomplished her goal but sprayed her shoes in the process. "Anything for the team", Nancy would joke later. While re-hydrating at the checkpoint, Team Illinois was passed by several other competitors as they moved through the checkpoint without resting. It was enough of a motivator to push them off on a running pace as they left the shade of the checkpoint tent.

The heat of late afternoon was just as intense as it was mid-day. Dave and Joel took turns again lightening the load on Nancy's back or carrying it when she needed a break. At one point, Joel produced a tow line from his backpack, similar to the one they had used in earlier endurance races. He tied it to himself and then to Nancy as a reminder that she would not be left behind. The symbolism of the life line was significant to Nancy as well, and she knew her team would help pull her through this stage even if it meant literally. This is what teams do. Words of encouragement continued to come from Joel and Dave and other individual runners as they passed Team Illinois by. The life line remained a gentle reminder that her family was there for her, no matter what.

Joel was the first to see the tents at the end of the stage on day three. He reflected on the fact that the unknown team from Illinois had stayed strong during this most challenging stage and knew the end of day three was near. "I've learned over the years that life events like this one are more about keeping one foot moving in front of the other and less about worrying about your (performance)." Team Illinois would finish stage three by doing just that, keeping one foot moving in front of the other.

Joel and Dave entered the camp and sought immediate medical attention for Nancy. She was so dehydrated that nurses in the medical tent had trouble raising a vein for an intravenous saline drip. A local Chilean ambulance driver stepped in and was able to start the IV line for the much needed fluids. In Nancy's words,

"Somehow, the IV incident became the lowest part of the race…I was exhausted, ashamed of myself for being weak, and devastated that I had let my team down. I sat in the med tent quietly, trying to envision the IV as new strength. Friends came in to check on me, smiling, telling me it was okay. Joel came to check on me in the tent and said 'Nancy, everyone here is physically wrecked. There's nothing physical that you have left (to prove). Now, it's all mental. You CAN get this together.' He was right. I slept fairly well after Stage 3, and woke up less worried. I was going to finish no matter what. Good thing I didn't know what was in store for me on Stage four."

Another friend of Team Illinois had joined them on their trip to Atacama as an event volunteer, and had been checking on Nancy from time to time while she lay in the medical tent. Denise Allman along with about 20 other volunteers had been busy setting up camp and distributing water and doing whatever else it takes to keep the RTP event running smooth. While Nancy recuperated, Denise and the rest of the volunteers were preparing to set up the course and distribute water on day four.

As Team Illinois recuperated in camp, Nancy finally had a chance to check messages received from well-wishers back home. One of the inspirations for Nancy running as hard as she did, came from a friend and cancer survivor who willed himself to running his first marathon a year after being diagnosed. Nancy read the words for the group that had gathered around the fire pit.

The miles will melt fast, they're no match for your feet
You will laugh at the rocks, at the sun, at the heat.

Your hearts will stay strong, your spirits stay light
You will shrug as you hear all the other teams fight.

You will sleep long and slow beneath blankets of stars
You'll rise fresh every morning, a queen and two czars.

There's always more left, just ask and it's there
All our love and support is an advantage unfair.

Hot legs, cool heads, always two others to trust
How grand an adventure, what causes so just.

The journey is sweet, the finish -- salvation
Bring it on, Team I, you are our inspiration

    Allan and Martha

Day Four

Joel Burrows came into the race as an experienced personal trainer, distance runner, and strong competitor. Nancy might claim that she was the one who talked her husband into the idea of the Atacama Crossing, but Joel wasn't the type of man who shied away from a challenge, especially when it came to running. Distance running and pretty much anything requiring physical endurance was in Joel's wheelhouse, to use a baseball term. Before Atacama, Joel had as much confidence and focus as anyone standing in the lobby of the hotel in Calama four days earlier.

RacingThePlanet desert challenges were different however, and it would not be the distance of a marathon through the hot desert that caused competitors to start dropping from the race. It would be something other than the physical challenge. It would be the mental challenge associated with the fact that one day's accomplishment would be met with another day's punishment. Joel describes the conditions of the race on day four.

"(Day four) was the hardest day so far. Dave and I are suffering from carrying the weight of our stuff and some of Nan's. We were only able to run a short part of the course today. We crossed over 10 miles in the salt flats and it took more than 3.5 hours to make that checkpoint. The salt flats were unlike anything any of us had ever been through. On the surface it was this hard crusty stuff and as you took a step, you could sink anywhere from the sole of your shoe deep all the way up to your shin. Because of that, we had to high step this section of the course. The heat was steady and hot. The radiant heat kept reflecting off the surface of the salt flats and bouncing off the bill of our hats and onto our faces. We walked out of this section with burned faces, but (no foot or ankle injuries)."

Day four would also be Dave's "bonk" day. Though everyone struggled through the heat and arid conditions of the salt flats at mid day, Dave had developed symptoms of Bronchitis. His sinuses were over producing and fluids normally used to hydrate the body were running down Dave's throat and clogging his lungs. Dave's body struggled to pull oxygen into his lungs, and his chest began to burn. Running and walking were difficult enough under desert and high altitude conditions, but breathing was now becoming a problem.

As Team Illinois reached the halfway point of the salt flats, Dave started to entertain thoughts of giving up. He had been strong through the first three days of Atacama, but his body was fighting with him now, trying to convince his mind to give up the race. He had described the situation in terms of water supply and dehydration.

"Nancy was out of water, I was out of water and Joel only had a little left. Nobody was talking, eventually the dehydration took the best of us. Our bodies could hardly move and we started to get disoriented. I stopped to lie down on the salt flats, like somehow that was a good idea, and had given in to whatever sickness that had taken control of me."

Nancy turned back to see Dave, prone on the desert floor. Perhaps it was Nancy's turn to be the strong one on the team. Maybe it was time to pay Dave back for conspiring with Joel to drag her sick and dehydrated body to the final checkpoint on day three. Nancy walked back towards Dave and kicked his backpack. "Get up", was all she said.

She was frugal with her words because speech took energy, but the look on her face carried with it a certain determination. Dave had decided to get up rather than get kicked again. Rolling to his stomach first then up to his knees, Dave put his weight on a single knee as he tried to push himself up from the flats. The shards of salt and mineral crystals cut through the skin of his knee and left him bleeding as he rose to rejoin his team.

Dave remembers thinking at that point that the Atacama must have been a place where God might have experimented with the concept of Hell. Dave joked, "When God was trying to think of a suitable place for the devil to call home, Atacama came in second and the active volcano at Kilauea had to be third." Dave looked back across the flats before continuing forward with his team and he thought he saw Attie standing off in the distance, watching.

Dragging themselves slowly towards the next checkpoint, they passed Mary Gadams who had stationed herself at the medical tent. Later that evening she would tell Dave that he was "looking as bad and as miserable as she had ever seen anyone." With one more checkpoint before the end of the stage, Team Illinois loaded up on water and continued off towards that night's campsite. Crossing the line together hand in hand, Dave who could now hardly breathe, separated from the team and laid down immediately in the back of their tent. It was Nancy who suffered on day three and Dave who suffered on day four. Joel had remained the strong one in the group during stage four and tried to lighten the mood before the 50 mile stage starting the following morning. "Well, at least tomorrow is flat."

As Dave tried to overcome the sickness that had taken hold of him earlier in the day, other competitors had picked up a survival trick on the evening of stage four. Word spread quickly around the camp and many were filling up empty water bottles with hot water boiling near the fire pit. Placing a bottle or two into the bottom of a sleeping bag tended to keep the feet and the entire bag warm. It would be enough to help take the edge off the 20 degree night air and help most fall quickly asleep. Attie had appeared again in camp, wandered around to check on everyone then curled up again by the fire pit overlooking Nancy's team.

Day Five

Team Illinois woke with a positive attitude the next morning despite Dave's Bronchitis, Nancy's constant intestinal troubles and Joel's blistered feet. Joel once again reminded everyone that "today was all flat", which is exactly the type of surface you would prefer if you had to run 50 miles. Dave mustered a bit of humor recalling their over-confidence in the Calama Hotel and all the sea-level training they had absorbed the previous year, "Nobody screws with a flatlander."

Team Illinois started with a strategy of running nine minutes and walking one minute. The one-in-ten walking approach allowed them enough of a break to recover from each nine minute running pace. By the middle of the day, Team Illinois was passing some of the other teams who had been leading the race since day one. Towards the end of the day and the first 25 miles, Joel could see the first place team off in the distance. The one-in-ten strategy was paying off and Team Illinois was catching up with the leaders.

Nancy had been vomiting again on day five as she struggled to keep any food or water down, but she would not stop the forward momentum of the team. Nancy had gotten used to throwing up in the altitude of Atacama. Like Dave's Bronchitis, or Joel's blisters, the vomiting was just another bio-physical hurdle to overcome. Call it what you wish. Whether it was mind over matter, determination in the face of adversity, strength of conviction, or pure will, Team Illinois had it in spades.

The 50 mile stage was set up so that slower competitors could take up to two full days to cover the distance. Those who could make the trek in a single day, were rewarded with a day of rest while the stragglers completed the 50 mile distance the following day. That meant if you chose to stop, it also meant that you had to bed down out on the open sand and exposed to the chilled night air. Those who chose to complete the stage in a single day would be doing so in the empty darkness of Atacama at night.

RacingThePlanet officials had planned for this contingency of course, and had begun to mark the trail back to camp with lime-green glow sticks. Race volunteers were told to mark the trail so that a direct line back to camp could be followed. The challenger's only light source would be mini lamps strapped to their heads and operated by tiny batteries. Glow sticks would be needed to keep runners from those minor little obstacles like the unseen edge of a cliff, or open hole in the desert floor. Still plagued by stomach trouble, Nancy remembered back to a conversation with the course designer.

"(We) had been looking forward to the 50 mile day because Ian (The Atacama course designer) had assured us that it would all be on roads. Ahh, finally. Mindless running. I finally was feeling good. Not that I felt great all day. After the 40k checkpoint, my stomach was acting up again, not happy with some of the hills and the heat. My teammates were so patient and, well, just wonderful…and then there was Greg, a walking/running pharmacy. What do you need? Tums, Coke, what? Tums it was and we were running again. That is why this race is extraordinary. The competitors are warm, encouraging, and wonderful and want everyone to finish. Team Illinois had agreed that we would push as far as we could before it got dark. Our goal was to make it to the 60k point, leaving only 12 miles to go in the dark. We made it. I was pooped, gagging at the 60k mark, but Sue the nurse, and race volunteers Emma and Mark, cheered us on. 'You can make it tonight' they told us. I cried every time I saw the volunteers. They were wonderful. Somehow, like we knew (what our fate would be), Joel asked just before we left checkpoint 21, 'Are there glow sticks out on the course?' Sue and Emma nodded, 'I certainly hope so.'"

As Team Illinois crossed into twilight on day five, dimly lit foot prints marking a trail in the sand were disappearing with the sun. Team Illinois had a general idea of where that night's campsite would be based on the direction they were headed, but glow sticks would be needed to guide them towards camp.

Absent of moonlight, the desert floor is a dark and ominous place. Team Illinois had already put on their hiking headlamps had cleared a canyon ridge only to find another wide open and barren plateau. There wasn't another headlamp or any other sign of human life for miles. Joel finally broke the silence remembering a pop song from the 80's, sung by Tiffany. Dave, without missing a beat (or a lyric) immediately responded.

> Joel: "I think we're alone now"
> Dave: "There doesn't seem to be anyone around"
> Joel: "I think we're alone now"
> Dave: "The beating of our hearts is the only sound"

A little humor in a tense situation went a long way for the team. Nancy smiled and shook her head, probably wondering why she married Joel in the first place. As they walked on further in the direction of the last seen glow stick, the lime-green light source had disappeared with no glowing marker in the distance. Team Illinois had been following the team sponsored by the British Broadcasting Company (BBC) and were eventually aided by a BBC cameraman who helped Team Illinois follow the posted marker flags until they could see the next glowing trail marker. Dave could finally see the faint green glow of the next marker in the distance. The first place team that had been within Team Illinois' grasp earlier in the day was now lost somewhere up ahead in the darkness. Joel struggled to look for telltale signs of headlamps bouncing in front of them, but there was nothing lighting up the desert floor.

It was the Atacama Desert version of a rave party. No teenagers or techno music could be seen or heard, but there was plenty of sweat as bodies bounced up and down to a synchronized running pace. The desert floor was lit up with their bobbing LED beams and the occasional glow stick rounded out the look of the desert dance floor. Glow sticks attached to the back of their packs bounced up and down in time with the imaginary music, and the muffled drum beats of their feet on the sand provided the percussion.

As they climbed up the next small incline, Dave spotted glow sticks placed now in two directions away from their current line of approach. Team Illinois had been walking in what they thought was a straight line, but now faced a larger incline where the glow stick trail clearly split to the right and left of their position.

Joel and Dave split temporarily to see where each trail led, but soon returned back to center to select a different strategy. Dave and another individual competitor who had caught up with them had attempted to climb a nearby ridge, but were pulled back down by the crumbling terrain. Dave managed to reach the top but no other glow sticks or campsite could be seen in the distance, ahead of their last walking line.

Two hours were spent looking for the right path before Team Illinois decided to bed down. No one could be certain of why the path was now split and whether or not the confusing glow stick placement was accidental or intentional. The mind tends to assume all sorts of interesting and evil scenarios when it's under stress and the confusing markers had provided the fodder for multiple conspiracy theories. While Team Illinois contemplated their options, eight more competitors had joined them during the two hour delay and all decided that it would be safer if they waited until they could be found. Some of the incoming eight were in bad physical shape, suffering from exhaustion and dehydration.

Stopping and resting was the necessary thing to do for many of them. "Attie" was apparently now guiding other runners as well, walking into their makeshift camp with the group of eight, and curling up with his old friends from Illinois. The friendly mutt had become the guardian angel of the Atacama Desert, and seemed to gravitate towards those in most need of help. The group of 11 competitors huddled together and waited for help while Attie watched over them. In Joel's words,

"After pulling out some snack food, we all started falling asleep. Gunnar (A new friend and fellow competitor) and Andrew (the BBC cameraman), figured out how to use the cameraman's GPS to try to radio latitude and longitude readings back to base camp to help them find us. While we lay out, we were able to watch shooting stars from the top of the sand dunes. The sky has never looked as clear and bright as it did in the silence and darkness of the desert."

It wasn't long before the sound of a truck engine could be heard in the distance. The group of 11 rose to their feet and began looking for the headlights of the truck against the desert floor. Signaling with tiny head lamps of their own, the rescue truck and one other vehicle found the group of 11 and took on those in the worst condition for a ride back to camp. Nancy was one of those struggling to keep any sort of pace with her own team, and she took a seat in the truck. The remaining group followed the small convoy on foot as it drove slowly through the sand. It would be a short run after all. Team Illinois and the others who had joined them, were only a few miles from their destination. Close but still far if you have no idea where you are in relation to the camp. Dave and Joel would finish the 50 mile day on foot, arriving in the worst shape any of them had ever been after an endurance race. Nothing would have properly prepared them for the rigors of the Chilean Desert.

As soon as the truck started moving in the direction of the tent camp, they passed an incline leading to the edge of a rock cliff.

Dave and Joel noticed that it was positioned along the same line they had started to run after they found the split to the trail. "We could have easily run off the edge of that cliff without ever knowing what hit us." Dave would later comment.

Team Illinois was exhausted and they all slept well that night, as well as they could have given the uneven desert floor and the almost non existent padding of their sleeping bags. The next morning they had heard that by 3:00 AM, all remaining competitors were rounded up by race vehicles and returned to the safety of camp. The mystery of the split trail would remain, but everyone was at least safe. Those lost in the desert were given credit for their finish time based on when they were returned to camp. No one should have been penalized based on trail markers that couldn't be found. Still, the multiple hour total delay suffered by Team Illinois and the other eight in their finishing group had pushed them all back from the race leaders who had finished the 50 miles despite the trail marker fiasco.

Friday July 9, 2004 – Rest Day

Casualties were everywhere. The previous five days of desert racing including the 50 mile challenge, had literally beaten the competitors into the ground. Many stayed in their tents, crawling out only for a short walk to the fire pit for some hot water to pour into a freeze dried meal. Others would socialize with competitors turned friends from other countries. Team Illinois would commiserate with the group about how they got lost and how Nancy's Ipod had run out of juice with no place to plug in and recharge. The same would be true for humans on day six. All any of them wanted was a way to recharge. A warm bath, soft bed, real food, clean water and tranquilizing views of green fields or open water would have been welcome, but there would be nothing to take the sting away from the previous five days. They ate as much of their freeze dried rations as they could hold down, took naps during the day and tried desperately to take care of their feet in the dirty conditions of their campsite. Toe nails had either been chipped or hammered off due to the constant pounding of the desert, and blisters were common on the heels and soles of their feet.

Despite the overwhelming exhaustion, a few of the RacingThePlanet entrants found a challenge of a different kind. One of the local volunteers had brought in a Boogie Board the night before. Showing the competitors how easy it was to surf the dune sand, the young man passed the board to Gunnar, one of the individual competitors and new friend to Team Illinois. Though he tried to stand up on the board at first, Gunnar took his first tumble complete with mouthful of sand before deciding to sit on the board and ride it to the bottom of the dune. A few others tried with similar results, but it was a good diversion to the day. Joel took the opportunity to conserve energy and do laundry.

"We've spent the morning eating, rinsing our clothes and bodies, and just hanging out. I have yet to take a look at my feet. I'm a little afraid of what might be lurking under my socks. Several day old bandages (wrapped) over trashed toes and oozing blisters can not lead to anything pretty."

Competitors would stroll out and back into their tents all day long, grabbing some water then returning to the light padding of their sleeping bags for a nap. Teams ate dinner separately that night, coming and going from the crowd assembled by the fire pit. Some were more talkative than others depending on the shape their bodies were in. Others shuffled out of their tents in flimsy hotel slippers, grabbed some water and then shuffled back without saying a word to anyone.

Before retiring for the night, Joel and Dave planned to remove everything from their packs that wasn't absolutely needed for the final day and the 10 mile dash to the finish line. For those things that weren't needed but the team still wanted to bring home, Joel and Dave decided to divide those items between their packs, lightening Nancy's pack a little more. Everything else not necessary for the last ten miles went into the trash.

They all were trying to think of a way to bring Attie home. He had spent the day in camp with the group, stopping by to see Nancy from time to time and feeding off the leftovers from each competitor. No one could figure out who he might belong to, or how he had ever survived out in the desert. As Team Illinois retired for the evening, Attie chose to wander out back to the fire and curl up in a warm spot on the sand. Nancy was reaching her own breaking point despite the rest day and wanted nothing more than to be finished running across the hot sands of Chile.

"The rest day was a mixed blessing for me. While other competitors played, I laid in the tent, wanting to be done. I was disturbed at the state of my feet. It still hurt to walk. The sun was too hot. I slept, ate what I could, and dreamed of being done. The will I had to finish was now diminishing. Could I really still go 10 miles? Dave and Joel were now talking about time. 90 minutes, Joel said. 90 minutes? I thought. Are you kidding? I told myself 2 hours. 2 hours 2 minutes tops. We agreed on a run nine minutes, walk one strategy. I fretted more and more about 10 miles than ever before. I reminded myself of the 10-miler I had done (a few months ago). 1:15, and that was easy. Every moment seemed like an eternity. Even looking at the stars through wonderful telescopes was stressful because I was cold, coughing and my bottom lip was starting to swell. I went to sleep Friday and awoke what must have been every hour just wanting to be done. When it was finally light and Dave and Joel were awake, the first thing I said was, I need to get out of here."

Final Stage - Day 7

Joel checked the posted standings that morning and found that Team Illinois could not possibly win in the team category based on their total elapsed time, but they still had a chance to win the stage. There would be no way to make up the hours that separated them from the leaders in a 10 mile final run. Based on the rankings and posted times Team Illinois could finish no higher than 4th place, but only if they turned in a solid effort to finish the day. Still, they had agreed that their collective strategy would be to muster as much inner strength as possible and run hard all the way to the finish line. It was a matter of pride and a way to prove the mettle of the team. Joel, Nancy and Dave would push the pace for the entire 10 miles.

There was never a focus on individual performance with Team Illinois, but it was also clear that Nancy would wind up posting one of the better individual race times in the Women's category, based on the overall performance of the team. Regardless of standings or the strategy of many other competitors on the course, Team Illinois continued to run at their maximum possible speed without pacing themselves with any other competitor. Others were content to hold onto their place in the standings, knowing they could not improve their overall finish in the race with a faster completion time. For many on the last day of Atacama, it was simply a social run.

Team Illinois had started to pass other individual competitors on the course as they kept their pace up. Some comments were heard along the way, encouraging them to take it easy and slow down. Everyone it seemed was well aware of everyone else's chances for improving or slipping a finish position or two. There was no real reason for them to keep pushing themselves, but they did anyway.

Attie was there again among the crowd on the starting line, but got lost somewhere back in the pack after the race started. Many of the competitors chose to run a modest pace with a larger group, and Attie stayed with them. Maybe he was making sure that nobody would be left behind. Maybe he was just looking for more freeze dried leftovers. Team Illinois pulled away from the initial group and never looked back.

The final stage would be another flat and technically easy course, but then again the final stage of the race was all about speed, if you had any left that is. The course was laid out fairly straight with much of their time was spent on a dirt road leading from one small town into the next. At one point in the 10 mile stage, Nancy had called out to Joel who was running well ahead of her.

"Slow down!"

Joel turned back to reply, "We ran your pace all week, it's time for you to run ours."

Nine miles into the final stage Nancy, Joel and Dave continued down a narrow dirt path that ultimately approached San Pedro and the finish line. The road would widen and run parallel to the city center walls, which were made from mud and brick. Passing one last length of wall, Team Illinois rounded the corner to see the causeway leading towards the city center and the colorful sponsor banners of the finish line. They would be the first team to see the finish in that last stage, and Nancy began to break down into tears at the sight. Dave would admit later, that all three of them were wet around the eyes, as the life and near-death journey and the mental and physical test was finally over.

Team Illinois finished running harder than they had started, and with 20 meters to go instinctively grabbed each other's hands once again. They crossed the finish line with hands clasped and arms raised in celebration of the team's accomplishment. This would eventually become their trademark in every race they entered as a team, and the photograph taken as they crossed the finish line at Atacama would become famous among the racing elite. It would become a symbol of what Team Illinois stood for; unity, self-sacrifice, and shared jubilation.

Joy and sense of accomplishment had overwhelmed them at the finish line. Dave could not stop shaking his head and smiling at the same time, as if still doubting that he had actually finished the 150 miles in the harsh Atacama Desert. Nancy would cling to

Joel as they celebrated together as a couple, smiling through the pain and coming to the realization that they could accomplish just about anything together. Everyone had individually sacrificed, and yet all three of them had done well as a team.

As other competitors crossed the finish line in smaller groups, applause would ring out across San Pedro's city center. Nancy and Joel looked back to see if they could see Attie running along with them, but there was no sign of him. Eventually Dave and Joel had asked a larger group of finishers if they had seen the group's new mascot, and finally someone confirmed seeing Attie running with the larger group but splitting off and disappearing once they reached the city walls.

It seemed odd to Dave that Attie would not be with them at their moment of triumph, to celebrate a desert crossing and to eat and drink with them. There was plenty of food and water after all, and Attie should have been as thirsty and hungry as the two legged mammals who had actually registered for the race. As the brotherhood and sisterhood of RacingThePlanet competitors celebrated the completion of a near impossible journey, their four legged guardian angel would disappear as mysteriously as he appeared to them six days earlier.

Pictures from the "Atacama Crossing" 2004

Photos provided by Joel Burrows. Team Illinois prepares for the first stage of the Atacama Crossing race with a pose for sponsors and smiles for the camera.

Photos provided by Dave Kuhnau. Attie the guardian angel (above) rests with the team out on the open sand. Dave's melted shoe (below) makes its debut on film.

Photos provided by Joel Burrows. Melting snow fed streams fill slot canyons across the trail (above). Nancy completed dehydrated (below) waits in the medical tent for an IV.

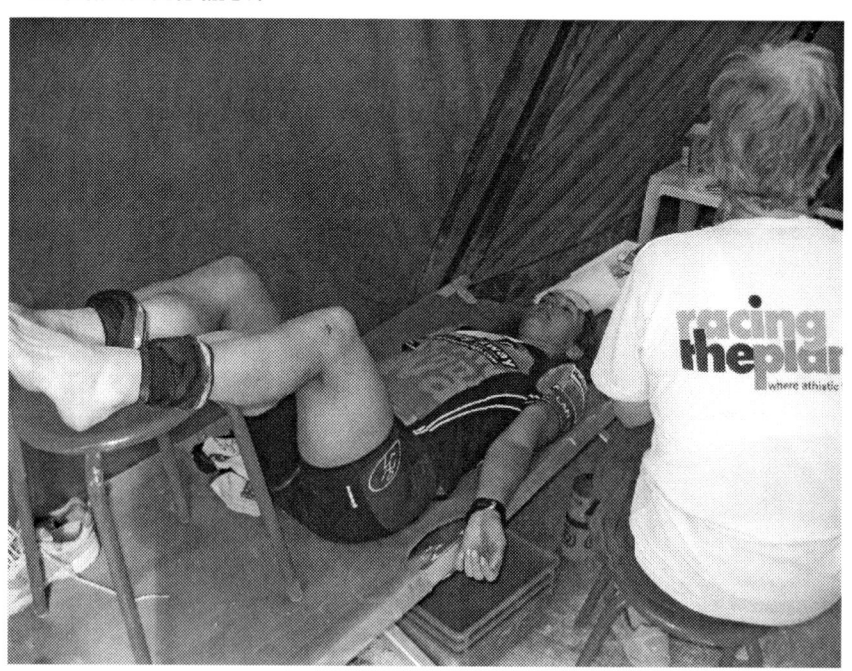

Photos provided by Dave Kuhnau. The jagged edges of the salt formations on the flats extend out to the horizon (above). Joel surveys the damage from multiple blisters on his right foot (below).

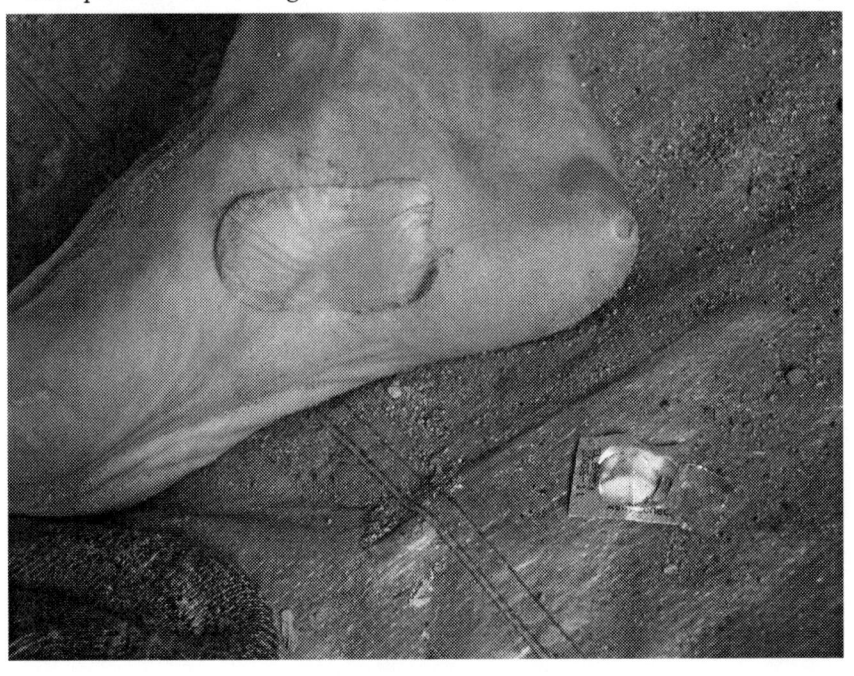

49

Top photo provided by Joel Burrows. Team Illinois follows the desert path towards the mountains in the distance.
Bottom photo provided by Dave Kuhnau. Emotion overwhelms all three members of Team Illinois after the arduous 150 desert crossing.

Photo provided by Joel Burrows. The awards banquet held after the race had completed, provided all with a chance to experience the joys of soap and running water for the first time in 7 days. With fresh clothes and new friends, Team Illinois enjoys the simple pleasure of cold water and professionally prepared food. Pictured from left to right: Dave Kuhnau, Nancy Fudacz-Burrows, Joel Burrows, Chuck Walker and Derek Kwik.

Chapter 4 - Atacama in Retrospect

Examples about how the human mind and body could be pushed beyond what it had accepted as its own physical or mental limit were nearly endless. When the body began to shut down, there always proved to be some gas left in the tank. When the mind was convinced that there was no longer any logical reason for continuing, a little push was all that was needed to turn things around.

Sometimes it was inspiration drawn from the memory of a family member or a friend or even a stray dog that kept the mind and body moving. In other examples, Team Illinois found inspiration within their own team. "If Nancy can gut it out, so can I". There was an unspoken air of trust and commitment among the three. No one person would leave any other member of the team behind even though the team had really just met six months earlier. No matter the circumstance, the members of Team Illinois would be there for each other, period. There was comfort and inspiration in that basic, mutual understanding.

Before even starting the race and before knowing all the variables that would impact their success as a team, Team Illinois expected to win a type of endurance race they had never participated in. Some would say that the goal was too lofty and unattainable. Perhaps it would have been a more realistic goal if Team Illinois had direct experience with that specific type of race. Estimating performance becomes more accurate after gaining experience with the type of endeavor being estimated. Still, given as many of the unknowns that faced Team Illinois in the Atacama Desert, they performed pretty darn well.

There were two distinct paradigms that can be drawn from Team Illinois' first attempt at that kind of race. First, the concept of being able to push the individual or team further than it could possibly imagine, applies to more situations than just endurance racing in the desert. Second and maybe most importantly, a team can accomplish more as a cohesive work group than the combined sum of their parts. Nancy may have never finished the stage on day three without her teammates. Dave may have never have pried himself up from the desert floor on day four if Nancy hadn't pushed his resolve, and Joel would have indeed bonked on day five if Nancy and Dave weren't there to pull him along to the finish.

Every member of the team had a bad day. Every person on the face of the earth has his or her own idea of what their personal limits are. Think about it yourself for a moment. How many consecutive hours could you spend working alone at whatever you do for a living? How many miles would you say you could walk or run right now, given the way you feel right now? How many hills could you hike over?

The lesson learned by Team Illinois at Atacama is that true personal limits are difficult to measure. For Team Illinois it was not just a matter of someone standing on the side, offering words of encouragement. A true definition of team means that each member has a personal stake in the other's success. You willingly help a team member because you've learned that their success with a task is also your success in the bigger picture. They know they can lean on you when they need a helping hand and you can lean on them in turn. There is mutual trust, shared workload and by default, mutual reward.

Joel summed up the final day of the challenge as Team Illinois finished fourth in the team competition among an international field, with Nancy taking best overall female finishing time.

"Today we ran as Team Illinois. For those at home who thought we could or could not (finish this race), WE DID. Although it was a short 10 miles, we ran it in 1:16 flat and put together a great last day. We finished the last stage ahead of the rest of the teams. It was the race day we wanted all along. Nan didn't feel great, but she ran strong. Dave and I were able to keep it together to carry us across the finish line. At this point, it looks like Nan will be the top female finisher, an accomplishment we are all proud of."

Still back at the San Pedro Square, the cheering continued and Team Illinois continued to applaud others as they crossed the finish line. New friends made along the way were quick to share hugs and cheers as they ran into Nancy or Joel or Dave. The pain had left them all for the moment, as elation became the common emotion for all in San Pedro.

The endorphins would fade eventually, and each member of the RacingThePlanet entourage was starting to feel aches and pains again. Nancy started to long for the simple feeling of hot and clean water running through her hair and down her body. After seven days of sleeping in their own sweat on dirty ground, the first order of business for most competitors was to wash off the stink and the stains that had collected during the last week. Nancy wanted nothing more than to stand in the running water until her mind would accept that the body was finally clean. Nancy stayed in the shower for what seemed like hours, but most of the pain wouldn't wash away. She would later offer a great quote referring to the effects of wearing the same clothes for seven consecutive days, "Eventually you reach maximum 'stinkiness', and it really doesn't get any worse." Thankfully, soap can fix that problem.

Some of the competitors had moved from the small town of San Pedro back to Santiago for some more rest and relaxation.

The first order of business in Santiago was a mandatory visit to Starbucks and then McDonalds. It was an unexpected reward for the three from Illinois to find a little Americana in Santiago, but fresh coffee and cheeseburgers it would be.

They continued on from there, stopping at local markets and buying trinkets and artwork before having to head off to the airport for the return flight home. It would be another long and brutal flight, but the members of Team Illinois slept through most of it, each body needing the recovery time and the sleep. The challenge and adventure of a lifetime would meet the harsh reality of a return to work the day after reaching the Chicago O'Hare airport.

When Joel and Nancy returned to the East Bank Club, the support, the kudos and the praise was overwhelming. Local public recognition was intense as well. Team Illinois had made news in the local papers and were featured in other local Chicago magazine publications.

Dave's first day back at work was also a blur. His work space had been decorated with things to remind him about an incident that had happened to his shoe. Everyone wanted to hear the story about how he could have possibly survived the grueling race. As Dave began to talk about the conditions of a particular stage, or a challenge that faced the team, he found that he wasn't truly able to describe it properly. He could not verbally paint the subtle colors of the sunset, or describe exactly how the lungs burned while trying to run at 13,000 feet. Then there was the team. Dave's descriptions of a particular event were always framed with the two-letter pronoun "we". Unconsciously, Dave would talk about a medical condition, or how the water ran out in a critical point in the mid day sun, but he always referred to that particular challenge in a way to show that it affected them all.

"We really needed to get out of the sun" or "Our new found friend Attie followed us from campsite to campsite." Dave was already missing his teammates, wanting them there to share in the story telling and the admiration coming from Dave's co-workers. It was a little thing, but a telling thing. Dave's adventure with Joel and Nancy had fundamentally changed him in ways that he could not yet fathom.

Nancy would describe her first few days back at home as "strange". Access to warm shelter, hot coffee, clean clothes, air conditioning, and unlimited varieties of food seemed difficult to absorb when they had learned to survive with so much less. She thought about the training that helped prepare them for the race. They had suffered so much and focused so hard on accomplishing their goal that when it was reached, home became just another shelter at a checkpoint. Joel and Nancy felt like they needed to be with their teammate Dave. They were frantically exchanging e-mails to make sure Dave was "OK" while Dave checked in with them to see if they were recuperating as well. The inseparable team of three was forced to separate in accordance with their own normal lives. Living and working only a few miles apart, their team was now just an entity on paper with a number attached to it. 40:54. Team Illinois' finish time at Atacama. Dave sent Nancy an e-mail after his first day back at work in the U.S.

"Nan, I got back to my client site today and found that they had decorated my cube to welcome me back. I have attached the photos of the cube. It was funny as it contained a Bob Dole puppet wearing burned up shoes, a cup full of money for "Dave's new shoe fund" and a top ten list of 'Why Dave did the race'. I have to say I was overwhelmed by the response. I have had so many people come up and say today, that they started working out again last week because what we were doing was an inspiration. Literally, I have had 7 people come up and say that. Blessings come in all shapes and sizes and I am just overwhelmed by the support and excitement from people I've only known for 60 days."

Nancy summarized the aftermath of the race by wondering if she would ever try a challenge like Atacama again.

"The question of the hour seems to be: 'Would you do it again?' Hmmm….sometimes I think about the pure torture. I think about the mistakes we made, and how we could be better, how I could train better. (How about maybe training off road once and a while…carrying less…did I really need that Ipod? Bringing more electrolyte, more salty food…how did I think I'd eat oatmeal every morning, yuk! And then, I remember the experience. How I was totally present during the good, and the bad. How everyone worked together for one common goal: TO FINISH. I am so proud of our team. I am so proud to have been a part of it. I worry that any 'next one' would never carry the same joy and excitement. I remember that we swore in blood that we would NEVER, under ANY CIRCUMSTANCE do one of these again. My daily mantra was, 'One and done'. We told the other racers they were crazy for doing more than one. I told my teammates that the next time I wanted to play in the desert, we were going to Vegas. I said, 'never'."

Measuring Success

This is a very subjective topic and the answer you might get from each person asked about Team Illinois' performance at Atacama would be different. For any team, success criteria needs to be defined at the beginning of the project or season or event. It provides a single goal for the whole team to focus on. Some might say that Team Illinois failed to achieve their goal of winning the team event based on their declaration of that goal back in January 2004. "We're going to win this thing."

The measure of success should be based on how well the team adjusts to these uncontrolled and unplanned circumstances, while still delivering a quality result. For Team Illinois, it was a matter of sticking together as a team no matter the hardship. They improvised and adapted to conditions that they did not plan to encounter. Even when their original goal of winning the team competition slipped away on Day 5, they still pushed hard towards the finish line to end the race as strong as possible.

Team Illinois returned home to both accolades and disappointment. Even some of their closest friends and acquaintances at Chicago's local running clubs had commented, "but you still finished fourth, right?" Despite achieving a huge personal milestone and finishing with a strong completion time, Team Illinois was left to stew on the fact that they didn't finish with a first place title.

Though Nancy was the women's champion overall, the team's performance was what mattered to her. The negative commentary was internalized as a bitter pill for all three members of Team Illinois. To anyone who sits as an outsider to the world of competitive running, what Team Illinois accomplished in their very first attempt at this unique competition was truly amazing. And in case you missed it, Nancy kicked ass.

Was their original goal achieved? No.

Was their endeavor a success? Absolutely.

Chapter 5 - The Gobi March

After Dave Kuhnau returned home and settled back into work mode, he took what little spare time he had and started to play back the short stories he had captured with his pocket video recorder. It was a chronological but sporadic series of images and short stories, but they seemed to frame the entire seven day adventure perfectly. The colors of the banners on the day one starting line blended with the excitement on the faces of everyone about to begin the arduous journey across the desert. As the race wore on, the images reflected the physical and emotional toll taken on those who chose to push on to the end.

Perhaps the most telling image was captured towards the end of the Atacama Crossing where Nancy Fudacz-Burrows rolled forward out of her sleeping bag to look straight into the camera. With matted hair and sunburned face, an exhausted Nancy proclaimed with as much intensity as she could muster, "I swear we are never doing this again".

In the two months following their return to the U.S. in mid-July, Team Illinois was heavily involved with wrap up activities surrounding their commitments to charities and sponsors. Checks were sent off to the charities they had collected money for, and they also participated in multiple events hosted by sponsors. Team Illinois had still finished the competition as the top team from

North America and coupled with Nancy's award as top female finisher, provided for great photo opportunities. There was plenty of medallion chrome and ribbon for the camera, and Team Illinois remained truly grateful to the sponsors who helped get them to Chile.

Post race doldrums started to haunt all three members of the Chicago based team soon after their return. Each was overwhelmed at work after having taken two weeks off for the race event, but once the day's activities came to an end, the "blahs" started to kick back in. Joel had described the feeling as "being dissatisfied with just sitting around".

Nancy and Joel stayed in contact with Dave electronically, but work was keeping them apart. Weekend social engagements were a rare opportunity to get together and laugh at the pain they had all suffered just a few short weeks earlier. Nancy and Joel had been talking about their next opportunity for a marathon, but for them it would have been familiar and uninteresting territory. Weeks after Nancy swore she would "never do this again", she and Joel were actually discussing the possibility of entering the next scheduled RacingThePlanet event in the Gobi Desert, aptly named "The Gobi March".

Unknown to Dave or Joel at first, Nancy began to e-mail Mary Gadams at RacingThePlanet about the possibility of signing up for the next event in China. Reserving a woman's right to change her mind, Nancy was preparing herself to do just that. Her phrasing had changed only slightly from "We're never doing this again" to "I want to do it again". In September of 2004, Nancy had officially signed up herself and Joel for the Gobi March race in China, knowing Dave would have to fall in line. Good teammates do that by the way, and Dave fell in line just as Nancy had predicted.

With another six months to find sponsorship, correct their training plans and improve their gear, Team Illinois had embarked on a new project. Their new target date was scheduled for April 22, 2005 to be executed in the searing desert heat of China's Gobi Desert, and Nancy was once again the one mapping out the strategy.

Learning from the Mistakes at Atacama

Team Illinois performed a little analysis into their own preparation and performance from Chile, and revealed some common mistakes that teams make when faced with a challenge for the first time. They were forced to make some assumptions about the proper training, about the desert terrain, about their equipment and about body chemistry in the rigors of the desert heat. These assumptions had to be made in lieu of actual experience. When Nancy and Joel first planned to build their team, Dave was selected for his speed along with his personality. Team Illinois was fast, on flat land without backpacks that is.

Experience from Atacama now told them that desert racing required other skills and other muscle groups not normally used in marathon running or bicycling in a triathlon. It became clear that their training in advance of their trip out to China would have to change. Nancy started to revisit the posted stage completion times of other teams at Atacama and she found that success in the desert seemed to be more about consistency of performance and strength rather than speed alone.

Training plans changed to include more off road work in the forest preserves of the outlying Chicago suburbs, more running on stair machines at the East Bank Club, and more weight training. They were forced to train individually during the week but met up on weekends to participate in other locally sanctioned races or mini-events sponsored by their favorite Chicago running clubs.

Team Illinois also seemed to start a training trend, at least in the Chicago area. Dave had commented about his weekend training later in the fall of 2004 and spring of 2005 where he spotted an occasional backpack on other runners. This was something never seen in previous years, at least among those running distance along the Chicago lakeshore. Some would still ask about his backpack from time to time, and Dave would politely respond. It was clear however, that others were catching on to the next incremental technique in physical endurance training.

Other adjustments were made to their equipment as the team looked for ways to decrease the weight carried in the Gobi Desert. Electrolyte packages and food combinations were reevaluated based on their performance at Atacama, and other trainers and dietary experts were consulted for recommendations on the proper mix. The trouble was that none of the people who could be consulted had any experience of a seven day, 150 mile run through the heat of the desert. Nancy and Joel were fortunate to have studied the same topic in college as part of their personal training curriculum and ultimately, they would need to build a formula specific to each individual human body.

Bio-Chemistry 101

Body chemistry or more accurately stated "blood" chemistry, is a wildly important aspect to the professional or amateur athlete. If we were discussing the average runner or cyclist or any weekend sports warrior, electrolyte balance is something that doesn't typically need to be addressed. When a 5K weekend run is over, water and food can still be easily processed by the body to balance out blood chemistry. Find a chilled bottle of water, nice salami on rye, a fresh beefsteak tomato and blood chemistry automatically finds its own equilibrium. It also happens to be yummier than an energy bar and tube of electrolyte gel.

When a body is stressed in a multi-day marathon, or multi-stage cycling event or any long term physical strain, muscles build up toxins and internal organs will eventually begin to shut down without the proper mix of chemical agents in the blood. Without the right amount of water, sodium, potassium and chlorides, internal organs are immediately impacted.

It does not take long for the body to experience muscle or internal organ stress. Nancy was faced with exactly that same scenario on day three of Atacama. Her body began to shut down from the lack of water and the associated imbalance of those same three basic blood chemistry elements. Unless sodium, potassium and chlorides are balanced properly throughout the stress of a seven day desert race, there is no chance of finishing.

Understanding the importance of that concept is the first step towards building a solution. Finding someone experienced in managing blood chemistry in an event like any of the RacingThePlanet challenges, is another story. Team Illinois would adjust their mix of electrolytes for the Gobi Desert race based on their own personal experiences from Atacama and each of them would have a different formula for keeping the machine that is the human body, running.

Spring of 2005

After January passed and Team Illinois had become tired of running on indoor tracks and the freezing temperatures on off-road runs, Nancy began to look for local competitions in March that would better prepare them for Gobi at the end of April. As it turns out, there was a scheduled 50K race for April 2nd along the Lake Michigan shoreline. The timing of the 50K put them almost too close to their departure date on April 19th. If anyone on the team took an injury, there may not be enough time to recover in time for the Gobi March.

Accepting the risk, Team Illinois registered for the Chicago Lakefront – George Cheung Memorial 50K and prepared for the 32 mile long race. Each reconfigured their backpacks to carry about 25 pounds and hoped that all the additional stair climbing and off road training would help them better manage the weight of the packs over a longer distance.

Warranting strange looks once again from the other competitors on the starting line, Team Illinois found themselves explaining the reason for the backpacks to a new audience. Though some faces were familiar among the crowd, the backpacks were still a conversation starter for those who could not imagine running the 50K distance with any equipment handicap, much less 25 pounds of it.

Team Illinois ran the distance as comfortably as they could expect given the flat, paved surface of the Chicago shoreline. "Mindless running" Nancy once referred to it when thinking about the luxury of needing only to focus on the direction her feet were pointed. There would be no technically challenging hills, rocks, streams or sand dunes to negotiate. The legs could just run.

Team Illinois completed the course in 5:26:18, crossing the finish line together and feeling about as good as they ever had following a similar distance. They could tell the difference the training had made during the last five months, where each of them felt stronger after that type of distance than just a year before without backpacks.

Flight to Beijing

13 flight hours from Chicago and located literally on the other side of the world; Beijing became the first stop for the next RacingThePlanet group of competitors before the last flight to a smaller town on the outskirts of the Gobi Desert. While Nancy, Joel and Dave stayed overnight at the Grand Hyatt Hotel in Beijing, most of the 98 entrants representing 22 different countries assembled in the race sponsored hotel in the final stop city of Urumqi, pronounced (Ooh-room-chi).

It wouldn't be good enough this time to finish well among the pack. Nancy, Joel and Dave had agreed when they began their new training regimen for Gobi back in September of 2004 that they had entered the competition to win, not just finish well. The original stated goal for China was the same as it was for Chile, "Win the team competition", but the team was stronger and more experienced the second time around. The stop in Beijing was just a simple overnight stay for Team Illinois and they looked forward to seeing some of the friends they had made at Atacama upon their ultimate arrival in Urumqi.

They completed the last leg of their journey and arrived the following morning into Urumqi and the Hoitak Hotel which also served as race headquarters. Joel began to scout out some of the other teams arriving and found the all-male team from Singapore looking very strong. It was clear that Team Illinois would have their work cut out for them if they wanted to be competitive in China. Some of the friends made in Chile were arriving sporadically too, and they spotted Chuck Walker before the group headed out to base camp for the night. Chuck had developed a bond with many from the Atacama Crossing and proved to be a strong competitor and great motivator. He had missed out winning his age bracket at Atacama by just over 4 hours, and he looked to have the determination necessary to win at Gobi. Chuck, a former "military guy" as Nancy referred to him, was affectionately described as a "bad ass". Nancy, Joel and Dave were glad to see Chuck had made the trek out to China for the Gobi March.

Drama in another form had developed on the streets of Urumqi the night before as well. Joel had started to look for his brother at the hotel but had no idea if he had made it to Beijing or Urumqi safely. Todd Burrows had signed up as a race volunteer and was supposed to be safely on his way to the Hoitak Hotel, but his original plane tickets that connected him from Beijing to Urumqi were invalid. After a cell phone call or two, the RTP staff was able to set up Todd with the next connecting flight into Urumqi and instructions to take a cab to the Hoitak Hotel.

Upon arrival at the Urumqi airport, Todd provided his best English instructions to the cab driver and headed off towards what he hoped was the right hotel. The driver apparently had other plans in mind, and made a stop to pick up a buddy who took up residence in the front passenger seat of the cab. Todd sat back and then watched as the cab started off again away from the lights of the city. After several attempts to explain what hotel he needed to be taken to without a response, Todd began to fear the worst.

Todd had explained to Joel later, that he waited for the vehicle to slow down in traffic, taking the opportunity to grab his bag and jump out the rear passenger door. The driver of the cab and his buddy stopped quickly and jumped out of the cab to chase Todd while he ran towards a small local hotel on the same street. As soon as Todd entered the hotel, the cab driver had disappeared. Todd immediately asked to use the phone so that he could call Joel, or anyone from RacingThePlanet who might answer, but the hotel clerk explained that Todd would have to rent a room first. Once Todd checked in, he was finally able to use a phone. He then contacted one of the RTP officials and politely asked to be picked up, followed by "Please?" They had agreed that a hotel sponsored cab would be a better choice in an unfamiliar town and the small hotel assisted Todd with directions and a reliable cab company. It was the least they could do after charging for a night's stay. With the right cab, Todd would arrive safely at the Hoitak Hotel a little shaken, but not stirred.

Urumqi was the meeting point for the Gobi competitors and was also noted for being the most physically land locked city in the world. Further away from the sea than any other city on the face of the Earth, Urumqi was a charming but soot covered city in the Northwestern Xinjiang Province of China towards the northernmost end of China's Silk Road.

Competitors were allowed to rest for another day in Urumqi before being taken off to the edge of the Gobi and the beginning of their 250 Kilometer, 150 mile journey. Dave Kuhnau had commented how readily available the sushi and other varieties of fish seemed to be in Urumqi. "For a city that's nowhere near an ocean, the sushi seemed to be everywhere. There was more fish and seafood on the buffet table than I could have found in Kennebunkport."

The following day, an entire line of busses and other vehicles gathered to transport the group to its final destination at a camp near a small farming village on the outskirts of the Gobi. As the line of vehicles made its way through the winding trails and dirt roads of Northwestern China, the caravan took on the distant look of a centipede as it followed the trail left then right then forward again. The small village of Donggouxiang, would eventually be the final stop for RacingThePlanet crew. It would also be the last supper for them before being forced to sustain their bodies with the joys and culinary excellence of freeze dried food.

RacingThePlanet was becoming famous for their banquets the night before the official race start. Last minute details for race rules and any changes in the course layout could be discussed over a hearty meal before all would turn in for the night. At Gobi, the meal would be barbeque, and appetites were healthy. Team Illinois was feeling confident in their adjusted training and looked forward to seeing what sort of pace they could maintain on the first day.

Before turning in for the evening, a few of the competitors climbed a nearby hill that overlooked their first night's camp. While the glow of the fire pit lit their semi-circle of tents, a cluster of sheep and goats were being herded through the campsite on their way to a different grazing location. It was a final reminder to all that food and water would be scarce in the Gobi.

Day One

As the group of competitors approached the starting line, they were treated to a ceremonial dance by local children all dressed in brightly colored costumes in contrasting shades of red and blue. The children continued their interpretive welcome dance against the backdrop of their local village and small single-story homes made from brick and mud. Chinese government officials carried the welcome further, and Ian Adamson thanked the local townspeople for their hospitality while his words were translated over a portable sound system.

Once the pomp and protocol were completed, a local village woman aided the official start to the Gobi March by pounding out the last remaining seconds on a drum. With her final drum beat, the starting pistol was fired and 98 determined competitors were off to seven days of adventures and challenges unknown.

At the beginning of a major endurance race, everyone on the starting line is confident that the outcome of the race will be positive for them. It seems to be a core attribute for most athletes and a driving motivator if you ever hope to complete a near-impossible journey like a 150 mile desert crossing. You have to believe down to your soul that you can accomplish the goal, even though it might be a lofty one.

Team Illinois believed that they could win at Gobi. The belief in the goal was based on a formula including careful preparation, experience from the Atacama Crossing, and the knowledge that they could rely on each other to help carry the whole team forward, no matter the circumstance. For Dave, there was an additional motivation that stung him like a bad paper cut. He remembered back to a personal exchange of words after returning from Atacama in 2004.

"The memory of a close personal friend calling our North American Team trophy from Atacama a 'bullshit' award was enough of a motivation for me. All I will have to do is remember those words, and I'll be able to keep moving."

Joel was still struggling with some minor injuries to his knee and groin from the Chicago 50K which made running painful over distance, but Team Illinois was becoming good at blocking out little annoyances like pain. Their pace was strong and each member seemed to be able to carry the weight of their backpacks a little more comfortably than at Atacama. Joel and Dave's packs weighed in at just over 26 and 24 pounds respectively, where Nancy's weighed in close to 22 pounds.

Everyone carried between 11 and 14 pounds of food on their backs depending on the calories each expected to replenish at the end of a stage. Dave had decided to go lighter and eat less which saved him about 2 pounds overall. Joel had hoped Dave wouldn't go hungry, but they also remembered back to Atacama where at the 50 mile stage they were all dumping extra food into the trash to lighten the load.

Team Illinois ran along side with some of their friends from Atacama including Chuck Walker from the U.S. and Jacob Nielsen from Denmark, as they all set a blistering pace (literally) from the starting line to the first checkpoint. The Gobi March would be like the Atacama Crossing in that race leaders would push forward and fall back depending on how the body felt at that point in time. As electrolytes become imbalanced and dehydration starts to kick in, the body will simply slow down. Team Illinois seemed to exchange leads with some of their friends frequently as body chemistry governed everyone's performance.

Through the second checkpoint, Nancy, Joel and Dave were leading the team competition though Joel was starting to hit the wall after mile 15 and Nancy's dry heaves were in full force. Dave continued to run strong but was suffering with the pace they all had set. By the end of the first stage, Team Illinois had maintained the lead in the team competition but lost some ground as their pace slowed in the last five miles. Joel had also logged a formal protest to race officials as some competitors took advantage of a flat road next to the marked race trail. Running on any flat surface is always easier than an uneven racing trail, but it was unclear how much time those competitors might have made up on Team Illinois. Joel couldn't let the infraction go unreported.

"We just filed an official protest because so many of the racers took the road instead of staying on the course. We spent hours in a twisting, winding, rocky, dry creek bed following the flags while some took the easier trail. Many people passed and finished ahead of us (in camp). We'll see what happens in the morning."

Day Two

Joel woke up in the middle of the night sick to his stomach, and vomited what was left of his undigested dinner outside of the tent. Waking up Nancy in the process, Joel had been looking for some sort of sympathy but given the amount of ribbing Nancy took at Atacama for her own digestive troubles, she offered no such support. "What do you want me to do about it?" Nancy had asked. Joel said later, "Served me right, but when I woke up in the morning I felt much better."

Joel's protest filed the day before was reviewed by race officials and an adjustment was made to every competitor's completion times based on their average elapsed time between checkpoints. It was an attempt to standardize each runner's pace that day, and apply that formula to the last segment of the stage when all were supposed to be running through the creek bed. Stage times were adjusted for all, but the hour or so lead Team Illinois had gained before day two was nearly gone.

The aches and pains suffered after the first day of desert racing weren't welcome, but they were familiar. It reminded them all that this was the price paid for being a race leader. Experience from Atacama taught them to block out the pain and discomfort and focus on the trail ahead. Nancy sometimes referred to it as "mindless running" but Dave characterized it in a different way.

"At some point I start to visualize my body as some sort of large machine like a ship at sea. I can picture myself walking into the control room on my ship with two big windows facing outward to the world. From there I can put the whole ship on auto pilot, and the body keeps running. I have the luxury of walking around to other rooms on my ship, each door leading to happy memories or images. When the ship starts to slow down, I visit a special room with motivating memories and the engine starts to pick up speed again. As strange as that all sounds, it works very well."

Day two found many of the competitors hit a wall of a different variety. Checkpoints are placed at various intervals to make sure nobody is left behind in the desert. Spaced sometimes as close as seven miles apart, sometimes more than ten miles, they are a place to receive medical attention and water and also a place to validate your bearings as you leave towards the next checkpoint. Somewhere after day two - checkpoint two, Joel and Dave were exchanging roles as front runner, setting the pace for the whole team and passing many competitors along the way. Eventually the flag markers disappeared and the team faced another series of hills and sand dunes in front of them.

In a matter of minutes, other teams and individual runners starting accumulating at the same set of hills and nobody was sure where they might have run off the trail. Instead of wasting any time guessing at the proper direction to advance, the assembled group of lost souls had agreed to send five volunteers up to the top of nearby hills. They knew they were close to camp and hoped to see it from a higher vantage point. Joel had picked a hill made up of "skree" or small jagged rocks and pebbles, and one of the European competitors commented that Joel looked like a spider as he used both feet and hands to paw his way to the top. Joel found no sign of camp or flags to mark the trail. The collective decision was made to wait until race officials could find them all.

Monitoring performance of the racers between checkpoints is critical to determining if someone might be lost or injured. Based on average elapsed times for any given race and knowing the distance between checkpoints, officials could calculate if someone was in trouble out in the desert. Ian Adamson, an internationally known professional endurance racer was also the course designer for both the Atacama Crossing and the Gobi March races. Minutes after the growing group of lost runners missed their checkpoint, Ian drove out into the desert looking for any sign of foot traffic left by those who might be lost. An hour later, Ian had found the group and loaded them all into trucks to take them back to the trail. They had all somehow missed a turn about two kilometers behind them.

Fighting Over Shade

The mid-day sun at Gobi was hotter than Atacama, but the elevation was closer to sea level in China. Parts of the Gobi Desert actually fell below sea level, providing the perfect topographical conditions to hold in the sweltering heat. Competitors had to trade cooler temperatures at Atacama without air to breathe, for more oxygen but hotter temperatures at Gobi. Nancy was getting baked, literally, in the open desert and it was clear that she was suffering from the heat again. The only member of the team with any hair, dark hair yet, Nancy's pace was slowing throughout the day and the boys of Team Illinois were stopping their running pace more often to walk and rest.

Dave had suggested that Nancy hold his small sleeping pad over her head when they were walking in order to give her a break from the sun. Nancy blew Dave's suggestion off and wanted no part of it. It would have only been for two minutes out of every ten, but Nancy did not feel that the little shade that Dave was suggesting would do her any good. In the heat of the moment (bad pun), Dave asserted, "You know, I am a member of this team too. I'm not a personal trainer and I'm new to this desert racing stuff, but I think you would benefit from a little shade when we walk."

Nancy was surprised at first by Dave's comments and Joel opted to stay out of the argument. She did however agree to use the folded pad as their pace slowed to a ratio of walking one minute out of every four. They continued to run four minutes and walk one while Nancy held the pad over her head during the walking segments. Dave would take the pad back from her after the minute was completed and stick it under his arm for the next four minute run. The overall pace for Team Illinois had picked up for the remainder of stage two.

Nancy approached Dave back at camp and apologized for the disagreement. "Thank you for being persistent, the shade really helped." The argument was really after all, a disagreement about the solution to a perceived issue while all participants are under extreme stress. Other teams would have imploded under the same set of circumstances, but Nancy, Joel and Dave had learned to work through challenges while keeping their friendship and working relationship in tact.

Bittersweet Ending to Day Two

One of the more heart breaking stories from Gobi came at the expense of the host country's Team Esquel. Team Esquel from China had been impacted by the desert heat and separated from each other on the course coming into camp at different elapsed times. Breaking apart the team on the course for any reason meant team disqualification. It didn't mean that any of them would be removed from the race, but they could no longer post race times as a team. Each would continue to race as individual competitors from that point on.

China was indeed proud of hosting the race and the desert challenge out in the Gobi. It was a great public relations move for them, and growing race coverage by magazines and television provided a forum to feature the charm of their small towns and the open friendly nature of the people there. In order to build a team for the desert challenge, a five kilometer race was held in China to determine the three fastest competitors. Two male champions and one woman champion were selected and this became the foundation of the privately sponsored "Team Esquel".

Accomplished racing athletes in their own right, the newly formed team would be inexperienced with the rigors of desert endurance racing and the equipment needed to perform well. Not necessarily their fault for a first time 150 mile event, Team Esquel had outfitted themselves with heavier running pants and jackets, and a rugged backpack that could have been lighter. They had shared a tent with Team Illinois on that first night, and Joel, Nancy and Dave could see the equipment first hand.

The female teammate had safely returned to camp later in the day, walking in the distance somewhere after that last checkpoint. Team Illinois never knew what circumstances came to pass out in the desert for Team Esquel. Perhaps they tried to run a pace too fast too soon, or they had been hit by the heat just as hard as Team Illinois was on their first desert racing event in the Atacama Desert. She may have suffered like Nancy had suffered in trying to keep fluids down. The heat offered by the Gobi Desert was hammering everyone.

Team Illinois took the opportunity to settle into their tent, but received more bad news from the grapevine inside the camp. One of their friends from Atacama, Gunnar Nilsson from Sweden was an individual competitor with multiple marathons and two desert challenge races under his belt. It was an accidental fall and an injured ankle that ended the race for Gunnar, but he refused to let a little set back like cracked bones stop him from participating. Gunnar turned into a race volunteer the next day.

As the rest of camp was fighting the wind that seemed destined to rip their tents off the desert floor, a few of the volunteers and race participants climbed up a nearby hill to confront the wind. Maybe the plan was to scream at each gust and ask the weather to cooperate, or perhaps the group was preparing to offer a human sacrifice to some ancient desert god at the top of the hill.

Joel's brother Todd, Derek Kwik, and a few others had reached the summit, struggling to maintain their footing against the 40+

mph winds. Derek had raced Gobi the previous year and had come along as a volunteer in 2005. Joel had noticed the small group from his vantage point back in camp and they looked as if they were enjoying themselves. Joel said,

"They keep striking poses like something out of a science fiction movie because the wind was holding their bodies up as they leaned forward. Nan and I have been concerned about Todd and whether he is having a good time. I know they are working him hard, but he is teamed with Derek Kwik (our good friend from Hong Kong whom we met in Atacama) and they seem to have really hit it off. Claire and Camilla (Race Organizers) told us Todd is a keeper. We knew he'd work hard, but he has really shown the RacingThePlanet crew what he is made of."

Reaching the end of day two, the camp was met first with a team tragedy then an individual tragedy. The true meaning of the race was brought into perspective for the remaining competitors and survival under these conditions was more important than anything else. At the end of day two, Team Illinois knew they were lucky but also prepared to be in the position they currently enjoyed. The training in preparation for the Gobi March coupled with the experience they had gained in Chile was serving them well.

As the tent shook violently from the gusting wind, Dave glanced over to the opposite side of the tent where the reunited Team Esquel had bedded down for the night. He hoped that they could pull it together and reenergize themselves for a better race on day three. Before retiring for the evening, Dave felt the need to take care of one more piece of personal business.

"For some reason the exciting dinner I had had eaten wasn't sitting quite right and I grabbed my headlamp and some toilet paper to take care of whatever needed taking care of. I wandered off from camp out on the open sand and dug a hole, which of course was what we all had to do as part of the exciting world of endurance racing. The wind was blowing hard and I tried to consider the wind direction when choosing my location but just then another competitor took up residence about 50 yards behind me, directly in line with the wind. I turned around to make sure they could see my headlamp but it was too late to ask them to move. I tried to drop the paper into the hole but the wind took it and blew it back towards the unsuspecting victim. All I heard was a yell and an expletive. It was not my intention to create a projectile, but it is what it is. I turned out my headlamp and ran back into camp to mix in with the crowd. My anonymity was assured."

Day Three

The previous evening had required the diligent watch of tent zippers and corner posts. Competitors were up all night wondering if their tents would indeed blow away. Joel, Nancy and Dave were up from time to time as well, as lightning storms were added to the wind just to make sure everyone was paying attention. "All we're missing are locusts", Dave had tried to break the tension. As the storms passed, they fell back to sleep.

The terrain offered to the competitors on the third day was perhaps the Gobi Desert's way of apologizing for the evening's wind and lightning storm. It would be a marathon distance of about 26 miles that day, but the race would wind through beautiful river canyons, water crossings, hills and piles of black rocks known as Gobi Stones. Apology accepted.

Team Illinois showed no signs of falling apart on day three like they had done at Atacama. Nancy continued to run through her own constant nausea and was as strong as she had ever been in any endurance challenge. As a team, they covered the distance well and in good time, taking the familiar run/walk strategy as they continued on. They started with nine minutes of running with one minute of walking. When their bodies started to show signs of stress, it might be four minutes of running and one walking.

Nancy started to feel the symptoms of heat stroke again, but Joel and Dave were there to help her through the worst of it. Based on their proposed solution however, Nancy might have just as well taken the heat without their solution. Since water was stored in a backpack plastic bladder it was easy enough to grab a drink from the tube attached to that water pouch. If you wanted to pour a little water on Nancy's head and neck to ease the heat, the only way to do it was to take a drink and spray it on her.

Let the visual of that example sink in a little. It was not a situation where Joel or Dave had bottles to pour over Nancy's head, nor did they have the convenience of a spray nozzle. Spray in this case involved air pressure from lungs, and a spray nozzle formed by human lips.

Some would call it spit, but in the heat of the desert we'll just call it a cooling mist. Under the stress of the desert heat, you'll do just about anything to survive the worst of it. Nancy gladly took advantage of the moisture provided to the back of her head and neck, regardless of the source.

Yellow Jerseys and Duct Tape

Team Illinois had been complimented by many at the Gobi Desert race about the color of their jerseys. Opting to pick something that would stand out among the crowd, it was the fabric blend rather than the color that fell under the closest criticism during the race. The yellow did look good after all, but the fabric turned out to be horribly dysfunctional.

Dave may not have had his pack straps adjusted properly or it could have been due to the extra sweat that Dave's body seemed to produce, but the combination of friction and dried salt that caked the jersey was rubbing Dave's lower back raw. The yellow fabric seemed to become crusty once infiltrated with sweat where other fabrics could remain softer and more flexible. For Dave, the backpack rubbed the fabric and the fabric worked like sandpaper to remove the skin from Dave's body. At some point, Dave's autopilot was interrupted by pain and he had to stop the team to address the growing problem.

Duct tape seems to fix everything and ultra-marathoners and endurance racers are deeply familiar with its benefits. The application of duct tape seems to vary depending on the type and size of the open wound, but it helps solve the basic problem of friction. The shiny side of the tape is naturally slick so that you can roll the tape onto itself and still peel it off. For as sticky as the adhesive side is, the shiny side must be just as "non-adhesive" to manufacture a roll of the stuff. Got that? OK, onto medical applications.

In the case of an open blister, some form of second-skin bandage is used to dress the wound and keep it moist where the duct tape is placed over the bandage directly onto the skin. The adhesive side reinforces the skin around the wound and the shiny side of the tape keeps anything like the heel of a shoe from abrading the wound further.

For larger wounds like back skin being sanded away, the treatment is different but the concept is the same. Once the tape is applied over the treated area, the shiny side of the tape allows for freedom of muscle movement under the tape while eliminating friction from the jersey outside of the tape.

Dave was tended to by his teammates and the "hamburger" as Joel had called it, was treated and repaired. Team Illinois headed back on the trail and continued setting a tough pace through to the end of the stage. It would be a good running day for Team Illinois, and they covered the distance in about six and a half hours. The elapsed time on day three was good but also aided by the fact that the trail markers were placed in better positions, cutting down on the amount of time lost by being lost.

Day three was also a day when Team Illinois seemed to trade the pace with another friend they had made at Atacama, Jacob Nielsen from Denmark. Pronounced "Yah-kob", Jacob would pass them by and say "Team Illinois, you guys look freaking awesome." As the race wore on, Team Illinois would accelerate their pace after a checkpoint and eventually pass Jacob by. He was always ready with a comment to cheer them on. "You guys look like a yellow train. You look awesome!" The lead changed several times and Dave finally took the opportunity to motivate Jacob. At the top of his lungs Dave called out, "Jacob, **YOU** look freaking awesome! Keep on pushing. You can do it!"

Towards the end of the stage, Joel was hitting his wall while Nancy and Dave were taking the lead and setting the pace. Joel focused on following his wife and new friend down the trail. Most days, Joel would be the strong runner, but today it would be someone else's turn on the team to help lead the charge. This is something else that successful teams do. One person should never, and can never carry the bulk of the load through the race or any long distance event. As they crested another skree hill, the camp could be seen off in the distance and Team Illinois accelerated towards the finish.

Nancy's mindless running, Dave's autopilot and Joel's zone had served them very well on this stage and Nancy achieved another stage win based on the team's overall elapsed time. As they all crossed the finish line and unplugged from their personal version of autopilot, their bodies started to ache and effects of other symptoms were brought into focus. As with other highly focused teams or groups, or even when an individual is deeply focused on something that interests them, little things that bother the human body at rest seem to disappear when you're in that zone. Athletes from most sports teams can describe the same condition during a game. Once the game or the stress condition ends, the body stops producing Beta-Endorphins and all the little aches and pains and sometimes serious injuries are only then detected.

Joel was still suffering from the heat and once his body started to wind down from the pace of the last few miles, he could feel the need for medical attention. Joel headed off to the medical tent overheated and energy drained and sat for an hour sipping on Tang orange drink and chewing on glucose tablets. The medical staff monitored his condition and Joel's body chemistry started to balance out again, taking him from drained and despondent to just sore with a hope that food and rest would help him recover further. Ian Adamson stopped by to check on him and made sure Joel had whatever he needed to get himself back into the race by stage four.

Day Four

Joel described day four in a single word. "Hot". Though temperatures are always lower in the morning, Gobi temperatures never really had the wide temperature swings found at Atacama. It was always hot in the Gobi Desert. Team Illinois was re-energized from an evening of food, rest and no storms. Their tent mates from Team Esquel were still hanging in the individual competition categories and making a solid effort each day.

Team Illinois felt strong and although the need for symbolic motivators was not as important as it was at Atacama, they all missed having Attie on the starting line with them. There would be no camp pet in the Gobi Desert, but Attie certainly would have appreciated Dave's beef jerky as well as the rest of the camp's leftovers.

At mid-day the temperature crested 118 degrees Fahrenheit. The marked trail had taken them all through another small town and surprisingly enough, a vineyard as well. They wondered what the local homemade wine might taste like. Inside the town, the course led them towards a large staircase which led up the side of a mountain. Joel was detached enough from his zone to count the stairs as they climbed them. With 758 steps in all, the three from Team Illinois were thinking about finding Ian (Their favorite course designer) after the stage, and beating the snot out of him.

The comments about Ian were made in jest. Nancy had known Ian Adamson's name for years, following his exploits as he was featured in several magazine articles. Ian was a professional athlete who also helped to pioneer the world of endurance racing. He was a legend in the world of competitive running and it was an honor, albeit a pain, to run one of Ian Adamson's endurance courses.

Reaching the first checkpoint was a challenge for all, where the distance came close to eight miles, but nobody was expecting to have to climb the stair equivalent of a 60 story building with backpacks in order to get there. Team Illinois was getting stronger and felt pretty good at checkpoint one, maintaining their small lead over the team from Singapore who were still just off the pace.

After the checkpoint they ran several ridgelines and eventually down onto a canyon road. The heat was so intense that Joel had described it as the "death road".

"The heat on the road was amazing and you could actually see the radiant waves coming up off the ground. There was no cover anywhere while on the road and it seemed to extend into infinity. Nan overheated and Dave and I were having a tough time keeping it together too. We thought the checkpoint was at the end of the road and kept hoping we would be able to see it. After an eternity on the road, the course took a turn back up monster sand dunes, mountains then back onto more ridgelines. This section took us over an hour to complete. We could feel our brains baking in the sun."

Before reaching checkpoint two, Dave was trying to record some scenery from the trail on his mini digital camcorder while they all had slowed to a walking pace. Removing his camera from his pack, Dave was attempting to walk and film at the same time only to trip over a rock. Dave described the event.

"I wanted to film more footage in our second race but it was difficult to do when running. We had some great scenery on day four and I was paying more attention to the viewfinder than the road. I hit a rock and started to go down when I instinctively held my right arm out to protect the camera and did a 'header' into another rock. Too bad that wasn't on film, it would have shown a nice face plant. It's safe to say that by the second race I had learned the art of stumbling and falling."

One goose egg sized knot on his head and a trickle of blood later, Dave and the team moved on towards checkpoint two which was again further than they expected. The distances were moved further apart because the day stage was under a marathon distance. Based on the heat and chance for dehydration though, Team Illinois and others would have gladly stopped at an intermediate station.

Once they arrived at checkpoint two, they were all ready for a break. Nancy was struggling again in the open sun with the disadvantage of her thick hair holding in the radiant heat. The pace Team Illinois had set was taking its toll on all, where the only advantage of completing the stage quickly was the benefit of getting out of the sun that much faster. Those who took their time that day would be baked. Literally.

It was a test of training and preparation really, to see which individuals and teams were truly ready for the conditions and the heat. The benefit of reaching checkpoint two, also meant that they were that much closer to camp. With only 2.5 kilometers (1.5 miles) left to run, Team Illinois moved on from the checkpoint motivated and moving quickly.

Finding camp and maintaining their lead overall, Team Illinois headed back to the shelter of their tent. Nancy and Joel discussed the need to offload as much weight out of their packs in preparation for the 50 mile stage the following morning, and Joel summarized the conditions at the stage four campsite.

"Thankfully we are back to camp. We have been eating as much as possible because we know tomorrow will be bad and we do not want to carry anything more than absolutely necessary. The camp is in this wide open desert valley and there is a gigantic sand mountain bordering one side of the camp. As the sun moves across the sky it seems like there are words spelled out on the giant dune wall. There is little to no wind movement here, so the heat is stifling. All we want to do is stay under the cover of our tent."

Dave had also told a story of one of their fellow competitors who experimented with cooking a bowl of instant noodles out in the open sun. Taking a lightweight aluminum pot filled with noodles and some water, the pot was placed on the sand out in the open. 15 minutes later, the noodles were so hot that they had to be cooled before eating. Complex laws of thermodynamics apparently apply everywhere including the desert. The heat of the sun and the sand had transferred to the cooler contents of the aluminum pot. Heat was exchanged, the water was heated and noodles were cooked. Perhaps a little sandy, but it was hot.

Team Illinois was tired and hungry, but it was clear that the change in training and electrolyte management had better prepared them for this race. The same was true for experienced individual competitors as well. Those who had experience with the extremes found in this specific type of endurance racing, were better trained and better prepared for the harsh conditions of the desert. Not everyone would be cooking noodles out in the open desert sun, but experienced racers had brought whatever food items their body types could tolerate.

Joel took another opportunity to check some of the current race statistics and found some of the individual elapsed times posted by their racing buddy Chuck Walker had also improved over his Atacama stage times. Based on elapsed times for the race through stage four, Chuck was closer to the race leader Evgeniy Gorkov from Russia than he had been to the race leader from the Atacama Corssing, Kevin Lin. Team Illinois had also drastically improved their time by the completion of stage four when compared to the Atacama Crossing.

Team Esquel returned to camp later that afternoon and none of them had dropped out of the race. It was great to see their group still competing at an international level, learning the intricacies of desert endurance racing like Team Illinois did their first time out at Atacama. Towards dinner time, one of the Chinese competitors tried to communicate with Dave regarding a trade for food. It was an offer for some of his canned food in trade for one of Dave's freeze dried meals. Dave couldn't make out the label on the can which was described in "Hanzi" Chinese characters. He thought about the risk of introducing something into his system that had not been tested before. Dave, like Nancy and Joel had done plenty of homework on which food items their individual bodies could tolerate and the list of those things the body would not handle. Dave tried his best to politely decline the offer.

Day four did not see many of the competitors socialize near the campfire in the evening, most were resting as much as they could and trying to tend to blisters and sores before the long day. Day five meant 50 miles, and nobody was looking forward to finding out what Ian had planned for the course. Nancy was hoping for more mindless running and Dave and Joel were talking about different running strategies depending on whether or not the course was flat.

Day Five

Team Illinois woke early to wrap new bandages where needed and replace duct tape on Dave's back. Last minute adjustments were made to their backpacks and extra food was tossed in the trash. Additional weight was distributed from Nancy's pack into Joel and Dave's just like in Chile, but the basic required survival gear stayed with her. Once again Dave and Joel had looked around the starting line for a sign of a guardian angel to help them through the worst stage of the race. Attie would have been a welcome sight on the starting line, though the memory of him would be enough to make them all smile when his name was mentioned.

Nancy knew that the 50 mile stage was the strong part of her team's arsenal. Apart from their added strength training for this Gobi March race, Team Illinois was still a team built on speed. A flat course would benefit them, but their bodies were also now prepared for a course that wasn't flat. They implemented the first part of their strategy which matched that of Atacama. Nine minutes running with a one minute walking pace. For the first few hours of the long day, Team Illinois had increased their lead.

At mid-day the temperature was posted at 50 degrees Celsius or 122 degrees Fahrenheit. If you're a science nut, that would be 323 Kelvin. With that increase, all teams and individuals were dropping their pace and changing strategies from speed to one of survival. Team Illinois had dropped their pace at first to a 4:1 ratio of running to walking. An hour later the ratio changed to 2:1, and eventually dropped to 1:1. The heat was going to claim victims that day and it would only be a matter of time. Thankfully finding the first checkpoint, Team Illinois was surprised by a greeting which included hot water bottles. There was no shelter to keep water in the shade. The team took their bottles, filled their backpack pouches and moved on.

Finding the open salt flats next, Joel saw that although it was a rough road, the flats at the Gobi March were smoother and harder packed than in Chile, but so much hotter. The radiant heat coming off the floor of the flats was worse than Atacama with a greater risk of sunburn on their faces. At one point they wandered across a Japanese competitor who had tried to find shelter near the small, broken wall of an old building, but the sun was directly overhead and there would be little protection. The next checkpoint was found later on the open salt flats and the truck driver had extended a small bed sheet stretched out from the side of the truck to provide some shelter from the sun. Joel described the scene once they arrived.

"The shade was able to give 4-5 people a brief respite from the sun. When we got there, Nan started throwing up and crying hysterically all captured by a Jeep film crew. As we sat under the shelter refilling our backpack water pouch, the film crew was asking us questions about the day. I was telling them how awful it was while Nan continued to cry behind me. Billy, one of the Ireland competitors was lying under the shelter pasty white and looking terrible. He was forced to drop from the race."

Dave also found his own challenge at the checkpoint when confronted by some sort of bee. Dave ran in circles to avoid the flight of the persistent insect, but got stung in the neck anyway. The swelling and the pain were immediate but they were able to secure some Benadryl from the checkpoint medical supplies before heading back out onto open ground. They laughed about Dave's futile attempt to swat the bee, while trying to figure out why they had to be subjected to yet one more natural challenge. The heat and dehydration and desert terrain weren't tough enough, and they wondered if Ian truly had the power to include insects as part of the overall challenge.

The salt flats continued on for miles. Each competitor was told that the next checkpoint would be found at the edge of a town but it turned out to be at the outer edge of the flats. It would have been nice to find some shelter from the sun in any small town but at least the checkpoint had a larger shelter set up. Team Illinois collapsed underneath it. Joel was overheating again.

"We stayed at this CP for about 45-60 minutes. The volunteers kept spraying us with water to try to get our body temperatures down. It worked for Nan and Dave, but not for me. I couldn't get my core temperature to drop. I had a very hard time getting food and liquids in (my system) all day. I was lying on the ground, miserable, as more competitors began to arrive. I just couldn't seem to get it together. As we were trying to get up and get moving, we saw the Singapore team coming in (from the flats). That was all Nan and Dave needed. They threw my pack on me and forced me back out on the course."

The Power Of Team

The next checkpoint and town were another seven long miles away and Team Illinois was down to a walking pace late in the afternoon. It would be a matter of training and preparation for them at that point. They had pushed the pace as hard as they could and their bodies performed above and beyond what they again thought possible. Those that could keep moving at a strong pace at mid-day were the ones who had prior experience in surviving the 50 mile distance.

Slowly approaching the next small town, Team Illinois drew strange looks from the locals as they passed by the entry way. The townspeople had apparently never seen taller foreigners, much less foreigners with matching yellow jerseys walking in from the open desert. Dave had spotted a small stream running through some farmland next to the town and they removed their "buffs" (a large square multi-purpose piece of fabric) to dip into the water and wash themselves down. Dave was taking his buff and drenching the back of Joel's head and neck to help cool him down and Joel finally started to feel better.

Further down the race trail, another small town was spotted in the afternoon where they found a community water station with constant stream of water being pumped into an open trough. It was another welcome chance to pour water over their bodies and let the evaporation take some of the heat away. Down the main street of this larger town, they spotted a small store which looked as if it sold bottled water. Dave pulled out some local currency which didn't amount to very much in U.S. dollars and bought some. Dave said something in English like "keep the change" but of course the language barrier would prevent that from being understood. Still, he waved and smiled and they were off again hiking up hill through the town and trying to find the trail again.

Several blocks later, the shop keeper had chased them down to give them change from the water purchase. The small amount of change would not have been a significant amount of money to a shopkeeper in China, but keeping the change would have tested their integrity. Sometimes we do not appreciate the cultural nuances found between nations, but honesty and integrity are still found across the globe. Living in North America we tend forget the value of certain things, especially when it is a commodity we have plenty of. Dave would bow and say "thank you" and Team Illinois continued down along the race trail.

Medical Condition Mayhem

Though the medical staff had been busy during the first stages of the race, medical emergencies were mounting after 12:00 noon on the long day. Checkpoints were starting to look like street side triage units in a war-torn country. Bodies were lying everywhere. Most competitors seeking medical attention were suffering from differing stages of hyperthermia, a condition caused by heat stroke where the body becomes so overheated it feels chilled. In the midst of the Gobi Desert heat, a hyperthermia victim would like nothing more than to be wrapped in a quilt. The medical staff could treat most cases with shade and fluids. Over the span of an hour or two, most hyperthermia sufferers were able to move on from the medical tent and head back out on the course. For some competitors, medical conditions were more severe on the long day. For one woman, her sunburn had become so bad that she was forced to drop from the race.

Where Nancy had suffered through severe heat exhaustion in Chile, others were having difficulty taking on fluids on the long day. Early into the afternoon during the peak of the mid-day heat, Dr. Brandee Waite was tending to multiple hyperthermia victims at one checkpoint while Dr. Brian Krabak was called to checkpoint 20 as another competitor was being set up with an intravenous drip. The IV would be a necessary course of action if the body refused to take on fluids orally. Gobi was claiming numerous victims during the fifth stage and the doctors on staff were kept busy driving between checkpoints well into the early hours of the following morning. The outstanding medical team supporting the RacingThePlanet event in China would wind up working as many hours as competitors would spend running the course. A doctor's work is never done, especially in the desert.

The Mandatory Health Check

The next town along the trail near the end of the long day was Chin Chin where all competitors took a mandatory one hour break. It was a chance for the RTP staff to take a health check, let competitors consume whatever calories they could hold down and hydrate themselves as best they could.

Three more Gobi casualties would be borne out of the heat but not be discovered until the mandatory stop. Wade Bloomer from Canada was a veteran distance runner and had finished well among his age group at The Atacama Crossing in 2004. He had also brought along his daughter Jodi, to share in the desert racing experience while Jodi had been posting Gobi March stage times consistent with the women race leaders. The youngest female competitor and a sure bet for one of the top finishing positions, Jodi had reached the mandatory stop distraught over news heard at her previous checkpoint. Separated on the course, her father Wade had not made it to his next checkpoint, was missing and presumed to be injured. Jodi ran hard to the mandatory stop knowing there would be more staff and potentially better information about her father, but there was no update on Wade's status.

Hearing about Wade's struggle in the heat and noticing Jodi's concern, Brent Weigner chose to stay behind with Jodi beyond his own mandatory stop time to make sure both Wade and Jodi would be OK. In contention for the overall win in his own age bracket, Brent sacrificed time on the clock to stay with a fellow competitor during a time of need. In the end, Wade was discovered behind the shade of a telephone pole out on the open salt flats. He eventually made it to the next checkpoint on his own, and a relieved daughter was only then able to continue the race. Jodi and Brent continued on to finish the stage, gladly absorbing a time penalty for news that Wade was indeed safe.

Team Illinois had reached the one hour mandatory stop close to sunset and immediately engaged in the fine art of foot maintenance, tending to new blisters and getting them taped up for the final push to the finish. Nancy was sure to check with RTP officials for the status of other competitors on the course and their arrival times at the mandatory stop. Some of the individual competitors Team Illinois kept pace with, had already crossed the stopping point and were released back into the desert. Nancy was anxious to get back out on the course.

Race officials continued to release competitors based on their arrival time at the mandatory stop. Team Illinois had broken out their head lamps in anticipation of the approaching darkness, and the sun had already begun to set against the horizon. The people of this larger town had never seen so many foreigners at one time. The local residents seemed to be in awe of the uniforms, the backpacks and the equipment. Crowds began to gather just out of curiosity, but it was a welcoming crowd. Joel had grabbed some of their extra glow sticks out of his pack and tossed a few into the crowd. Cheers were offered in return.

Nancy, Joel and Dave were finally released and started off on a running pace with everyone feeling recharged. The temperature had cooled off a bit as the sun disappeared for the day and they began to follow the foot trails in the dark. Headlamps were a poor substitute for sunlight, but everyone made the most of the situation. The next checkpoint was scheduled at another 10 kilometers out, but it measured more like 12. Team Illinois wondered again if they had missed some sort of trail marker. Missed markers meant more elapsed time and Team Singapore had never been that far behind. There was a concerted effort to catch up with Chuck Walker and Lisanne Dorion, who were leading their respective categories and who had left the mandatory stop 25 minutes earlier. Once out on the flats again, Joel could see the faint light of Chuck's and Lisanne's glow sticks hanging from their backpacks.

Motivated by chasing a new goal, Team Illinois followed the white painted arrows on the desert road and focused in on the glow sticks in front of them. Almost up to the next checkpoint, Team Illinois caught up with another group of athletes and they all ran together towards a small town but without a view of the next glow stick marker. At the top of a hill they could see some sort of truck traffic in the distance, crossing the road with yellow flashing lights engaged, but the group could not see the next glow stick marker. It was another tense moment for Team Illinois, not wanting to give up any more ground to Team Singapore.

Eventually they decided as a group that there was no other option but to run towards the top of the hill and the yellow flashing lights of the crossing truck traffic. It turned out to be the correct path after all. They finally arrived at the next checkpoint and Chuck Walker was there waiting for them. Lisanne had apparently split off alone. Chuck's headlamp was completely dim and it would have been more dangerous to attempt the run on his own. Chuck decided to team up with the small band from Illinois and share the safety of their working headlamps. It was near midnight and Joel had been struggling physically since the eighth hour of the race. With the end nearly in sight to the long day, Joel prepared himself mentally for the last 8 kilometers of the race through the national sand dune park and the punishment his body would have to endure.

Chuck and Team Illinois had stumbled across four more competitors who had been maintaining a similar pace all throughout the Gobi March stages. Ben Ferguson, Jan Luedekke, Mark Blick, and Jacob Nielsen were pulled into the growing group of day-five sufferers as they approached the dunes. Each human body tended to react differently to exhaustion and dehydration, and the growing group with Team Illinois found themselves in pain as they crossed over the first few dunes. On one climb, Ben

Ferguson was heard slightly off to the left of the group, suddenly having a conversation with himself. Ben had apparently walked directly into a bush growing out of the side of the dune and claimed that the bush had spoken to him. Ben then explained to the group (after being convinced) that it must have been the "burning bush". Dave and Joel had experienced hallucinations in the desert on previous stages when the body's blood chemistry became imbalanced. Ben was beginning to show the signs of heat stress, and falling into projected mental images from either the Old Testament or movie images of Charlton Heston on Mount Sinai.

The soft dunes were endless and based on the direction of the trail markers; there would be no way around them. Ian Adamson had designed the last few miles of the 50 mile stage to humble even the best prepared athlete. Chuck Walker, Team Illinois and the rest of their group were humbled. Stopping at the bottom of almost every dune descent, the small group was gasping for air and struggling to remain on their feet. All the body wanted to do was collapse, but there was always a teammate's health and motivation to consider. No one person on the team or in their little group was prepared to let the others down, so they continued on. Chuck seemed to remain the stronger one in the clan, but Chuck also seemed to be motivated by something else.

Finally breaking his normally supportive tone and quiet strength of will, Chuck had reached the summit of yet another four-story dune only to find one more glow stick on another distant dune climb. Throwing his head back and yelling at the sky Chuck screamed, "IAN, YOU BASTARD. I'M GOING TO FIND YOU IAN."

Chuck continued as honorary team leader, heading the charge up each dune and symbolically pulling Team Illinois, Mark, Jacob, Jan and Ben along with him. Once at the next summit, Chuck found that the torture would continue and another glow stick could be seen at the top of another dune. Chuck again proclaimed his fondness for the course designer. "IAN, YOU (insert your favorite expletive here). I'M GOING TO GET YOU IAN."

Chuck Walker had been generating enough motivational energy for the entire group. They all rested briefly at the bottom of the last few remaining dunes then charged up each sand hill to the apex and the next awaiting glow stick. Soft sand remained the most difficult surface to climb, but the sound of drums could then be heard off in the distance. The group knew they were getting close to camp. Joel, Nancy and Dave had experienced the drums from the base camp at the end of the 50 mile day at Atacama. It was a tradition now on the long day for RacingThePlanet and a way for stragglers who might be lost to find their way home.

Finishing 50 Miles

Somewhere after 19 hours and 40 minutes, the entire group crested one last huge dune and could see the camp. At 19:51:16, they all grabbed hands again as they had in every stage of every race since they met, and crossed the finish line together. Joel and Nancy collapsed together in the sand near the camp entrance and finally noticed that it was Gunnar, injured ankle and all, beating the drum to welcome them in. Chuck doubled over and caught his breath and Dave also fell to his knees and then rolled over onto his back. Jan, Mark and Ben collapsed in their tents. Nancy and Joel had the strength to pull themselves up after 15 minutes, but Dave lay near the finish line for 40 minutes looking up at the sky.

Todd Burrows had been everything a volunteer needed to be the previous five days, but especially to his extended Illinois family. He kept asking Dave if he needed anything and finally convinced him to get off the sand and into his tent. Todd helped them all get hot water for food and assisted in the meal preparation. Nancy thought that this new brother-in-law guy would fit in well with their team, since he was a member of the family anyway.

Some time shortly after the meal, they had all dozed off in their tent, exhausted from the day. Joel slept for about three hours and woke just after midnight to hear the sound of the drums still pounding in the background. Gunnar was in the midst of his own endurance challenge on the drums it seemed, and the homing beacon would be there for any and all late arrivals into camp.

Joel looked across the tent and found the entire side open from the missing Chinese team. He slid his sleeping bag over to gain a little more room and dozed off to sleep again. Sometime early the following morning, Dave was startled by something and woke to see one of the Team Esquel members huddled close to Joel on the floor of the tent. One had returned without his sleeping bag, but the others were still out in the desert, trying to bring an end to the long day.

Day Six – Rest Day

Dr. Waite was called on later that morning to check out the health of the Team Esquel lone returning member. She had explained to Team Illinois the concept of hyperthermia and why the body feels chilled even in extreme heat. Despite the 90+ temperatures at night, the Chinese competitor was displaying signs of extreme dehydration and chills from hyperthermia. He would fall into the hands of the good doctor and recover later in the day.

A few missing competitors started to trickle back into camp in the early morning. RacingThePlanet sent out trucks to look for anyone else who could not complete the distance. The 56 mile stage was designed to be a two day event, though top finishers completed the distance in a day. The benefit to finishing in a single day was that you were rewarded with a day of rest. Day six was rest day for many already in camp.

Day five had indeed been different that other desert races or maybe it was just simply more difficult. Where the Atacama Crossing found all competitors completing the 50 mile distance by 3:00 a.m. on day six, the heat and the dunes of China would impact everyone's completion times.

The other male member of Team Esquel had walked into camp separately, as the female in the group had to drop from the race and was retrieved by truck. Others in camp had mixed emotions about the situation surrounding this team from the host country. Nobody wishes ill will for any competitor in an endurance race, but everyone hoped that this would be a learning race for the new team. It was good to know in the end that all would be safe on day six.

Chuck Walker, Kevin Lin and Team Illinois were out in the commons of their base camp talking about the last stage and laughing about Ian's brutal course design. Dave had commented, "I thought the steps on day four were bad, but those dunes at the end of the stage yesterday were murder."

Dave added, "Do you guys find it weird that Ian's name makes up three letters of the word 'PAIN'?"

Joel fired back, "And we left the 'P' out in the desert."

Throughout the rest of the day, the heat had peaked to its highest point during the race at Gobi. Dave talked about those still lost in the desert.

"The whole day was a mess. By three or four in the afternoon there were at least six to ten people lost out in the desert. Mary had sent trucks out to help find those who had not made it back to camp. Some had wandered far off the trail and required transportation back for medical attention."

Dinner was once again the excitement of whatever was left in their packs, but everything else other than mandatory gear was removed as extra weight. Team Illinois would be running as light as they could on day seven, but knew that they had all but sewn up the team championship at Gobi, that was if they could avoid getting lost on the last day of the race.

Day Seven

RacingThePlanet conducted a full group race meeting in the morning and the collective group of competitors had convinced the race organizers to change the final stage design from an endless dune climb to a flatter course. It would be the dunes that had ended the race for many of the competitors on day five and it was felt that the final day of the race should be a day of elation rather than a day of punishment.

RTP officials had agreed and the course was moved away from the dunes and towards a dry riverbed and road flats all the way to the finish line. Three sets of starting times were assigned based on average stage times for each competitor. Slower racers would start at 7:00 a.m., an average speed group would start at 8:00 and the race leaders would begin at 9:00 a.m. This staggered start time would see most of the competitors cross the finish line together for a much more exciting end to the day and the event.

The group of surviving racers were trucked to the new starting line and pointed towards the direction of the finish line. In advance of the start, lead vehicles went out on the 16K distance to set the course flags, but the trail would follow pipelines and roads all the way into the welcoming town of Shanshanxian.

9:00 a.m. and the race leaders were finally released from the starting line. Team Illinois adopted the same strategy they had implemented during the last stage in Chile. They would run as fast a pace as Nancy could handle, and drop to a 9:1 run-walk ratio if needed. 16K would still be a long race given the 56 mile distance two days before, but this was the day where Team Illinois performed their best. Flat trails and a fast pace were welcome.

Once past a marked trail along a pipeline, Team Illinois turned into the first of a series of vineyards leading to town. It was an odd site to find grape vines growing in the barren desert, but grapes will apparently grow just about anywhere there is water supplied to them. Eventually they reached the first and only checkpoint for the day and by then had been pacing only a few runners in front of them. Everybody else was behind, but not too far behind. They all loaded water and pushed on with two other individual competitors, Mark Blick from the U.K. and Jan Lueddeke from Germany. Jan and Mark had been running about the same pace as Team Illinois all six days but sometimes separated in the pack. Today they would finish the pace together as a group of five.

Mark and Jan were fellow sufferers of Ian's course design but they had proven themselves to be well trained and experienced competitors. It was an honor for all to be working together to help set the pace and support each other when one needed encouragement.

Nancy would be the first to falter. At one point Jan could see Nancy struggling and starting to dry heave. He called out, "Why run so hard? Who are you running from? No one can catch you! Maybe we should slow down." Nancy didn't go into the long explanation of how this was a normal stress-induced body response for her, but Joel finally said, "We just want to be done."

One kilometer away from the finish line, Jan and Mark told Nancy that she should go ahead of them and cross the finish line first. "You all have earned that right this week."

Nancy would have none of that. Apart from this being a significant accomplishment for the team who suffered miserably in Chile, and that most would look for individual glory in a situation exactly like the last day at the Gobi March. Nancy replied, "No way, we cross together."

Team Champions

It was a statement that Nancy had made near the end of The Atacama Crossing as well. "I just want to be done." She would suffer through one more vineyard in front of the town and make one final stretch to the finish. For the members of Team Illinois, part of the personal reward was proving to themselves that their bodies could be pushed further than Atacama. Nancy and Joel and Dave just wanted the punishment of the Gobi March "to be over". It was clearly less of a need for glory, and more of a personal accomplishment for all three. The team that had grown to five members including Mark and Jan, all held hands together as they crossed the finish line with raised arms.

Nancy, Joel and Dave along with Jan and Mark shared hugs and celebrated with high-fives and the celebratory spray of beer. Team Illinois knew they had won the race by virtue of staying in front of the tough Singapore team late on day five and running a hard pace through to the last stage on day seven. There was no doubt that the amateur running team from Illinois was indeed champion of the Gobi Desert.

The elation and excitement of the finish lasted until everyone had crossed the line. Competitors made it into town in clusters as many of the near 100 finishers had decided to run in the final miles together in groups. It was a testament to what a race like the RacingThePlanet series could do to a person. It humbled them. It inspired them. It forced them to cross cultures and language barriers and then cross finish lines together as fellow sufferers of a near impossible desert challenge. This race brought out the best in most people. Ian Adamson should have been proud.

More hugs and handshakes were offered to Chuck and Jacob and other friends who had battled through the dunes of the Gobi Desert. It was good to see so many of their fellow veteran racers from Atacama do so well. Each seemed to improve on their placement in the finishing field when compared to The Atacama Crossing. It appeared that everyone had improved on their training curriculum.

Team Illinois would win the team competition in 42:13. It would wind up to be a 3.5 hour lead over the second place team. It was quite an improvement from Chile where Team Illinois finished 6.5

hours behind the race leaders. Six months of improved training and a better balance of food, water and electrolytes were enough to take Nancy, Joel and Dave over the top.

Evgeniy Gorkov won the overall individual competition at 35:43, while Chuck Walker won his age bracket finishing in 39:40. Lisanne Dorion won the women's individual competition at 42:00, Nancy's team time placed her only 13 minutes off the women's lead for a finish in second place, and newcomer Jodi Bloomer placed third despite waiting at the mandatory health stop for news of her father on the long day.

Dave was reminded once more of the memory locked away in his head. It was reserved for him in a room on board his ship when he needed inspiration. When his body was on autopilot and his mind had wandered from memory to memory, Dave knew of a door that he could always open to find that one motivating memory. "It was a bullshit award" the voice had said in Chile.

"Not this time." Dave muttered with a smile.

Pictures from the "Gobi March" 2005

Photos provided by Lester Lim-Framewerkz. Wade and Jodi Bloomer (above) represented Canada as their only father and daughter combination to race in the Gobi March. Course designer Ian Adamson (below) knows what the competitors will be facing in the hours and days ahead.

The Power Of Team

Photos provided by Lester Lim-Framewerkz. The unexpected sight of vineyards were found along the race trail (above). Joel and Dave take the lead (below) at the start of the next stage.

Peter Wortham

Photos provided by Lester Lim-Framewerkz. Hamish Morrison enjoys an afternoon desert snack (above), while other competitors run alongside sheer face walls as they navigate through a Gobi Desert canyon (below).

The Power Of Team

Photos provided by Lester Lim-Framewerkz. Hot on the heels of Nancy's U.S. team, Team Singapore raises their hiking poles in salute for the camera (above). Jacob Nielsen (below) picks up his pace alongside a desert road.

Photos provided by Lester Lim-Framewerkz. Chuck Walker from California pushes hard on the flats of the course (above). Ben Ferguson takes a break from the heat (below) by dousing his head with a little bottled water.

The Power Of Team

Photos provided by Lester Lim-Framewerkz. Competitors needed to keep their wits about them as they balanced on the razor back ridge lines of the mountains in the Gobi Desert.

Chapter 6 - The Learning Race

So much had changed since Atacama and the results of those changes led Nancy, Joel and Dave to a well deserved victory. It would prove to be a combination of experience, modified approaches to training and better nutrient management that helped put them over the top.

Many of the things Team Illinois needed to learn were things they could not learn from anyone. To reach the peak of anyone's performance, physical preparation and blood chemistry management would have to be uniquely developed for each individual competitor. Even if Nancy was able to contact Ian Adamson for advice on food and electrolyte management, Ian's body chemistry might require a completely different combination of fluids and nutrients to keep him in peak form. The same combination might cause Nancy's body, Joel's body or Dave's body to fail.

Body chemistry and physical training are only part of the story. It was clear that without a core set of values mutually shared by the team, without a genuine concern for the health and welfare of your teammates and without agreement on the common goal, Team Illinois would have failed to win the Gobi March race. The little group from Illinois had the team-thing down pretty well their first time out, but just needed to adjust their preparation a little for the next race.

Team Esquel struggled on many fronts, but especially because they were asked to enter the Gobi Desert race at the last minute and had little experience with longer distance endurance races. Based on Team Illinois' experiences from Chile, they were confident that Team Esquel would probably perform better in their next RacingThePlanet challenge. Better team preparation and race strategy along with enhancements in equipment and nutrition management would help the Chinese team in their next challenge.

Class Dismissed

What Nancy, Joel and Dave learned about their little specialty team, was that their original goal was still an attainable one. The RacingThePlanet series of desert races included four continents and Team Illinois had done well in their first, but dominated in their second attempt. Original goal achieved, thank you for playing. They never gave up on that original target and used experience and determination to prove to themselves that it could be done. Dry heaves, dehydration, and duct tape repaired wounds would not stop the yellow train.

Good teams like the three from Illinois learn from their mistakes and did things better the second time around. They even helped each other on their homework. Team Illinois was content to celebrate with their friends and even enjoy the four hour bus ride back to Urumqi. Some dozed off on the trip but most were energized from the day and stories flew back and forth to fill the bus with laughter. Nancy was dying for a shower, but then again so was everyone. Dave was closing the door to his motivational room. Joel was just looking forward to a meal not cooked over an open fire. Joel summarized the accomplishment.

"People always ask us why we do these races. It is hard to make them understand. We won this team race by over 3.5 hours. This wasn't done because other teams weren't in shape for the race. (The difference was) our hard work. We spent a lot of time preparing on our own and training how we as individuals felt we needed to. Additionally, we spent at least one day per week running together. At the end of the day, I guess I have to say I am proud. I am proud of winning with my teammates, proud of our hard work and completion time, and proud of representing my country."

Dave spoke about learning from their first race.

"Chile for us was a learning race. We became aware that the flat road training was not working well. We learned that electrolytes needed to be balanced differently for each of us. Even the food combinations were changed based on what each of us could tolerate. Gobi was the race we did everything right. It was by far my best race."

And finally, the story of the attractive yellow jersey comes to an end. The color had indeed made them stand out in the crowd and they were easily recognizable from a distance. "The Yellow Train" did make its mark in the Gobi Desert, but the fabric also left its mark on Dave's back. It was a collective decision to dump the jersey in favor of another fabric type that could handle the built up of dried sweat and salt. If they turned out to be yellow, so much the better, but comfort would be a driving requirement for any jersey selected in the future.

Welcome Home

Nancy was rewarded locally soon after their arrival back at home. The news of the Gobi March championship had started a buzz around Chicago. Nancy was interviewed and then honored in a local magazine as Amateur Athlete of the Month. Friends and athletes back at the East Bank Club were full of praise and congratulations followed by a single question. "Are you going to do it again?"

On the flight back home before the accolades had even begun, the three teammates were discussing the feeling of relief coming from the accomplishment. Joel and Nancy both talked about the preparation and the sacrifice made at work in order to get to Gobi, and all three had agreed that the increased training regimen had been a strain on them all. All three agreed that the goal had been accomplished and, "That was it". Dave reminded Nancy of her quote from Chile, "I swear we will never do this again."

Two weeks later, Nancy took it upon herself to sign them all up for the Sahara Race in Egypt September of 2005. Somewhere after that phone call to Mary Gadams, Nancy knew she would have to break the news to her husband and running partner. "That can wait. There's still time to break the bad news."

Dave was met with a slightly different albeit a congratulatory welcome home. Many who had listened to his description of what the desert race format was like, doubted that any amateur guy (like Dave) could actually win such a race. Those same people at work and around town were the first to approach Dave and offer their congratulations.

News of the race spread quickly around Chicago and all of Illinois. The RacingThePlanet series was also grabbing some national attention and growing in name recognition around the world. With more than 20 countries participating in the events now, it was hard not to sit up and take notice of the drama attached to the race. The Mayor's office in Chicago had apparently also noticed and helped to provide a little home town recognition for Team Illinois' accomplishments.

On July 27, 2005 a resolution was passed by City Council after it was presented for their consideration by the Mayor of the City of Chicago. It reads as follows:

The Power Of Team

OFFICE OF THE MAYOR
CITY OF CHICAGO July 27, 2005
To the Honorable, The City Council of the City of Chicago:

LADIES AND GENTLEMEN – I transmit herewith a congratulatory resolution concerning Team Illinois, winners of the Gobi March 2005.

Your favorable consideration of this resolution is appreciated.

Very truly yours,
(Signed) RICHARD M. DALY,
Mayor.

Alderman Burke moved to Suspend the Rules Temporarily to permit immediate consideration of and action upon the proposed resolution. The motion Prevailed.
The following is said proposed resolution:

WHEREAS, An extraordinary organization called Racing The Planet was founded in 1996 to inspire people to explore the world's rich and varied cultures through participation in world-class athletic contests; and

WHEREAS, The flagship event for Racing The Planet , called the 4 Deserts, consists of a series of one hundred fifty mile footraces across the world's largest and most forbidding deserts, including the Sahara in Egypt, the Atacama in Chile, the Gobi in China and Antarctica; and

WHEREAS, On Sunday April 24 of this year, nearly one hundred competitors from twenty one countries lined up ion the remote village of Dong Gou, China for the start of The Gobi March 2005. Dubbed "The Race of No Return" by the locals, this contest required contestants to make their way through one hundred fifty miles of China's Gobi Desert in seven days, carrying all the food, gear and clothing they would need for the entire distance; and

WHEREAS, Among the participants in the Gobi March was Chicago's own Team Illinois, consisting of Joel E. Burrows, a kick boxer, endurance athlete and Master Trainer at Chicago's East Bank Club, his wife Nancy Fudacz-Burrows, an elite triathlete and director of exercise programs at the East Bank Club, and Dave P. Kuhnau, a software consultant, entrepreneur and world traveler; and

WHEREAS, The members of Team Illinois undertook this grueling challenge not only to test their bodies and minds, but also to raise funds for Operation Smile, a charity which provides surgery for children with facial deformities; and

WHEREAS, The members of Team Illinois pushed themselves to the limit, facing temperatures that soared to one hundred twenty degrees, driving rain, stinging dust storms, sleeplessness and intense physical pain; and

WHEREAS, Team Illinois completed the entire course, an impressive accomplishment in itself, but when the results were tallied, Team Illinois stood at the forefront of world-class athletes, for they won the Team Division, and its three members placed in the top ten finishers overall; and

WHEREAS, Equally laudable, the efforts of Team Illinois, along with other race participants, helped raise one hundred fifty thousand dollars to sponsor a mission in Xian, China and made life-changing operations a dream come true for one hundred sixty children; now therefore,

Be It Resolved, That we, the Mayor and members of the City Council of the City of Chicago, assembled this twenty-seventh day of July, 2005, do hereby congratulate Team Illinois members Joel E. Burrows, Nancy M. Fudacz-Burrows and Dave P. Kuhnau on their astonishing feat of physical and mental endurance, which helped to provide much-needed operations for children; and

Be It Further Resolved, That suitable copies of this resolution be presented to the members of Team Illinois as a token of our admiration and esteem.

On motion of Alderman Burke, seconded by Alderman Ocasio, the foregoing proposed resolution was unanimously Adopted.

Chapter 7 - Sahara

Registering for the Sahara Race was not a necessity for Team Illinois. They had proven that they could win; in fact they had all agreed on the plane home from China that the Gobi March victory would be enough. Nancy had even made the same now famous statement she did while unfolding herself out of her sleeping bag at Atacama. Once again Nancy would exercise her right to change her mind from "I swear, we are never doing this again", and this time the boys would not put up an argument.

She might have gotten a different reaction had they been beaten into the Gobi sand and lost again by six hours. Even with improved training and better equipment at their side, it would have been difficult to agree to Sahara if they had lost after so much additional preparation. Not that winning is everything and of course winning was not the reason Team Illinois had decided to come to Sahara. There were two other things to be found in the desert. Two important rewards for Team Illinois could only be found in a place like the Sahara. Family could be found there. Joel, Nancy, Dave, along with Chuck and Derek and Mark and Jacob and Jan. These were people who had suffered life threatening journeys with them and survived. This was extended family that could only be visited in the Sahara Desert. After Gobi, their friends had all returned to Germany and Singapore, Hong Kong and California. Even the three amigos from Chicago had a hard time seeing each other with Dave's travel and work schedule and the East Bank Club's demand for Nancy's time.

The main reason Sahara was a quick decision had to do with the personal experience of something so indescribably difficult, that overcoming the obstacle is a reward equally indescribable. For years Nancy had been looking for something a little more difficult than a marathon or a triathlon. Based on the speed at which she had signed up her team for each race it would be safe to say that she had found what she was looking for.

Dave and Joel felt the same way about the elation of just completing a race as mentally and physically taxing as any of the desert challenges. Each desert had a different look and feel and different pain points. The mountain elevations of Atacama and the rock formations of Gobi were beautiful but painful reminders of what had to be paid in order to see those natural wonders. The dollar cost was high of course. Entry fees for the race, airfare, equipment and everything associated with training for each race would be costly. Sponsors thankfully took some of the sting out of that requirement.

The real cost to see the desert however, was that you had to pay with sweat, and muscle failure and nausea. You had to drag yourself to the next water station and stay on your feet in order to survive. You needed to pick yourself off the sand and continue moving when every muscle in your body is begging you to just stop and roll under anything that provided shade.

Team Illinois began to thrive on the life altering challenge and drama to be found only in the desert. Nothing much lives there, but yet humans can cross 150 miles of burning sand in a little over 40 hours on foot. Aside from water made available roughly every 8 to 10K, each competitor remained self-supported. The water was a necessary evil as well, whether Ian wanted to provide it or not, because it would be physically impossible to carry enough water to last a 25 mile or 50 mile (85K) trek across the desert. Figure 2 to 3 liters of water available per stop, each liter weighs 1 kilogram or 2.2 pounds. On the 50 mile day, each competitor would have to carry up to 52 pounds or 24 kilograms of water on their back to make it through the distance. It would be the equivalent of running 50 miles while carrying a small teenager, and a 30 pound backpack. Reluctantly, Ian would need to provide water checkpoints along the race trail. Even Ian recognized that the backpack handicap of near 30 pounds was enough of a challenge at a marathon or greater distance.

Cairo, Egypt

Anxious over the potential for a repeat performance in Egypt, Nancy remained restless through the long flight from Chicago but calmed once spotting the pyramids from her window upon approach to the Cairo International Airport. It was one of the few land based features on Earth that can actually be seen from space, and easily viewed from her window seat. Bags were gathered and Team Illinois found transportation to the Movenpick Hotel about one kilometer from the airport. Check-in to the race committee for returning competitors was open after 8:00 p.m. that evening while the newbees would be checked off in the morning just before the busses left for the desert.

Competitors arrived and checked themselves into the hotel while race organizers were beginning their own internal training session for new volunteers. Helpful advice was offered by race veterans including Ian Adamson, who suggested that volunteers needed to be careful if taking a break out on the open sand. Avoiding small piles of rocks was recommended since they seemed to be the favorite hiding place for scorpions.

The check-in process was the same for every race and it was nice for returning competitors to get some preferential treatment. The mandatory equipment checklist was reviewed and each competitor was audited for the required gear. A quick health check up was provided in order for competitors to be cleared for the race, and each stepped up on a scale to determine a starting weight, partly for a study being performed by the medical team.

Nancy, Joel and Dave didn't make big plans for the evening, but then again the flight was hard enough on everyone. It would be better to rest and become acclimated to the time zone change during the next 24 hours.

The lobby of the hotel was buzzing the following morning with check in activities for new desert racing competitors. There was still time in the morning to relax in the lobby before boarding the bus at noon and Team Illinois met up with old friends also waiting for the bus. It was clear that the word had spread about the RacingThePlanet series of challenges, because the newbee body count in the lobby had grown since Gobi. Team Illinois wouldn't know until race day what sort of team competition they would face. Many looked good enough to be in shape, but Nancy, Joel and Dave all knew that being in shape had nothing to do with surviving a race in the desert.

Dave thought back to his first marathon accomplishment and smiled. He had decided that 26 miles on flat pavement was hard back then, but his perspective on many things had changed. Relationships and friendships and the things that he considered important in his life had all changed since Atacama. Dave was truly a different man one short year later.

In many ways Nancy and Joel had not changed except for the strengthening of the personal bond between them. Both had become reenergized about the ability to push the limits of personal training and learned to reach beyond the goals that were once thought to be too high. This was a message they both could take back to their clients and athlete-customers and one they could internalize as well. The two desert races had taught them that they could accomplish more than they ever thought possible.

The Power Of Team

Noon came quickly and the growing throng of competitors was pointed towards the waiting busses. Ranging in age from 22 years old to 73 with small backpacks in tow, they each took a place on the bus for the seven hour ride out to the desert and the first night's campsite. The ride was long but not too bumpy and most continued to share stories of past races and the associated comedy of errors.

Tent camp was waiting for them upon arrival and the smell of Middle-Eastern food was beginning to waft through the campsite. There would be no barbeque tonight, but the local cuisine was beginning to smell excellent. Hunger abounds after a full day on a bus and a short time later, the dinner meeting was called to review race rules and guidelines.

Joel had looked around the campsite once more to try and spot people that he had recognized, and found two members of the team that had won in Chile. He found out later that the newly formed team was a blend of two members from the Atacama Crossing plus a new teammate. They would be contenders for the team competition, Joel was sure.

Race details and rules were mostly a repeat for those who had run one of Ian Adamson's desert challenges before. Team Illinois listened, but knew what the story would be. They were even better prepared as a team, and the training for the Sahara Race had started early in April. More weight training, more hill climbs and more weight in the backpack would be the training regimen through the Illinois summer of 2005.

Nancy and Joel had been playing catch-up at work with their individual clients who were looking to continue their own training programs after their return from China. Both Joel and Nancy's coaching and personal training careers were taking off especially with the press coverage they had received. Much like Dave's friends and co-workers, everyone wanted to know the secret to pushing the mind and body to the next level. Their summer remained busy seven days a week as they caught up with work and home responsibilities. The Sahara Race would back everything up once again.

Nancy had clearly started to view the desert competitions as a quest. RacingThePlanet was a series of races after all. Four different continents and four of the world's harshest deserts would complete the series, and the last desert would be by invitation only. The Sahara Race provided a chance to accomplish two personal goals. First to prove that the win at Gobi was not a fluke, and second to qualify for an invitation to a desert that was surrounded by, and covered in frozen water. Antarctica was the destination for the last race and despite it having a ready supply of ice and snow, Antarctica still qualified as one of the driest, windiest and by default, coldest places on Earth. It was a desert by definition, but chances are that t-shirts and shorts wouldn't be appropriate running gear in that climate.

Ian went over some of the same information about the reptiles and other smaller creatures that could be found in the Sahara, sharing the same story about rock piles and scorpions that he described for the volunteers. The meeting was nearly over and there was still some socialization time left before the competitors took off to their tents for the evening. Team Illinois circled back with Jacob Nielsen and Chuck Walker and a few others from the previous two races, but it was getting late and all decided to turn in for the night.

Joel, Nancy and Dave had decided to give up their padded bed mats to save a little more weight, and they were all trying to mold the sand under the floor tarp of the tent to cradle their bodies. Most seemed to fall to sleep quickly, but Joel kept getting disturbed by the snoring of a couple of newbees on the other side of the tent. Joel never slept well that first night.

Day One

The official start to the Sahara Race would be 9:00 a.m. local time from the day-one camp "Farafra". Joel was eager to hit the 32K first-day course as is looked to be relatively straight and flat. Expectations of an easy run were common among those who had never attempted this sort of endurance challenge before. They would of course, be mistaken.

Nancy's strong race was the Atacama Crossing, though she would never admit that. Dave's strong race was the Gobi March, but Joel sensed that he might have to step up and be the strength behind Team Illinois for the Sahara Race. If all three were gathered in a room discussing who bonked or who was strong for a particular stage, none of the three would admit to being the glue that held the team together for any particular stage or race. Each would point to another member of the team to say that he or she was truly the strong one. It was like that in the Fudacz-Burrows-Kuhnau family. They had indeed grown to love each other over the course of the previous year, and no one person would claim credit for success in any race. It was a team after all.

Despite the health issues Nancy ran into at Atacama, it was her drive and never-quit determination that proved to be the inspiration for the whole team. Better prepared for Gobi, Dave continued to be a pace leader and a workhorse for the team, helping to drive them to the finish line each day. Sahara would be Joel's race to shine. Joel had positioned himself for leadership partly through his enhanced training regimen and partly due to dietary changes, but mostly due to the fact that it was simply Joel's turn. Good teams might have one consistent leader at the top of the team structure, but great teams have people who share and shift the responsibility for leadership based on skill sets or experience or even based on a point in time. Joel was feeling great coming into the Sahara Race and not that he planned to become the strength of the team in Egypt, but it would just work out that way.

The mystery of the team jersey color was settled on the starting line, as Team Illinois did find a more functional fabric blend though it didn't happen to be yellow. Team Illinois could be seen as the Electric Blue Train while trudging through the hot sands. Joel and Dave had apparently decided that a new hair cut or more accurately stated, a lack-of-hair cut would absorb less heat than longer darker hair. Both had ventured into what appeared to be the same hair stylist, Joel receiving his number two blade buzz cut and blonde dye job while Dave opted for the clean look, shaved right down to the scalp. Nancy opted out of the buzz cut decision as well as the dye job, preferring to keep her slightly off the shoulder length brown hair.

While some of the individual competitors and newbees ran hard out of the gate at the starting gun, Team Illinois began their typical brisk but controlled pace. They had done the calculations and determined what their pace might need to be per kilometer to keep themselves near the top of the leader board. Joel knew that if they could stay with the leaders or even keep the team lead overall, they would be able to pull away from the pack on the 50 mile "long day".

There would only be two middle checkpoints between start and finish the first day at Sahara, leaving approximately 8K between water checkpoints. They had started the race late (in temperature terms), where by 9:00 a.m. it had already climbed to 105 degrees Fahrenheit or 40 degrees Celsius. As they passed 10:00 a.m. on day one of the race, the temperature climbed over 115F / 46C.

On the way to the first checkpoint, Team Illinois began to pass many of the individual competitors who had blasted out from the starting line. Five kilometers into the race and people were already beginning to have difficulty in the heat. Joel wondered what their training could have possibly been like, or what their expectations would be for running in this kind of environment. In either case it was clear that some of the first-timers in the pack were not prepared for the conditions of a long distance desert race, and were dropping off the pace quickly.

The landscape was becoming beautiful about five miles into the stage, and the terrain remained relatively hard-packed and flat which was always a good surface for running. It wasn't a bad way really to ease everyone into a seven day race. The RacingThePlanet course designers did well to open up the Sahara Race on a good note. Team Illinois began to pass rock structures that included deposits or large formations of white rock-like material that they later learned were a form of chalk. Boulder-sized formations popped up from the tan desert sand floor, like misshapen white mushroom caps.

The heat would remain oppressive all day but that was part of the challenge after all. Shifting from a hard packed surface to something a little softer than running on skree, the trail would change to take some of the energy out of each stride. Running on softer soil or sand was brutal over a long distance, but the terrain varied enough to include some harder packed chalk and salt flats for an easier run. Quickly approaching the first checkpoint, Team Illinois was running strong and keeping themselves hydrated and chemically balanced in the proper way. Each team member had determined the right mix of electrolytes and nutrition in order to combat the heat and keep the muscles and body organs working. The Electric Blue Train's engines seemed to be working well during the first stage.

Seven Degrees

They had learned so much since the Atacama Crossing, especially about the importance of keeping the body chemistry working under the stress of heat conditions. Heat stroke can attack quickly unless team members keep a close watch on themselves and each other. All it takes is an additional seven degrees Fahrenheit in the body's core temperature to prove fatal.

When the body core temperature is raised from 98 degrees to 105 degrees Fahrenheit, body and brain functions are severely impacted regardless of how the body chemistry is being managed. Even at rest, the human body will process and lose one liter of water every hour in heat stress conditions. Without water and the ability to keep the body core temperature under 105, a human will typically become incapacitated in 12 hours, and fall into coma in 24. Individual competitors in the desert need to watch themselves for signs of heat stroke, but by the time some of the symptoms occur, it might be too late for them to take corrective action. Symptoms include:

> Headache
> Dizziness
> Disorientation, agitation or confusion
> Sluggishness or fatigue
> Seizure
> Hot, dry skin that is flushed but not sweaty
> Loss of consciousness
> Rapid heart beat
> Hallucinations

Not to make light of a potential grave situation in the desert, but once you experience the symptom of losing consciousness, it's a little too late to do anything about the root cause of your ailment.

It was an advantage to run with a partner or team under the worst of conditions. Nancy could monitor Joel, Dave could monitor Nancy, Joel could monitor Dave. If the situation called for it, you took the initiative and spit water on your friend's head and neck to help bring her core temperature down. You could see if your teammates are becoming disoriented or fatigued and take action to find shelter.

Watching the Train Wreck

As Team Illinois continued their fast but comfortable pace, they had maintained the lead in the team competition but were starting to see individual competitors along the way struggling to even keep moving forward. They had spotted several individuals who were off to a fast start, now down to a walking pace. One who was close to the second checkpoint looked to be slightly disoriented and had trouble walking in a straight line. Thankfully, shade and water were close at hand. The story would be the same for many wandering on day one of the Sahara Race, but the complete story of devastation wouldn't be known until the end of the day back at camp.

About mid point between the second checkpoint and the finish line for day one, Team Illinois seemed to be hitting their individual walls at the same time. Nancy was back to her usual but always unpleasant nausea while Joel and Dave were experiencing muscle fatigue.

They kept themselves hydrated and slowed their pace to a point where they could continue to move forward. They still held on the team lead position in the race and slowing down would have been the safe thing to do, but Team Illinois was not comfortable just walking it in. The last few kilometers had them alternating from running to walking pace and their completion time for the day would not be particularly stellar.

When the heat had started to get the best of them, Team Illinois took a tip they had learned from Dr. Brandee Waite during the Gobi March. Dr. Waite was a returning member of the RacingThePlanet medical staff and was experienced in the training, and medical management of endurance athletes. An accomplished athlete herself, Dr. Waite had advised Team Illinois to carry small water spray bottles and use them on each other's head an neck to dispel heat more quickly. It was the same technology used to break the heat while waiting in long lines at most any Florida theme park.

Instead of large fans blowing water mist over customers waiting in line, Team Illinois shared the job of misting each other's head to cool it off. This method also eliminates the need to spit water on friends and family.

Team Illinois crossed the line in five hours, seventeen minutes. One of the regulars from the Atacama Crossing and Gobi March, Kevin Lin, had turned in a time just over three hours for the day. Performance on day one varied greatly between team and individual and the heat was proving to be the worst of any desert race so far. Word was spreading in the camp about the unseasonably high temperatures in Egypt for that time of year, and further reports of race drop outs were spreading around camp.

That evening Team Illinois had learned that some teams were struggling to keep their teams together and depending on the posted status the following morning, might have been disqualified from the team competition on the first day. One team was found to have separated in the desert for unknown reasons and had come into camp at different finish times. It was unclear what circumstances had caused them to split apart but that action would be enough to be taken out of the running from the team competition. Team after all, meant "team of three". The rules had specified that teams needed to be in plain sight of each other on the course, and cross all checkpoints and finish lines together as a group.

A total of nine people would drop completely from the race after the first day. Those teams who disqualified could still compete as individuals and post individual stage times for the remainder of the race, and most of them would wind up standing on the starting line for day two.

Team Illinois returned to the shelter of the tent where it was still hot, but any shade was better than no shade at all. They tended to new blisters (always on the first day of any race), and took on as much water as they could hold down. It takes the body a while to cool down after any workout, under the best climate controlled conditions. In a tent on the Sahara Desert floor, it takes forever. Sometimes the lungs will help to cool the core body temperature down, assuming that the temperature of the air taken into the body is cooler than the actual body's temperature. Not today. Team Illinois would have to continue using the evaporative qualities of water to help cool them off until the sun had finally set for the day. It was still mid-afternoon and sunset wouldn't come until 5:17 p.m. It was best for them all to relax in the safety of the tent and wait for the surface heat of the desert to cool off.

Day Two

At just over 20 miles, day one had claimed the largest single-day percentage of drop outs compared to Gobi or Atacama. Day two would be a marathon distance at 26.2 miles and would not be a pleasure cruise for anyone who had struggled on day one.

Joel was feeling strong on the starting line despite his lack of sleep. Noise in the tent would be a common disturbance thanks to the endless snoring of at least two people who shared quarters with Team Illinois. Joel grabbed onto as much sleep as he could, but he and Dave were talking about the alternative of sleeping under the stars later that night. Nancy seemed to drop like a stone once she had fallen asleep and was not as affected by the stereo snoring effect in the tent.

The posted start time for day two was set at 7:00 a.m. in order to provide some sort of break from the mid-day heat. Taking advantage of that two hour difference in start time was only beneficial if you could get yourself out of the sun before you had to suffer through the afternoon bake. For many on day one who came in after the sun had set, they had suffered through the entire day of sun exposure. As slow as Team Illinois' five+ hour finish time was, they were still out of the sun by 2:30 p.m. Dave summarized the predictability of the Sahara temperature swings.

"It was like turning on a light switch. At ten O-clock every day, the heat would climb twenty or more degrees and stay there all day until sunset around five. Some of the individual racers who could complete the distance in four hours or less would have the advantage of avoiding most of the day's punishment."

Day two obstacles would include more of a mix of terrain, including a stretch of smaller sand dunes to negotiate, right about the time when legs were begging to stop. Ian had again found a way to challenge those who thought that a marathon was too easy.

As the day wore on and Team Illinois had passed two checkpoints, it was clear based on their interval times between checkpoints that this would be another slow race day. It would not be clear until they made it back to base camp, how their overall time would compare to the rest of the competition. They managed to keep the lead in the team competition during day two; at least they knew that they were not passed by any other team along the race trail.

After the second checkpoint, the heat had begun to rise and Team Illinois took advantage of some shade cast by a large truck found along the race trail. It was still over 110 degrees Fahrenheit in the shade, but it was cooler than standing out in the open desert. They rested and cooled themselves as best they could before hitting Ian's sand dunes another mile away.

Team Illinois chose to stay at the next checkpoint for more than 10 minutes, able to take on fresh water and cool down their body temperatures as much as they could, but knew that they had to move in order to finish the day. It was another seven miles to the finish line and despite the muscles that wanted to lock up and stop working; Team Illinois forced themselves back onto the course. Nancy had said it best in previous races; they all "just wanted to be done". There was something to be said for getting out of the heat and the sun as quickly as possible.

Punished by small dunes and with only one mile left until the finish line, Team Illinois had to stop near a rock with a small overhang and curled up on the ground under the shade. Both Nancy and Dave had thrown up the little amount of remaining liquid in their stomachs, and Joel lay on his side away from the group, without the strength to get up and relieve himself. Joel continued to lie off to the side while Nancy and Dave dealt with their stomach issues. Dave talks about the interesting events at their unplanned stop.

"As I lay on my side puking, I could hear what I thought was running water and began to believe I was hallucinating again like back in the Atacama Desert. I began to look around and noticed that Joel was laying on his side with his back to us and that there was a trickle of water running down the hill from him. In my scratchy dehydrated voice I said 'Dude…what are you doing?' Joel responded with, 'What does it look like I'm doing…I'm too tired to stand up and pee. Besides this works really well on a hill'. How can you not love a teammate that conserves energy every chance they can."

They would eventually force themselves to their feet to finish the day walking. Their bodies could not be convinced to run. Team Illinois finished the second stage in 7:37. Nancy and Dave were absent of any remaining energy and Joel was still overheating and suffering symptoms of heat exhaustion. He sat in the medical tent getting sprayed down with water until his core body temperature started to drop. Joel drank as much water as he could hold and still felt sick as he walked back to his tent. It took all afternoon through to sunset before Joel could start to feel normal again. For the average person, the concept of feeling normal takes on the connotation of sitting in a comfortable chair, possibly with remote control, in an air conditioned environment, with clothing that isn't sticking to their bodies. For Joel, normal simply meant he might have the luxury of not throwing up the water his body was begging for him to retain.

By 5:00 p.m. there were more than 20 competitors left out in the desert and by 8:30 p.m., ten were still more than a mile away from camp. Those who spent the entire day out in the sun would pay a significant price for the slow pace. As the stage race times were posted, Team Illinois was shocked to hear that three of the five teams entered for the Sahara Race were either disqualified or had already dropped from the race altogether. Though the high elevation at Atacama and the dunes of Gobi were challenging for any experienced endurance racer, the heat of Sahara was claiming more casualties with each passing day. One team remained in the race along with Team Illinois. Made up of members from three different countries, the international team was pressing Team Illinois but remained more than 3 hours back from them in the standings.

Even the water bottles were hot. After coming in from an extremely long day of running through the hot sand, a cool drink is all that anyone would ask for. Despite being stored in the shade of the tents, the ambient temperature alone would bake the water up over 100 degrees. Dave and Joel had met a military survival specialist from South Africa on the first day of the event, but noticed him stuffing water bottles into his socks and then wetting his socks down. Neil Reynolds had just finished a tour of duty in Iraq as part of an international military force and had learned the trick of evaporation as a means to cool off just about anything, provided there was a breeze.

The slight wind that day provided enough of a means to cool off the bottle while the water evaporated from the sock, the whole process taking some of the heat away from the contents of the bottle. After ten minutes or so out in the sun, sitting atop the burning sand, the wet sock did the trick and the water inside had indeed cooled down. The process did not stay secret for long, and other bottle-shaped socks were found standing erect out on the open sand. Given the nastiness of a two day-old desert racing sock, they probably could have stood up on their own anyway, but in this case water bottles were reaping the benefits of the newly learned cooling process. "Just don't smell the bottle when your drinking from it", an unidentified voice called out from a neighboring tent.

Shade found in the tent was also proving to be treacherous commodity for competitors as well as a necessity. While the afternoon sun could be avoided underneath the tent ceiling, it also provided the same benefit for any creature looking to hide from the sun. Dave describes an encounter with a tiny but unwelcome visitor.

"Gunnar Nilsson had spotted a small Black Scorpion on the ceiling of our tent and knocked it down into the sand. As Gunnar and others tried to step on it and kill it, the sand gave way to cover the creature. All it did was pop back up out of the sand even more angry. Surprise!"

As the day wound into twilight, everyone looked forward to sunset and then a potential break from the heat. A planned evening of recuperation wound up to be nothing of the sort. The late evening produced a storm that was as intense as the heat of mid-day. A massive sand storm had appeared sometime after midnight, and was pounding the foundations of most tents in camp. The wind in conjunction with the weight of the sand worked to pull up corners of two tents, and collapse poles. The RacingThePlanet volunteer staff braved the abrasive storm to secure the tents, but the two in peril had been completely blown over in the wind. Most occupants chose to remain under the collapse, covered at least by a layer of tent fabric, but a few of the competitors and some of the remaining staff sought shelter in open trucks used in the daily camp-migration convoy.

Joel and Dave had agreed before the storm that they couldn't take another night of stereophonic snoring. They had grabbed their sleeping bags and went out to a nearby dune incline to lie out under the stars. The wind was just a breeze at first and it felt good running across the body as they fell to sleep. As the wind mixed with sand and became more violent, Dave and Joel stayed on the dune but zipped up their bag hoods to help keep the sand out. There was one benefit to the wind for Joel and Dave, it erased any evidence of the evening's activity on the sand around them. The significance of that benefit would not be realized until the following evening however. The storm would never completely end, carrying the wind up through the 6:30 a.m. starting time on day three.

Day Three

Reacting to the unseasonable heat, the RacingThePlanet organizers pushed the start time for the stage up another half hour in an attempt to give everyone as much a break from the mid-day heat as possible. Stage three was set for 32 Kilometers or 20 miles and would include sights of more hard packed flats and dunes, with a welcome surprise at the midpoint of the race.

Joel was running strong again on day three with Nancy close behind. The husband and wife duo had done well to interpret the needs of a complex desert endurance race and adjusted their training schedule as needed. The mistakes made at the Atacama Crossing had been recovered from, and Joel was reaping the benefit of a better training program, more experience and the support of his teammates.

Where Dave ran strong the entire Gobi March, Joel was shifting roles to become a leader when the team needed one. On any given day it could be Nancy or Dave as well, but Joel had recovered from his "bonk" on day two and was ready to be the motivational leader on day three.

Day three was also the first opportunity to cross paths with Jacob (Ya-Kob) Nielsen on the course. Jacob was always running in or around the same pace of Team Illinois now for two races. Joel had decided that it must be because his training, body type and metabolism were similar to their own, but in any case it was good to see him running well. He had passed them with his traditional "Team Illinois, C'mon keep going. You guys look freaking awesome!"

Team Illinois ran hard for the first two hours including a stop at the first checkpoint complete with a natural oasis. The race volunteer staff had added a few new members including a couple of guys who had to drop from the race on day two. The camaraderie between everyone at the race was stellar. New volunteers were helping competitors to dip into the cold spring water of the oasis and poured it over their heads.

A reptile incident had apparently been avoided at the oasis earlier in the day as Egyptian Tourist Police were called to dispatch a large viper that was found near the water. The police were diligent in their monitoring and protection of the entire RacingThePlanet group and removing large snakes was just one of their services. Nice job fellas.

Back again out on the course near the last checkpoint for the day, Dave had told Joel that he was "done" and that the race and the heat had finally beaten him down. Nancy was suffering too, but Nancy would never admit to Joel that she was weakening. Joel commented on Dave's condition.

"After the last CP, Dave and I had a heart to heart. He said this race had finally broken him. He was very upset that his reserve tank was constantly empty. I told him this was why we race as a team. We work well off each other and need to look out for each other."

Before reaching the finish line, Dave was beginning to fall apart fast. The team found a parked truck near the trail and Dave rolled under it enough to take advantage of a little shade. Team Illinois would rest there for ten minutes then walk to complete the last mile and a half to the finish.

Finishing the stage and arriving in camp with an elapsed time of 6:01, they worked together with Jacob and other new few friends from the Gobi March as an extended team to help motivate and carry each other to the day's goal. It was a decent finish time when compared to the previous stage, but not a great time. Team Illinois remained significantly behind the individual race leaders, but still held command of the team spot.

Once in camp they learned that the only remaining team in the competition had imploded before day three had even started. One member of the multi-country European team was still seeking medical attention on the morning of day three, and had missed the starting line with his teammates. Instead of waiting for him, the two other members of the team took off without him. At that moment, the European team had disqualified. The abandoned team member in the medical tent could still choose to run an individual race, and he was offered no other choice than to run alone on day three. His now former teammates would be running individual stage times for the remainder of the race.

Team Illinois arrived in camp later that afternoon, wrecked as usual but Dave especially would struggle to recover from the third consecutive day of 120 degree heat. Nancy wasn't as bad off as Dave, but she returned to the shade of the tent as well, waiting to feel better from the stress of the day. Two hours later, they all started to improve and reclaim some energy, enough to stand up without feeling dizzy that is. Dave ventured out of the tent and bumped into one of the individual competitors in the women's division. He describes the story of an unwelcome visitor to her tent that afternoon.

"One of the race leaders in the women's division, Theresa Schneider, was telling me a story about a Camel Spider that had made a home in her tent, looking for its own place to get out of the sun. They had to toss the spider out of the tent to try and get rid of it only to see it scamper back inside to find shade. Since the spider was about the size of a ten inch dinner plate and ate scorpions for lunch, no one was happy to play the role of exterminator. A local volunteer managed to squash it inside the tent. It was further affirmation for me that sleeping outside the tent was a good idea."

The boys of Team Illinois chose to return to the sand rather than the tent later that evening, while Nancy opted to endure the noise until she could doze off. While the rest of the camp retired to their tents with flashlights scanning the corners and ceilings for nasty crawling things, Dave and Joel's sleeping bags were unrolled again and they both relaxed to views of the stars and the occasional sight of a high altitude jet liner, complete with vapor trail.

Day Four

Different from the other two deserts where the heat index would only spike above 110 degrees Fahrenheit then cool down late in the day, at Sahara the temperature stayed consistently above that mark all day long. A cool evening meant that the ambient temperature was only a couple of degrees cooler than normal body temperature. In other words, it was never cool in Sahara unless of course you are talking to a teenager and they are referring to the sights of the desert rather than the heat.

Race start time was again pushed up another hour to 5:30 a.m. to cut more heat out of the day. Dave and Joel woke to the noise of the camp and also to find a surprise waiting for them near their sleeping bags. What they couldn't see the morning after the wind storm was now quite clear the morning of day four. Critter tracks were found encircling both their sleeping bags as various reptiles and other multi-legged walking creatures left footprints (if they could be called footprints), all around them. Curved repeating furrows in the sand were clearly a result of an unknown snake passing by and the scattered repeating pattern of two-track foot prints could have been left by scorpions or spiders. It was best not to elaborate on the possible species they had both unwittingly encountered while they slept.

Based on the tracks and their position relative to their sleeping bags, neither Joel nor Dave could determine if they had actually been crawled on, but they were definitely crawled around. Both were quick to share the news with Nancy and she was glad that she chose the entertainment offered to her by the snoring, rather than by the local residents of the Sahara desert.

Day four would turn out to be another marathon distance of 26.2 miles and people were starting to line up. While three of the teams had already dropped from the competition by day two, the only remaining team in the competition had disqualified by leaving a teammate behind on the starting line of day three. The multi-country European team had been the only remaining competition for Team Illinois on day three, but now Team Illinois was running unopposed for the team trophy. Day four would be a day where Team Illinois would be forced to change their strategy, now without a competing team to chase.

The European team had all appeared on the starting line for stage four. Joel wondered if they had patched up whatever issue had caused the two teammates to leave the other behind on day three. Despite being officially out of the team competition, they could still provide a support system for each other out on the open sand. To Joel, that seemed like the logical thing to do.

It was evident to Joel and Nancy that the multi-country European team had been put together for speed. Nancy had spotted the body type and she and Joel noted the speed with which they attacked the start of every stage. Joel and Nancy had already learned from Atacama, "The race was not only about speed, it was all about strength and consistency over the seven days of the race." Team Illinois also knew that there was strength in the team structure and breaking up the team from Illinois, regardless of the circumstance, would never be a consideration.

Speed was no longer a requirement for Team Illinois on day four. All they would have to do was finish the race on day seven to be crowned champions for the second straight desert challenge. It was a position that they had not experienced at any team race. There would be no one to chase, and nobody chasing them. Two factors they had used as motivators were now gone. Dave admitted, "A real moment of fear had settled into each of our guts. The real question was, what do we do now?"

The strategy that they had implemented well in the past now had to change. It required a re-think about the goal and what the daily motivation needed to be. Without the combination of the goal and the motivation to reach it, Team Illinois would struggle just to finish the race. In most all team leadership situations the absence of a firm goal and lack of motivation will kill the productivity of a team.

After the start, Team Illinois was only able to run through the first two checkpoints or 12 miles before needing to slow to a 4:1 minute run to walk ratio. Later that morning the ratio was reduced to a 2:1 pace. Dave and Nancy had been suffering all day in the heat, and Joel was left to anchor the team, become cheerleader, and dune climbing lead. The course on day four was sandy and soft and provided for horrible conditions to run in. Legs and feet would move forward and half their energy would be lost digging body weight into the sand rather than pushing their bodies forward.

Joel decided to slow the team's pace down conceding that it would be more important to keep his team alive and active rather than lose them to heat stress. The Sahara had produced conditions that removed more competitors from the race each day, and finishing became the new priority and the new goal. Joel would help drive their team but also make sure they were healthy enough to finish on day seven.

Wandering Alone in the Desert

Team Illinois got a mental boost when they ran across Jacob again. Dave tried to muster up his best greeting in a dry, scratchy voice, "Jacob, you look freaking awesome!" They walked together as an expanded team again, making as much progress in the soft sand as they could. The thermometer on their backpack strap was reading 50 degrees Celsius or over 122 degrees Fahrenheit. In the midst of the sweltering heat the same lone member of the mixed-country (European) team that was left behind on day three, was now seen wandering alone along the marked trail. Though the European team members were all were back together on the starting line for day four, the group had separated once again and the same man had been left to run his own race out in the open desert.

From a distance they could see that his legs were taking him left and right instead of forward. As they got closer to him they could see that he was showing signs of being overheated and dehydrated. The combined group of Team Illinois with Jacob Nielsen stopped him and sat him down while covering him in a reflective space blanket, a lightweight foil/plastic blanket used by emergency rescue crews. In this particular situation, the foil blanket provided shade for the man barely able to speak.

Enough cover was provided by the blanket while they forced some of their own electrolyte packets and water into him. A staff truck could be seen off in the distance and Jacob helped flag the truck down for assistance. While the lone European teammate sat in the shade of the truck, Team Illinois pulled out Dr. Waite's handy spray bottles and began to mist the man down, helping to reduce his body temperature. They all waited with him to see if he could recover and eventually he did. No one wanted to see a fellow competitor drop from the race if they could make a conscious decision to move on. It would be left up to the man who they found out was Stefan, to make the decision when he was of sound enough mind to do so.

The Power Of Team

Racing Sahara would be a very personal journey for anyone who attempted it and aside from the team aspect of the race, it was still a significant personal accomplishment for anyone to have punished the body and the mind to its limits and still conquer the challenge. Stefan, the lone runner from the now defunct European team, had decided to finish the race after all. Joel describes the last few miles to the finish.

"About 5 km from the end of the day, Jacob's nose started bleeding. At the same time, Nan started dry heaving and we had to wait for her to get her breathing and stomach back under control. We helped Jacob pack his nose, and then he and Stefan took off ahead of us. Nan got sick a few more times on the way to the finish but we finally crossed the line."

Dave and Nancy went directly to the tent to off load weight and try to cool off. Joel was exhausted but still able to stay on his feet to check with some others from the course on the damage from the day. As the sun set and the temperatures cooled off, Dave and Nancy returned to the commons of the tent area but the breeze was still hot from the mid-day sun. Chuck Walker and Derek and a few others were seen walking in and around the tent areas and everyone looked to be dead from the heat. Joel and Jacob, Nancy and Dave and a few others had gathered to talk about strategy for survival on the long day. Day five would be scheduled for another 50 miles in the same heat that was causing competitors to drop the race in distances less than 27 miles.

All were in agreement that they were going to try to gain as much ground as they could early before the heat of mid-day started claiming casualties. After the 20 to 25 mile mark in the stage, Joel planned to slow the group down and coast through the heat of the day. After that it would be a matter of water and "heat exhaustion management" until they could get to sunset around 5:00 P.M.

Joel and Dave would turn in for the evening again out on the open sand. Nancy would have no part in sharing her evening with the "critters". Dave and Joel figured that they just needed to keep the zipper closed on their sleeping bag and everything would be fine. Considering that Team Illinois had proven to be pretty good at setting strategy in the past, the whole "we'll be fine out here among the scorpions" decision, was escaping Nancy.

The Long Day

The Atacama Crossing and the Gobi March had already taught them that the 50+ mile stage in the seven day race was all about survival though the long day. It had also been a strong suit in the past for Team Illinois. Not that their speed had been spectacular on the long day, but they had managed to find a formula that allowed them to carry a consistent pace and still rest along the way. The simple allocation of work load, for lack of a better term, was the ticket to managing the distance and the productivity of the team.

Basic ratios for running and walking were applied for the day and Team Illinois would indeed try to cover as much distance as quickly as they could before the sun got hot again. It would be the now famous 9:1 minute ratio for running to walking at the start. The minute of walking seemed to allow the body a chance to gather oxygen, to process water and to cool off. It is truly a non-scientific observation of why the running/walking splits had worked for Team Illinois, but the strategy did work. While many of their fellow competitors pushed hard from the very start of each stage non-stop, Team Illinois usually caught up with them by the mid point of the 50 mile distance.

There were athlete exceptions to the rule as well. Past individual winners and top finishers of the RTP challenges had indeed run most of the course with very little walking. In some cases their individual performance could have been attributed to more intensive training, or a better physiological body type that was better suited for distance running. It would be difficult to say if any of the three members of Team Illinois would have posted better individual times than they did as a team. Somehow the team structure for Nancy, Joel and Dave had served them well. Where all other teams had come apart by day three in Sahara, they had managed to keep it together. No one would know if Nancy in Atacama, or Dave at Gobi or Joel in Sahara could have contended for the individual lead. Perhaps individual competition was not their strongest play in this new game they had found in the desert.

For Team Illinois, there was a greater satisfaction for all within the team structure, that is to say when the structure is formed well. It was a family experience and there was satisfaction to be had when helping a teammate excel beyond their individual expectations. It's a different kind of competitive satisfaction. Still, guys like Kevin Lin (Taiwan) and Ray Zahab (Canada) had posted monster individual times in the previous Sahara stages and were to be admired for their individual accomplishments. They had survived out there alone in the desert, relying only on themselves to get through each checkpoint and to find the motivation to keep pushing further.

Group motivation would be difficult to find for Team Illinois during stage five. They had already won the team competition and there was no need to push any harder on the 50 mile day. The lack of motivation can kill the performance of a team, and Joel knew that Dave was already out of gas from the previous day. Nancy was still holding up well enough, but she had taken a long time to recover from her heat-induced sickness the day before. Joel would have to be the task master and pull his team through the brutality of the heat on day five.

There was no need to be reckless and push a pace that couldn't be maintained, but Joel knew that some sort of goal and pace had to be set in order to keep Nancy and Dave from just giving up. The climate would assist Joel a little on day five, providing a bit of a cold snap during mid-day which brought the temperatures down to a crisp 109 degrees Fahrenheit, 43 Celsius. Joel describes the ground conditions on the long day.

"The terrain was not too challenging early on. We were able to move around a 9 minute run, 1 minute walk for the first hour. We worked with a small group of people and covered a good amount of ground. The second hour we kept running, but a little slower pace then at the start. The landscape was pretty soft at times, which slowed down our progress. Portions were quite pretty, even spectacular, but after awhile the long day becomes monotonous."

Nancy and Dave were not all that talkative throughout the day while they were alternating with each other as to who would start to feel sick. They had made the first two checkpoints and moved on quickly trying to cover ground before mid-day, but their team pace slowed as they approached checkpoint three for the day.

Team Illinois had partnered up with a new acquaintance from Canada, Sandy McCallum, who was posting similar stage times to Team Illinois all week long. It was good to bring in new faces and friends in a mutual struggle towards the same goal, and the four of them had started new conversations and joked about events of the week. It was good to focus on anything other than the brutality of the desert, and in its own small way helped to keep the Electric Blue Train moving. Sometimes the simplest gesture or positive activity can be a strong motivator. Sandy would stay with Team Illinois all day long.

Walking the back half of the long day meant that they would be passed by individuals and small groups along the marked trail. It was hard to be on the receiving end of a "pass" when they had been so strong on the 50 mile day in the past.

As the day crept into night around 5:00 p.m., everyone was pleased to get another small break from the heat, but the temperature was still hovering around 100F / 38C. Nancy struggled again to keep water in her system. They waited longer at each checkpoint for Nancy's stomach and Dave's legs to recover. It took longer for the benefits of water and electrolytes to kick in, and they waited until it was safe to move on to the next checkpoint.

The Sahara Race had been one of changing goals, forcing Team Illinois to set smaller and more achievable targets in order to keep making progress. Joel had set a finish target for the 50 miles at midnight that night in order to give their small group something tangible to shoot for. Joel found himself to be a clock-watcher as they continued on past the second-from-last checkpoint for the day. The midnight target time drifted closer but Joel remained focused, trying to be the strength for the team when they needed it most. As Joel looked away from his watch and refocused on the desert, another wandering desert soul was spotted walking in front of their group.

Team Illinois along with Sandy had brought Hamish Morrison from Australia into the group and they started another conversation to take everyone's mind off the heat and the pain. Something as simple as a conversation where everyone shares in the story, is a strong motivating tool. When one member of the team is down or focusing on the wrong kind of thing (like sour stomachs or tired legs), refocusing attention on the pain of Ian's Gobi dune course or Attie the guardian angel would keep the body moving.

Glow sticks framing the front of the last checkpoint could finally be seen and the group of five entered to find one of their favorite RTP staffers, Jan Richardson, with treats for everyone. Nancy was continuing to battle her sick stomach and Jan pulled her off to the side and helped to take care of her. During the short stay, Jan had provided some chocolate and carbonated soda for everyone and the simple sugar rush of a little soda seemed to boost everyone's internal engine including Nancy's. With backpacks on, the new expanded group of five pushed on towards camp and the finish line.

It was only a 7K short run into camp from that last checkpoint, but the motivator remained a simple one. For all intents and purposes, the bulk of the Sahara Race would be over once they arrived. Day six would be a rest day though a shortened one, and the final stage of the race on day seven would be more of a symbolic run rather than any challenging distance. Dave talked about the mood of their expanded team now that everyone was mentally and physically "spent" towards the end of day five.

"Conversations would come and go with longer moments of silence in between for quiet self motivation and reflection. Similar to a hermit crab that emerges from its shell to forage for food, individuals in our group would emerge during their personal suffering to eat, chat a little or share funny stories about life. After a while the need for silence would overcome the group and each person would retreat to the safety of their thoughts while continuing to run."

The last few miles were not made easy, and glow sticks were becoming more difficult to find along the trail. New honorary team members Sandy and Hamish were helping to provide additional sets of eyes to spot the markers and keep the group moving in the right direction. As they approached more dunes near the end of the stage, Joel and Dave wondered what Chuck Walker might have said as he approached them. At the top of the dune climb, they finally saw camp. Luckily for the group, it would be the last dune to climb for the entire Sahara Race.

Nancy, Joel, Dave, Sandy and Hamish all exercised Team Illinois' tradition of holding hands as they crossed the stage-five finish line. It was an extended group effort and they all shared responsibility for helping carry the other team members through to the finish.

The extended team crossed the line close to midnight, but others had completed the 50 miles in only ten hours. For Team Illinois, finishing the 50 miles in a single day meant rest on day six. There would be time to mend blisters, take on calories and relax. The final stage on day seven would map out to be only 10K or just over six miles. The proposed distance for the final stage was not much of a burden given its length compared to any other day of the Sahara Race. Team Illinois and everyone else for that matter would happily take on a six mile run to close out another memorable adventure. There was no point to pushing any pace on day seven. It would be a day to enjoy the sights, revel in their accomplishments, and appreciate the hard work that each member of Team Illinois had invested during the past year.

While Nancy and Dave and Joel co-mingled with their old and new friends during the early part of day six, others were sill coming into camp. The final two competitors crossed the stage-five finish line at almost 2:00 p.m. in the afternoon on day six. It would be a long 31 hour day for them, and it was good to see all fellow sufferers had finally made it back to camp.

The Final Stage

At midnight on day six, camp was disassembled and all competitors were bussed back to Cairo for an exciting finish to the Sahara Race. It would be another long bus ride but the payoff would be found the next morning as they would race along a 10K path leading to the Pyramids at Giza.

The race started in the city as they all ran along a canal leading out of the city and back towards the desert. Joel and Nancy had determined that the pace should be reasonable but not too slow and Dave's energy had been returning with the extended break on day six. For many in the race, there was no reason to set a fast pace. Regardless of how much time they might make up against another competitor, the short distance would prevent most in the pack from improving on their current placement on the stat sheet. For the individual and team competitions, the winners in each category were locked by the end of the long day.

Team Illinois was surrounded by friends and fellow sufferers as they started their run through the city finally approaching the edge of the sand. From about 5K on, the pyramids could be seen in the distance. Everyone in the pack was uplifted from the sight and the pace picked up for all without anyone consciously choosing to run faster. The adrenaline seemed to be supplied equally for all in the group.

As Joel and company approached the first pyramid, a CNN film crew was spotted shooting the competitors while using the pyramids as a backdrop. Joel slowed to touch the corner of one of the base stones, and the team rounded the same corner to see the finish line down hill from a road leading to the Sphinx. Quickening their pace, they could see and hear the RacingThePlanet staff, volunteers, and some of the faster finishers applauding each competitor as they approached the banners and the finish line. Team Illinois crossed the line in typical fashion, holding each other's hands and raising their arms to the sky. They completed the 10K stage in 1:03, with a total completion time of 40:54. They were once again team champions.

Other friends and colleagues did well on the finish line. Chuck Walker put up a tremendous number of 33:59, but missed out on first place in his age bracket by just over an hour. Derek Kwik struggled in the heat of Sahara, but still finished and qualified for The Last Desert race in Antarctica. Other new faces were grabbing the top of the leader board. Ray Zahab from Canada posted a winning time of 26:24 time to take the men's overall competition while Kevin Lin took second place with a 27:33.

In the women's division, newcomer Theresa Schneider from the U.S. took the championship with an overall time of 32:18, while another newcomer, Kazuko Kaihata from Japan followed in second place with a time of 34:08 with Lisanne Dorion finishing third.

Joel reflected on the Team Illinois victory after all competitors had made the finish line:

"We've won the team race. That makes two overall wins. We've maintained our friendship, maintained our original team concept of strength in numbers. It's about the team, not the individual. It's worked. We've proven it works. We are champions, and friends."

Pictures from the "Sahara Race" 2005

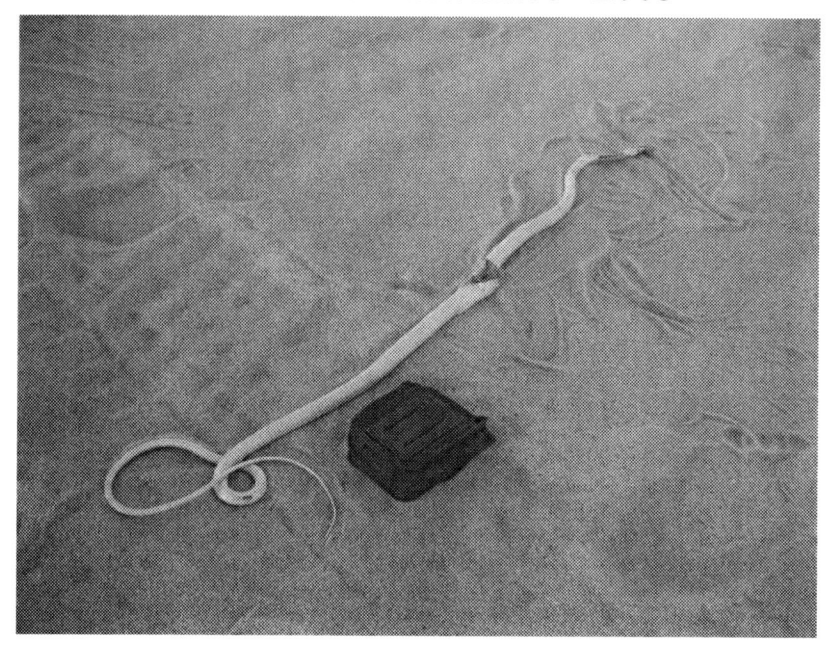

Photos provided by Dave Kuhnau. A large white viper attempted to move through the camp (above) only to be killed and eaten for lunch by local volunteers. Some of the competitors commiserate about the rigors of the course (below), while resting up for the next day's stage.

The Power Of Team

Photo provided by Dr. Brandee Waite (above). Dr. Waite finds some rare shade up under the overhang of a large white rock formation.

Photo provided by Derek Kwik (right) World class competitors come in all shapes and sizes as Derek Kwik grabs a photo with Gunnar Nilsson.

Peter Wortham

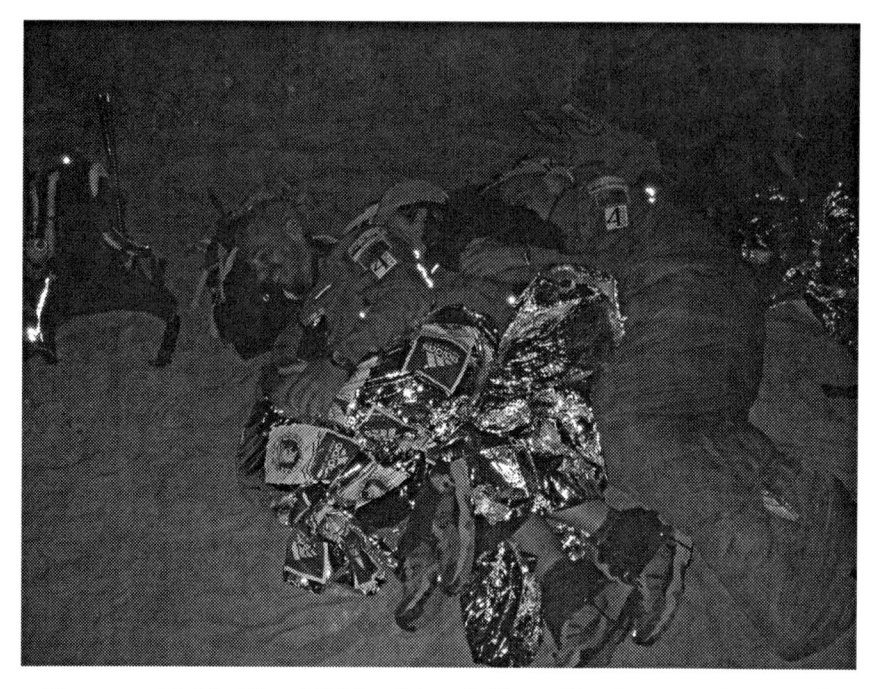

Photo provided by Chuck Walker (above). Team Illinois spoons for warmth while trying to fend off some of the lasting effects of hyperthermia.

Photo provided by Derek Kwik (below) British competitor Gary Johnson finds his own way to cool off in the mid-day heat.

The Power Of Team

Photo provided by Derek Kwik (above). The eerie sunset in the Sahara Desert is courtesy of a distant dust storm.

Photo provided by Chris Lusher - Framewerkz (right) Dave Kuhnau takes advantage of an irrigation pipe and takes a break from the 130 degree temperature.

Photo provided by Dave Kuhnau (above). Joel Burrows is monitored in the medical tent after becoming dehydrated and disoriented at the end of a stage.

Photo provided by Joel Burrows (below). The endless dunes on the 50 mile day remained perhaps the most difficult surface to run on, pulling the energy out of each step as competitors attempted to push forward.

The Power Of Team

Photo provided by Mark Ning (above). Team Illinois runs the final sprint to the finish line with another team victory assured.

Photo provided by Joel Burrows (right) Apparently everyone required shades in the Sahara Desert. Team Illinois poses with their finisher medals.

Chapter 8 - Celebration and Tragedy

Team Illinois enjoyed a brief respite from desert and spent a little time visiting Cairo before returning to the United States. They would have time to see more of the sights in the Middle-East, and to enjoy the food before needing to board their plane home.

They had regarded the victory in Sahara to be a bittersweet accomplishment. This attitude was coming from a team who had just proven that Gobi March win was not a fluke, but at the end of the race they weren't really competing against anyone. It was the first time that the team had difficulty in finding a goal to chase after and the lack of that significant goal had hurt their overall performance.

What they failed to realize at first, was that they literally destroyed the competition. On the first day of the race, Team Illinois hit the sand with a huge burst of maintained speed that could not be matched by any other team. They had seen this strategy before from other teams and individuals, but many of those competitors would prove to be one-day-wonders. The first stage delivered at high speed was done for glamour, but a consistent and repeatable pace was required for glory. The high speed, glamour seeking teams were typically out of each race after day one.

Team Illinois' training and preparation had put them in a position to post another strong, but not necessarily record setting pace. After day one when other teams had struggled to keep up with them, they posted a second day of solid running which distanced them from every other team in the competition. If they could maintain that pace from day to day like they had proven they could at the Gobi March, the Sahara Race would be theirs. The overall strategy worked and for all practical purposes, the team competition was over by day two.

It would be a blessing and a curse. Team Illinois had to adjust their strategy for the rest of the race and the end goal was adjusted as well. It was difficult to invest any more energy into an endeavor when you have already accomplished the original goal. Team Illinois had to find a way to keep motivated and deliver a quality result all the way through to the finish on day seven, once the original motivators were lost. Despite both Dave and Nancy suffering badly on days 3 through 5, Team Illinois did what they needed to do to make it through to the break on day six. With the help of some new and old friends, they all were able to finish strong through the long day and finally into a short sprint ending at the Pyramids.

Personal Glory

Where Nancy, Joel and Dave had never considered breaking up their team for personal glory, other teams had done just that and had lost an opportunity for team trophies. Joel was clearly running strong after day two. After he had hit his wall at the end of the second stage, Joel recovered and fell into his zone from the start of day three on to the finish at the Sphinx. Joel could have broken away from his struggling teammates and contended for a victory in his age bracket or for the overall win.

Joel could have abandoned his team, but he didn't. Integrity and commitment were not just words to be found in a motivational book, they represented a binding personal contract Joel had figuratively signed with his teammates. The same was true for Dave and Nancy. On any given day in any given race, one of the three teammates from Chicago would feel as if they could conquer everyone on the course. Nobody chose to abandon the team because it was never even a consideration.

The multi-country European team had separated from their teammate Stefan twice over the course of the seven days. The circumstances surrounding the decision to break up the team were never known. The decision could have even been mutual, but some would argue that it was not wise.

If the team had stayed together and worked with Stefan as he struggled, the multi-country team would have taken second place in the overall team competition with some pretty nice awards to take home at the finish. More to the point, Stefan may not have needed aid from another team to help stabilize his declining medical condition.

Because the pace set by both Team Illinois and the European team was so strong, they had both helped to eliminate the remainder of the competition by day two. It could have been a great team race as both groups struggled with the health issues of their teammates along the way. Honoring the original team commitment and sticking with team members regardless of the circumstance, would have provided a better race, a real goal, and guaranteed trophy hardware for both teams at the finish line.

Although all three members of the mixed European team still turned in excellent finish times, they missed winning in any individual age category. There could have been so much more to the story if the team had simply found a way to stay together.

A Chilling Decision

Along with a handful of other competitors, Team Illinois had qualified for the final challenge in the RacingThePlanet series. The Last Desert challenge would be by invitation only, provided an individual or team had successfully completed the series of challenges in the Atacama, Gobi, and Sahara deserts. Based on the difficulty of the climate and the course in Antarctica, competitors would need to have proven they could manage health and injury issues as well as the technical aspects of running through differing terrains. Of the last three desert challenges (Atacama, Gobi and Sahara), Team Illinois was the only team to have successfully completed each race.

Antarctica would be perhaps the most challenging and most expensive race when compared to any of the other three. Estimates from the RTP staff placed Antarctica about 300% over the expenses of racing in a hot weather desert. It was a temperature extreme on the other end of the spectrum, which meant that competitors would need to wear more layers of clothing in order to run. They had hoped to leverage the publicity of their recent win at Sahara to help fund the trip to the South Pole.

Nancy had already given an indication of her decision before leaving Egypt. She was interviewing with a staff member from the RacingThePlanet team where she commented, "We are now officially retiring from hot weather racing." Joel was more optimistic and commented in the same article, "It's all about icebergs now."

There would be only three and a half months to prepare for the race before Team Illinois needed to pack up and leave again. The race in Antarctica was scheduled for January 23, 2006 but Nancy had already decided on behalf of her team while still in Egypt. She was always the one who instigated the races, always the one who was ready for the next challenge, and always the first one to forget the pain and agony of the previous race.

At Home in Chicago

For some strange reason Dave thought it would be a good idea to commit to running the Chicago Marathon two weeks after his return to the U.S. It was the sort of thing Nancy had been famous for, but she chose to enter the competition world a little more slowly than Dave. For the Chicago Marathon, Joel and Nancy chose to watch from the sidelines. She had jokingly created a to-do list upon her arrival back at the East Bank Club. Number two on Nancy's list was:

"Watch Chicago Marathon runners from warm vantage point. Cheer on Dave while sipping on Venti Mocha Latte with whip." Nancy's priorities seemed to be in the right order, but nobody was sure what Dave was thinking when he agreed to the race. "At least he doesn't have to carry a backpack." Joel tried to support his teammate's decision.

Nancy had allowed herself some considerable time to recover from the physiological damage she had endured at Sahara. Her next competition wasn't scheduled until November 4th, a whopping 4 weeks away. Instead of easing back into competition with a 10K or even a marathon, Nancy had decided to do Ironman Florida again, but only after Joel and Dave had convinced her to sign up for it. It's just a short little triathlon including a 2.4 mile swim, then a 112 mile bike ride, and finally a 26.2 marathon run. Ah well, so much for easing back into training. "Honey, did I forget to mention that you're racing the triathlon in Florida? Honey? Nan?" What Joel didn't elaborate on was that the Florida triathlon was actually Dave's idea in the first place.

Nancy had assigned an acronym for the remainder of her training for Antarctica, "OAT – Official Antarctica Training". It made everything sound so much more official after that. Nancy would plan to start the OAT program on November 20, 2005 with a running/cycling partner competition, followed by three weeks of weight lifting and leg work, while putting in about 40 miles of road work per week. From there, Nancy would ramp up the mileage to 50 per week, then closer to January she planned to peak between 60 and 70 miles of road work per week.

Dave's body was still suffering some lingering effects from the Sahara Race; though he was gaining back some of the body weight lost to the desert heat. He prepared for the Chicago marathon with some intermediate runs but nothing at marathon distance. Despite his non-peak physical condition, Dave still posted a 3:40 for the marathon two weeks after his return in October, 2005. While Dave was finishing his marathon, Nancy was contemplating the reason for picking a triathlon to start her training for Antarctica.

"I don't want to admit that my training is somewhat half-assed (it is), but not because I don't put in the time, it's because I am so distracted by various other races and my work that's it's hard for me to focus on one thing. The best I ever did at a one-race focus was Atacama, and it did pay off, because I was in way over my head and I did get to the finish line. But training for Sahara was a mish-mash of short triathlons, trail runs, running stairs, and the random swim workout. This is why I told myself that an Ironman race would not be all that bad."

Nancy and Joel fared pretty well down in Florida. Two weeks after Dave's marathon finish they had entered and finished the triathlon in decent time, each beating more than half the field in their individual age categories. Joel had placed 123 out of 270 competitors in his age bracket with an 11:56, and Nancy finished 37 out of 92 competitors in her age bracket with a 12:35. With everyone back into a training curriculum and then with only two months to go before flights to the extreme south, Team Illinois needed to start focusing on sponsorship.

Tragedy in December 2005

Dave had been busy getting back into the swing of work. After being gone again for two full weeks to compete in Sahara, it was all he could do to catch up on work commitments after his return. Along with the Chicago Marathon, Dave had also signed up for the Las Vegas Marathon which was newly scheduled for early December 2005 and would require even more time away from his customer and everything else that needed attention before the end of the year.

The end of November would be busy for the man running his own consulting company and trying to stay in shape for the upcoming race in Antarctica. As the Thanksgiving holiday approached, Dave was also busy trying to avoid the topic of a trip back home to visit his family. It was not because he didn't care about them, and it was not because he was so overwhelmed with work that he could not make the trip. Dave seemed to get along well with his father and mother, but he also preferably avoided extended conversations with his sister Tamara for fear of a repeat confrontation.

When Dave talked with his mother on the phone the week before the holiday, he had used "preparing for the Las Vegas Marathon" as the reason for skipping the trip to Iowa for Thanksgiving with his family. It was part of his planned training, but he could also avoid any uncomfortable encounters with his sister.

Dave's five year battle with his sister had centered on her chosen course of medical treatment for breast cancer. Tamara had been diagnosed five years earlier with a form of breast cancer that her doctor suggested would most likely be aggressive. The entire family took the news hard, but Dave heard the news and prepared himself to help Tamara battle the disease. He immediately began making suggestions about her coming to Chicago to hunt for advanced treatment centers, and volunteered to research new medicines and programs to help Tamara get past what he was convinced was a manageable health issue.

Tamara objected to Dave's aggressive involvement mostly because of his assertion that she needed to be doing more to fight her own disease. Dave would admit later that he felt, "Tamara had just accepted her fate and refused to look at newer medical alternatives".

Tamara benefited from a strong faith in God and sincerely believed that her own chosen course of action was the correct path. Tamara was actively exercising more homeopathic methods, and did her own extensive research into alternative methods of nutritional and herbal treatments. From Dave's perspective, her approach was a waste of time. It was however, an approach that Tamara strongly believed in.

For the next few years, Dave and Tamara would barely speak to each other except during Holidays and major family events. When he learned of any downward turn in Tamara's condition, he was quick to suggest that she find another treatment option or specialty center. Dave was still angry over what he felt was his sister's unwillingness to listen to the people who cared about her the most. Whatever Tamara's reason, the treatment or lack of it, would be her choice.

Tamara had always been an active woman and excellent athlete. She had continued her career at Waldorf College in North-Central Iowa as their Director of Student Activities and strength conditioning coach after the diagnosis, and continued to keep physically fit as part of her own treatment program. What Dave never knew until later in 2005, was that Tamara was fired along with other long standing employees from Waldorf College after a change in the college's leadership.

In early 2005, Tamara's condition worsened and Dave had checked in with his parents on how she was doing. Without being overly judgmental or aggressive with advice, Dave had accepted the fact that he may never be able to influence his sister's decision.

News of Dave's racing exploits would make it back home and the news would be shared with Tamara and older sister Twila. Dave had accepted his fate that 2005 would be a busy year requiring non-stop training and then of course, two 150 mile races on two different continents. It was not a planned avoidance of his family that year; it was just a side effect of all the training, work commitments and travel.

After he missed the Thanksgiving holiday with his family, Dave received a call from his mother simply asking him to "come home". "I think you should come home and see your sister. She's not doing well." Dave cancelled his upcoming weekend trip to Las Vegas for the marathon and headed back home to see Tamara.

Conflicted on the drive home to Iowa, Dave had started to think of ways to apologize to Tamara for the years lost. He began to realize that many of the decisions that Tamara made, were hers alone to make. While Dave hated the thought of losing his sister and childhood best-friend, he knew she was an intelligent woman and that she had the capability to weigh the options and make her own choice. It is the right we all hope to have when faced with a similar challenge and Dave was finally beginning to understand that simple fact.

Dave returned to his sister Twila's home where Tamara had taken up residence now in hospice mode. Tamara was dying. His older sister Twila walked into her room first to wake her, and Dave was finally able to see her body. Tamara was just a shell of the strong woman he had grown up with and fought with as an adult and Dave felt like someone had punched him in the stomach.

That Saturday was spent with his mother, Twila and Tamara, and Tamara was alert most of the day. At one point Dave helped lift Tamara out of bed so the sheets could be changed, but she weighed what seemed like less than 80 pounds. Dave broke down and was overwhelmed with guilt for not having any sort of relationship with her these last five years. He realized that all the pride and all the arguments with Tamara were a waste of precious time.

During the afternoon when she was awake, Dave stayed by her side to talk about whatever Tamara wanted to talk about. She started by telling Dave that, "God told me in a dream that I'm not going to die. I am going to beat this." She finished by saying, "I'm sorry we let so many years slip by."

Dave simply replied, "I'm sorry I've been gone so long Tam."

Tamara then asked, "If I get out of this bed, will you help train me to do a marathon? I had a dream about Dad and I running a marathon with you."

Dave replied, "Tam, If you get out of this bed, you and I will run a marathon together."

She faded in and out of sleep for the rest of the day, and Dave was as destroyed emotionally as his sister was physically. He continued talking with his mother and his older sister Twila and tried to get his mind to accept the fact that his sister was fading away from him. Dave's mother and his sister never gave up hope of Tamara's recovery. Knowing Tamara's strength, it was hard to see things any other way.

Dave had made a commitment with his client to be back and available early Monday morning, and would have to leave in the late afternoon on Saturday to avoid a snow storm. He spent more time in Tamara's room when she was awake. She spotted Dave and asked about his new car, then a little while later told her brother, "I'm really tired and I can't talk much. Can you please tell me more stories about the desert?" As Dave remembered people and stories from the previous year, Tamara had closed her eyes then reopened them to look at Dave. She continued to fade in and out of consciousness but managed to ask one last question about the upcoming race at Antarctica.

Dave continued to talk while she faded to sleep again. He was sure she had heard at least some part of the description, and Dave was wishing that she could join him there among the penguins.

That afternoon while Tamara slept, Dave packed his bags. He woke Tamara up one last time to say goodbye. He wanted so strongly to believe that Tamara could overcome anything, including the cancer that had taken her body over; he believed that he would see her again. It was a difficult ride home for Dave, but there was nothing else he could do.

That Thursday, Dave received a call from his sister Twila simply telling him, "She's gone Dave, she's gone".

Dave's personal time with his family dominated the following two weeks where he only then learned about Tamara's job loss and the lack of medical insurance. He was devastated once more knowing that he could have helped Tamara with COBRA insurance payments or whatever she needed. In the end, it would be Tamara's decision to deal with her situation in her own way and part of that was not telling Dave too much about challenges that surrounded her. Though she would be at peace, Dave would struggle with guilt long after December of 2005 over the things he could have done to help her. Asking for help was just not Tamara's way.

Antarctica Preparation

While Dave tried to insert himself back into some sort of normal work and home life, the lack of training for Antarctica was looming over him. There was simply no time or motivation to get up and go out and train. Dave had shared the news with his extended family back in Chicago. Joel and Nancy were on the phone with Dave when he got back to town, "We will do whatever you need us to do".

Nancy and Joel had discussed cancelling the Antarctica race for the team, but Dave remembered Tamara asking to be taken on a marathon, and wanting to see the Antarctic. Dave had agreed that the trip and the race would be best for him because he had also made a promise to Tamara to go and bring back more stories.

The RTP crew understood completely and was willing to work with Team Illinois on whatever contingency planning they might need to make. Mary Gadams was extremely supportive and offered to put up a notice on the website saying simply that, "Dave was dedicating this last race to Tamara". In order to do that however, Dave would need to get back out on the road and start running again. The flight south was leaving in a little more than five weeks.

Nancy and Joel continued with scheduled races and Nancy's OAT training schedule through December. Nancy also suffered through an annual event where most women would admit to dreading the outcome. It was Nancy's birthday. One of Joel's presents to Nancy was a new MP3 player with upgraded memory and a longer battery life for long distance training. On the back, Joel had engraved "IronNan the Desert Rat, puke and rally. Run on."

Nancy wondered if all husbands talked to their wives that way, with inspirational messages involving rodents and vomiting. You would have to meet Joel and Nancy to know that it was a compliment, albeit a comment better suited between drinking buddies than husband and wife. Joel and Nancy were simply friends and drinking buddies long before marriage. Joel's words were meant for his best friend and running partner, she just happened to be his wife.

Towards the end of December 2005, Nancy and Joel had signed up for the Huntington Ultra Frosty Fifty race in Huntington, Indiana. When they arrived to the parking area, the local temperature was settled in nicely at eight degrees Fahrenheit. It was perfect training weather for Antarctica and excellent swimming weather for penguins.

Nancy and Joel had started the race running together, but as the miles wore on and autopilots were kicking in, Joel had started to run at a pace that pulled him away from Nancy. It was an unplanned event, but Nancy was not happy about being left behind. Joel probably expected Nancy to push her pace harder, but she was busy digging her shoe into a small hole in the ice about mile 14, twisting her ankle and tumbling off the race trail into a pile of snow. She checked herself for injury and got up from the snow drift, wet and sore from the fall. She began to bawl and feel sorry for herself and considered walking back to the starting line to give up on the day, but remembered the training advice she had offered her students as their coach.

"Anyone can finish on a good day when they're feeling strong. It takes real strength to finish when nothing goes right. So I remembered so many of (my triathlon students) this summer, suffering through swims, falling on the bike and getting back up, and running when their legs wouldn't move, and I remember I wouldn't let them quit. So, I couldn't quit. As long as my feet were moving, I couldn't quit."

Nancy finally finished the H.U.F.F. in 6:25 placing her 13th out of 37, and Joel finished 39th out of 140 with a finish time of 5:48. There would be hell to pay for leaving her behind during the race, but Joel had been in trouble before. He was still pretty sure that his martial arts training would come in handy if Nancy decided to attack him with some sort of blunt object. Then again, she might save payback for a time when he least expects it. She knew Joel would have to sleep sometime.

Nancy had also found a reasonable combination of clothing layers that seemed to work well in the wet snow and cold of the 50 mile race. Through trial and error, she had found that a base thin clothing layer, followed by a thin fleece, then Gore-Tex fleece lined jacket worked well over tights and a lined set of Gore-Tex running pants. She wore a pair of gloves, covered with a mitten, two pairs of socks on her feet and waterproof running shoes. It would be a considerable handicap to running any sort of speed in a cold-desert distance race, but she could stay warm and relatively dry.

New Year, New Beginnings

Dave was still involved with settling the modest estate that his sister had left behind and not running much at all. In the midst of all the racing activity in 2005, Dave was also trying to grow his small consulting business in Chicago, wrap up a number of legal details and prepare for the tax man. All this activity was added to the worry about his lack of training for Antarctica, and possibly letting his teammates down.

Nancy was plagued at the East Bank Club with hundreds of new members, many of whom had joined the club and sought out Nancy's personal counsel on how to prepare for their first marathon, or first triathlon. New Year's resolutions would overwhelm Nancy with more requests for her time at work, all while she was trying to increase her weekly training mileage to 70. Happy New Year.

Joel was faced with similar challenges for his time as the local notoriety Team Illinois had received from Gobi and Sahara meant that many people were looking for both Burrows' to become their personal trainer. Work and other responsibilities were cutting into training time for all three members of Team Illinois, and there was nothing much that could be done.

Nancy reflected back on the three previous races and the stress that had faced them each and every day. Her perspective wasn't only based on the challenges experienced during a given race but also during most any day requiring training, fund raising, or any other activity connected with Team Illinois. She talks about the long journey her team had taken and how they dealt with adversity.

"I wonder if we could have ever made it to this point without each other, and I look at all the other individual competitors and am amazed by their courage to do all this by themselves. Don't get me wrong. Teams have their own challenges. We have to stay together all the time (by the way, we also travel together, are in the same tent together) so once we start our journey, it's pretty much about the three of us. In three races, we have fought only once, when the stress of the heat in Gobi pushed us to disagree on a strategy, and it lasted about 5 minutes. We have a way of dealing with each other with humor that makes us laugh in the face of a challenge."

It would be humor and their mutual dedication to each other and the team that had carried them successfully through three deserts on three continents. Prior to leaving for Punta Arenas in Chile, Dave had purchased commemorative tee-shirts just for the occasion. Nancy's shirt said simply, "It was my idea". Dave and Joel's tee-shirt message almost matched with "Innocent Bystander". Innocent? Hardly.

Chapter 9 – Antarctica

Nancy had done most of the work in testing and gathering up the clothing needed for the entire team at Antarctica, and made sure the Team Illinois uniforms would match before arrival at O-Hare International Airport. There were delays of course and a missed connection along the way, but after 22 hours of travel, the three amigos from Chicago had arrived at the Southern-most point of South America in Punta Arenas near Cape Horn and the Tierra del Fuego. Revisiting Chile for the first time since 2004, Team Illinois wondered if they might be better off heading a little north and racing the warmer sands of the Atacama.

While walking towards the connecting gate out of Santiago heading towards Punta Arenas, Dave stopped Nancy and Joel and pointed towards the gate number posted near the door. Dave said, "Hey, do you realize that this is the same gate where we started the first part of our adventure?" Nancy replied, "It's kind of funny that it all started and ended with this gate." Joel commented, "Who would have ever thought that we would be back here at the same place after all that has happened." Everyone had conveniently forgotten Nancy's quote back in 2004, "I swear, we are never doing this again".

The last leg of the flight down to Punta Arenas was perhaps the most interesting. After connecting out of Argentina, Team

Illinois boarded a plane full of passengers and a small group of Eastern Europeans who did not apparently have the chance to bathe within the last seven days. Joel mentions the details:

"The final two flights went fine, except for the very full flight of smelly men going on an expedition. The stench of old sweat mixed with the bottle of Vodka they were passing around was almost overwhelming. Twenty-plus hours of plane food probably didn't help our stomachs either, so there were a few slips (mostly from Nan) on the last flight. Puke and move on."

Pre Race – Day of Arrival

Day one of the trip was just a chance to reacquaint themselves with friends and fellow athletes they hadn't seen for months. Derek Kwik and Chuck Walker were there as well as Gunnar Nilsson and Brent Weigner, who they had commiserated with at the last three races. Most of the RacingThePlanet organizers were also there including Mary Gadams who kept the journey and the challenge rolling now for more than two years. Notably absent was Ian Adamson who had to decline the trip due to a scheduling conflict. Ian was probably the only smart one in the bunch.

A small group of competitors headed off to find a secluded lunch spot in town complete with what they hoped would include a reasonably priced wine list. Well into the second bottle, stories would fly about placement of the flags on a particular day or about the food. Chuck Walker gave up a little secret he had learned about carrying the extra weight of freeze dried food. The trick was simply to not carry any. Aside from packing powdered milk and dry cereal in zip lock bags, Chuck dined each night on whatever leftovers the other people in camp couldn't eat. It was the survival strategy of a scavenger, but the strategy also meant that Chuck could cut significant weight out of his backpack. Those military guys are no dummies.

Later that afternoon after a little shopping around town, Team Illinois had returned to their hotel to start giving credit to the sponsors who once again helped to fund their trip to The Last Desert. Dave and Nancy had laid out a series of embroidered patches that still needed to be attached to their brand new, matching outer jacket shells. Since packing a full size sewing machine was not a real option for the team, Dave had brought along some liquid fabric glue to help set up the patches on the jacket. It would have been good to check first if the glue would work on all types of fabric, or in all conditions, but that story comes later. Nancy talks about the joys and risks of fabric glue:

"Dave kept telling us how his patches were perfectly holding on, so although we were a little skeptical, we followed his lead. Later that afternoon after all my patches were glued on, I read the label on the bottle 'Keep from freezing'. I think I screamed. I proceeded to stitch on what I could, and figured I would, like Dave, take the chance that my patches would indeed hold."

After the sewing and gluing fun was over, the three of them all met in the hotel restaurant for dinner and ended the day with a fantastic meal including a little roasted beaver for Dave. Nancy wasn't sure she had heard the waiter explain the evening's specials properly so she asked him to clarify. The waiter promptly said the word "rodent" then spread his arms out wide to apparently indicate large, followed by sticking out his two front teeth to make sure they all understood that it would actually be beaver coming to them on a plate. Dave gave the beaver a try and commented that it tasted like liver. Nancy was glad that she decided to order off the regular menu.

Pre Race - Second Day

Team Illinois had bumped into the rest of the competitors with Mary G. at another hotel which also served as the official checkpoint for mandatory gear. It would be a small crowd of competitors for Antarctica so gear-check went quickly after which a group of them decided to go out to lunch again, looking for more good food and wine.

The race hotel was only two blocks away but Team Illinois still had to lug their 60 pound duffel bags to Mary Gadams' hotel so the RacingThePlanet staff could validate the equipment. After making the trek with large duffels in tow, Nancy couldn't find her large safety pins (a required item) in her duffel. Joel had extra, so Nancy was officially checked in. She later found her safety pin stash buried in a small pocket on her backpack.

Mary had organized a dinner that night for all competitors and everyone was excited about the meal as a kick-off for the journey ahead. Nancy was placed next to Scott Smith who had been one of the front-runners in all three warm desert races and was an Army ROTC instructor from New Mexico. Before dinner had started, Scott got up from the table to get everyone's attention in what looked to be a toast. Instead, Scott told the story of how he had visited a Navaho Indian healer before leaving on his flight to Punta Arenas. He had gotten each member of the 15 competitors a protective symbol called a "Talisman" as they began their last journey into the frozen desert.

Nancy opened her small gift box to reveal the symbol of a bear carved out of white stone. Others who knew of the Indian traditional symbol were genuinely touched, and Scott went on to explain the significance of the protective symbol. Nancy was immediately taken back to just before the first race at Atacama. Her close friend Maria had given Nancy her first Talisman to protect her as she ran through the harsh climate of Chile. Maria's Talisman gift was also carved in the likeness of a bear. Since then, Nancy had taken the Talisman with her to each desert race. When Nancy saw the bear that Scott had given her, it was as if the moon and the stars had aligned and the small troop of 15 competitors and friends would be protected for this, their last race of the series.

Scott had finished handing out the talisman to each competitor and then finally stopped to announce to everyone that there was one more competitor who had already run her race. Scott had brought an extra special talisman for Tamara. Scott proceeded to explain to everyone that Tamara's talisman was of a bigger white bear staring into the distance. The size and color represented Tamara's strength and that she had moved beyond this world and finished running her race. Scott presented Dave with the talisman to carry on behalf of Tamara.

As the group broke from dinner, Team Illinois headed back to their hotel for one last attempt at repacking their duffels for the final leg of the trip to Antarctica. As Nancy faded off to sleep, Dave and Joel were rethinking every item in the duffel on whether or not to leave it behind in the hotel to be picked up on their return back to the U.S. During the discussion about which critical items to take with them, Nancy woke up and threw a tantrum, "That's enough. I just want to go to bed." Dave stared back at her with a straight face, paused and responded, "Well, I just want a pony."

Pre Race – Third Day

The group all gathered back at the Isla Rey Jorge Hotel, Mary Gadams' semi-official headquarters, for news of the flight schedule to King George Island in Antarctica. There were known weather delays frequently along this flight path, so they all waited until later that morning to leave for the airport. Most had gathered outside the hotel with their gear in anticipation of a late morning departure to the airport. Nancy was double checking to make sure all her equipment had been stuffed properly in her duffel.

She had selected the same GoLite endurance racing backpacks that had served them well in the past, and Nancy found no reason to change pack design for Antarctica. As for outer clothing, Nancy had found a layering system from Patagonia to work well as they would change from fleece to outer running shells depending on the temperature or wind conditions on any particular day. Outer jacket shells were from GoLite as well. Legs were protected by CW-X Pro Tights as Team Illinois' base layer with a thin fleece pant layer over the top, and a water proof wind breaking shell pant for the outer layer. Faces and heads would be fully covered at times by multi-layer protection and hands were covered by a combination or inner layer glove and an outer mitten. She checked the contents twice, but still wondered if she had missed something when packing.

As Dave sat with Vincent Carroll (Ireland), Gunnar Nilsson, Scott Smith and Chuck Walker, they were approached by a dog casually walking up the street towards their hotel. It was a German Sheppard mix with a curled up Husky tail but had a surprisingly familiar look to his eyes and ears that flopped over at the tips. The dog approached the small group without fear and looked at Dave for a moment as if he were a long lost friend. Dave produced a small piece of beef jerky and the dog took it without hesitation. Curling up near their feet, the friendly and familiar dog took up residence in front of the hotel and watched over the strangers wearing colorful jackets with over-stuffed duffel bags. Dave wondered if it was the same guardian angel with perhaps a different tail, sent to watch over them before the arduous journey in Antarctica began. It was "Attie" at Atacama, perhaps this was "Anti" for Antarctica.

At 11:00 A.M. local time, the group boarded busses and traveled to the airport with duffel bags, backpacks and Talisman in tow. All were excited to see that the posted departure time to King George Island was scheduled a little more than an hour and a half away. "Anti" was seen watching the group board the bus before he casually strolled away.

For those of us who travel or have traveled for a living, we've come to expect that there is a direct relationship between the chance that a flight will be delayed, and the desire to actually fly to your destination. Forced to fly out of town on business to a city you

The Power Of Team

don't want to visit? That flight always leaves on-time. Dying to get home for Thanksgiving dinner with your family? Here's a great Scrabble word for just this occasion: DELAYED.

The Talisman was doing its job and keeping them all protected. King George Island and all of Antarctica for that matter was known for its freakish and unpredictably strong winds. If the board said DELAYED, it's probably best not to question the reason why. It's just time for another beer. The disappointed group did just that, with fries on the side of course.

After hours waiting for the flight status to change and a small conference with the gate agents about the possibility for travel to King George Island, it was clear that no flight was going to happen that day. The group had to find new lodging somewhere near the airport because although their extra equipment was being stored, their original rooms at the hotel were now gone. Nancy, Joel and Dave managed to find a small hotel with a nice $200 room rate. Their room had three small twin size beds and not much else. It was cozy, but that was OK for the small family from Chicago.

Dave, Chuck Walker, Scott Smith and Nancy all decided to go for a run, for lack of anything better to do. Opting for a path that took them along the Straights of Magellan, they all ran with heads up to catch the view. Nancy was stiffening up at the early stages of the run and she felt as if the boys were reducing their pace just to accommodate her. Dave and Nancy decided to run just a warm-up distance of about 30 minutes and then peeled away from the group to head back to the hotel. Thoughts quickly turned to food again and Joel decided to make the suggestion.

"A group of us went out for burgers and ice cream. The burgers were great. I ate one and a half cheeseburgers. Dave had ordered two and gave me half of one...I gave half of that one to Derek. We went back to an ice cream shop we had found the day before, Chocolotto, and brought our group with us. Seven of us ordered ice cream - Chuck Walker, Gunnar form Sweden, Scott Smith,

Dave, Derek Kwik, Nan, and me. They kept screwing up both Dave's order and my order. It took a while, but we finally were all served. Dave was really funny. His Spanish isn't any good, so as he gets more frustrated, he raises his voice and keeps speaking English. The wait staff has no idea what he wants, but he keeps getting louder. It's actually funny to watch."

Later that night, Nancy was channel flipping the small hotel television while other competitors were wandering the hallways looking for something or anything to pass the time. Joel was already in full recline and Dave was close to nodding off when Derek Kwik, Chuck Walker and Scott Smith stopped in to say "hey". Nancy stumbled on to a surprise by finding of all things, American Idol being played in English on one of the hotel cable channels. Once again reveling in a little Americana found at the southern-most tip of South America, Nancy retained control of the remote and made a decision on behalf of the group. Bad interpretations of 90's pop songs would be the entertainment for the evening. "What no popcorn?"

The following morning the combined RTP group met again at the airport in advance of the first available flight out to King George Island. After two days of delays, the group was clearly getting anxious from all the sitting and waiting and needed to burn off a little energy with some sort of physical activity. For the group of 15 at Punta Arenas Airport, that meant a short little 150 mile run.

From the lobby of their temporary hotel, they boarded a bus for the short ride to the airport. While Nancy's excitement energy levels were peaking, Dave was a little more worried about the lack of training and how his body would react to a longer challenge. Some of his concern was overstated. The body would remember how to manage a longer distance run, because it had been there before. It was also true that nothing prepares a body for running like running, and Dave had not been able to invest as many hours on the road as Nancy and Joel had.

Antarctica would be a completely different race and format to consider as well. Dave knew that the race wasn't really a race at all for Team Illinois. There would be no competing team, and based on the past performance of some of the individual competitors, Team Illinois would not be able to compete for the actual top finish time. It would not be likely that Joel or Nancy would be in contention for the fastest overall time. That was not to say that given the right circumstances and best health conditions that Joel or Nancy wouldn't be able to contend for the top spot at the finish, but their strength had always been to combine efforts as a team.

Dave found it hard to latch onto the same motivational spirit that had enveloped the rest of the competitors on the bus. The race at Antarctica would be another test for Team Illinois to find the right motivation and keep them moving, when there was no other team to compete with. Dave was trying desperately to forget about the events of December and focus on the task at hand, but it was also clear that Dave would most likely struggle with both the physical and mental aspects of the race, for the entirety of the race.

A Change in Race Format

The final race in the four desert series would sway from the typical format found for the other desert challenges. Six desert stages were compressed to four stages where the bulk of the race would be run in a single 100 mile stage spanning up to three days, though the competitors did not yet know.

King George Island would be starting point for the historical endurance race, as RacingThePlanet would be the first sanctioned multi-stage race to be held on Antarctica. King George Island is also the largest of the South Shetland Islands, where several countries from around the globe had anchored research stations there.

Stage One on King George Island was set as a warm up run of only 6 miles or 10K, but it would be a chance for the competitors to test out clothing combinations and running conditions. It would also be a chance to get used to the wind that could be dangerous near the southern tip of the world.

Stage Two would be held near Hope Bay at the tip of the Antarctic Peninsula, close to one of the Argentinean base stations named "Esperanza". The stage was originally scheduled to be close to marathon distance but depending on weather conditions might also serve as the long stage of the race. Unknown to the competitors at the time, Mary was planning to make stage two a little longer than a marathon.

Stage Three would be planned at the marathon distance of 26.3 miles, to be held on Deception Island. The final distance of the race would also be run on the main island in Antarctica, just off the mainland.

Stage Four represented the remaining mileage to be held on King George Island and incorporated a short distance across the glacier there. Covering 18 miles, the final distance to the race finish line incorporated two loops of nine miles.

Lodging would be different in Antarctica as well. Aside from the long stage where RacingThePlanet could take advantage of a permanent building on the Argentinean research base, competitors would all return to the safety of the Dap Mares ship at night. The temperature in January stayed warmer during the day at about zero degrees Fahrenheit, or -17 degrees Celsius, but the winds could also kick up to 60 miles per hour without warning. The ship would provide protection from the unpredictability of the elements, and it would be a necessary evil for those who enjoyed making the desert challenges hard on the competitors. Non-reinforced cabin tents would have been a bad idea out on the frozen gravel in a wind storm.

An Actual Departure

As the members of Team Illinois and the rest of the competitors would learn, the reason for the never ending flight delays had everything to do with the unpredictability of the force and direction of the wind on Antarctica. In order to safely navigate a plane to the continent, a pilot would need to be confident in the predictability of the wind's activity for that particular day, at least during the duration of the flight.

The issue is all about the ability to plan. Back in the good old U.S.A or Europe or anywhere North of the equator, the patterns of weather activity and wind direction can usually be established. As the world turns on its axis, (picture it spinning from left to right) weather tends to float in the same direction pulled with the rotation. In North America we tend to refer to the weather patterns as prevailing westerly because the weather tends to come from the West. Not so in Antarctica. Because of the Katabatic winds created by downward force of heavy air past the curved slope of the polar ice cap, the ground speed of the wind can be treacherous. You can look that up.

That day, the Katabatic winds were playing nice and the flight that had been delayed indefinitely, was about to depart. The whole of the RTP staff and group of competitors were hurried off to the plane with gear in tow to make the short window of opportunity for the flight.

The flight would take multiple hours though the distance had deceived most of the people on the plane. Nancy was expecting something in the neighborhood of a 30 minute trip. When looking at a standard world map, the southern tip of South America looks to be a stone's throw from the Antarctica northern peninsula. In actuality it's about the same distance as a flight from New York to Minneapolis. The deception is also the fault of almost every map and every globe found in just about every school or college. For centuries, Cartographers were heavily lobbied and paid to make their own countries look larger when world maps would be created. This is why Western Europe looks to be huge in comparison to Greenland, and Africa looks relatively small in comparison to all of Europe and Asia. Greenland is actually massive, and so is Africa when calculating square miles. Take a look sometime at a Peters Map and compare it to any standard map you've grown up to know and love. The Peters Map will be an accurate representation of land mass and its placement relative to other continents. South America was a little further away from Antarctica then most maps indicated. Too late to avoid rambling on for that topic, but it also explains why the flight took longer than most had expected.

Nancy knew they were close when Derek Kwik's handheld GPS monitor had lost its satellite connectivity and represented the ground below their plane as a large question mark. They started to come in on approach to King George Island but noticed that the airport was just a rocky patch of flat land. The plane would be landing on a gravel runway and the experience was less than fun for all. Nancy managed to keep her stomach in check for the entire flight, although nobody really wanted to volunteer to take the seat next to her. Joel had reluctantly agreed, because as her husband he was obligated.

The landing was a little shaky but then again any landing that does not require the involvement of a search and rescue team, is a good landing. The group disembarked and tried to get used to the fact that they all were actually near the continent at the bottom of the world. King George Island provided a transfer point from small airport to ship anchored off shore awaiting their arrival. The ship would finish their journey to Antarctica. While waiting to board ship, nearly everyone on the plane dug for their cameras stashed away in duffel bags and began almost immediately to snap as many pictures as they could of the surroundings.

After the rest of the equipment was offloaded from the plane, the entire group made the short 1.5 mile walk to the island's coast line in the direction of their awaiting ship. They would then wait for the inflatable "Zodiac" boats to arrive from the ship and pick them up on shore. While they all waited, the first penguins were spotted both on and off shore. The islands around Antarctica were home to many penguin rookeries as they made their nests up on the rocks. Nancy fell immediately in love with the flightless birds as they went about their business feeding in the open sea and returning home.

The inflatable rubber boats with outboard motors could be seen coming to shore and the group wondered how exactly they were going to get off the island, into the boats, out of the small craft and up the side of the ship. Dave had thought back to a consulting engagement in New York where a trip from the airport to your destination was easily and commonly afforded by private limo. Taxi cabs from LaGuardia to Mid-Town would cost $37. A Limo would cost $48. Nobody was expecting to have to rock and roll with the waves, take water in the face and hang on to prevent getting tossed into the Arctic Ocean. "Uh Mary, where's our limo?"

Once they had made it to the side of the exploration ship "Dap Mares", a ladder was attached to the side of the ship leading up towards a hole in the deck overhang. Nancy couldn't figure out how to get herself and her gear through the hole at the same time, but it would be a matter of pushing the bag through first, followed by climbing through.

The rooming list had already been announced and in their little split room cabin which slept 4 people, Team Illinois had been paired with Chuck Walker which Nancy thought was pretty cool.

"We were given our room assignments on the boat and found that poor Chuck was going to be our roommate. Of course, I was thrilled. Chuck is amazing, kicks all forms of ass, and is cool as hell. Secretly, though, I hoped that he was as happy to be rooming with us as we were to be rooming with him. He didn't complain, and I tried to ease his pain by telling him that we had more snacks than anyone else on the ship."

The Dap Mares would remain their shelter for the following week, providing them real protection and a place to stow their gear and snack food while they engaged in the business of running. It was another departure from cooking and sleeping arrangements on other continents with hotter climates. The RTP crew recognized that they could not invoke the same restrictions for the race on Antarctica, because the conditions were potentially more life threatening than in the desert heat.

In the desert without water, the body could survive up to 24 hours before potentially falling into a coma. The effects of heat stroke with a seven degree rise in core body temperature is very similar to the symptoms of hypothermia experienced when the body is reduced by only three degrees. Within minutes of the body being exposed to extremely cold temperatures, hypothermia can set in and cause unconsciousness, cardiac arrest or coma. When a human's core body temperature falls eight degrees, it experiences organ failure and clinical death. The warning signs should sound familiar if you come from a cold weather climate. When your core body temperature drops just one or two degrees, you will experience goose bumps on your skin, shallow breathing and eventually uncontrollable shivering. It's time to put on more dry clothing because you're truly freezing.

Clothes that were both dry and heat retaining were all that stood between the athletes and a certain life threatening situation. If anyone took an accidental fall into water or wet snow or had saturated their clothing with sweat, they ran serious risk of hypothermia. This was why competitors were allowed to bring extra clothing and gear but would not be required to carry everything on their backs. As soon as the material around the body gets wet, the insulating properties around the skin are lost and the cold travels easily through the clothing and next to the skin. Team

Illinois and the rest of the competitors would need to stay dry and the RTP staff had allowed the needed safety measures.

Stop, Eat, Go – Stage One

While everyone was unpacking their gear, lunch was being served just before they were all carted back to the island for the short warm up run, and the beginning of the Antarctica challenge. Joel and Chuck played a game of chess where Chuck summarily wiped up the board with Joel. Chuck was trying to ask Joel about his strategic decisions on the game board, but Joel was just hoping to protect the pieces that Chuck easily took away. Nancy came back in the bunk room and declared that they all needed to be back on deck in fifteen minutes for the boat ride back to shore. The first stage of the race would begin within the hour.

Joel packed up his gear for the run, taking the required equipment with him and of course, the Talisman Scott Smith had given him. Chuck and Joel met Nancy and Dave on deck and they all climbed back down through the hole, to the ladder and an awaiting Zodiac boat for the rough ride to shore. Everyone had gathered on shore and started adjusting their packs while Mary was looking at her watch for a good incremental start time.

Once Mary had marked the start time for the short loop on the island, she quickly declared "Ready, set, go", and the race was officially underway. As soon as Team Illinois left the starting line, Nancy could hear the distinct sound of fabric ripping, but had initially assumed it was just her strap or her jacket adjusting to the load of the pack as she started. A second later, Nancy was holding one shoulder strap as it had torn completely off. She continued to hold onto the strap while the weight of the pack was distributed fully to the other shoulder. Nancy would continue to run the entire distance of the first stage holding onto the strap.

As their collective pace led them to their first mile, Dave was off in his own world, letting his mind wander as he tried to find some sort of "auto-pilot" for the run. Running was now a curse for Dave, forcing him to think about things he didn't care to remember. Daily activities, staying busy at work and at home tended to occupy his mind and force him to concentrate on the issues at hand. Running provided time to reflect on things and time to recall memories that he just assumed forget. Perhaps it was one of the reasons Dave had not trained as hard as he usually did before any of the other races. Perhaps Dave was forcing himself to stay busy so that he wouldn't have to run. As they ran on with the group of 15, Dave's mind finally wandered back to the news of early December, the memory of his sister and of the dedication he had made before the race in Antarctica.

"Dear Tamara,

I wanted you to know that I am dedicating this next race, The Last Desert Race to you.

Your energy, love for athletics, passion, faith in God, humor, crazy diet and overall love for life will never be forgotten. You told me in your last few days that you wanted to be able to run with me again someday and this time, do a marathon. Well guess what, Tam? You will be with me on this race and I have news for you...."we aren't doing a marathon.... we are doing six of them back to back". I have always admired your drive, passion and willingness to bend and sometimes break the rules. It is some of the common traits we've always shared as siblings.

You will always be loved and forever missed.

This race is for you Tam…

With Love….Your Little Brother"

Joel continued to run close with the team on that first short stage but there was very little conversation between the members of Team Illinois. Nancy was dealing with her new found shoulder strap hardship, Dave had been quiet all day and Joel was just trying to get into the rhythm of the run. He remembered back to the group dinner and took a moment to reflect on the significance of Scott's gift.

"The other night at dinner, Scott gave us all little animal statues made by a Navaho shaman in his hometown. He explained the meanings of each and told us the color, animal, point to which they gaze were specific to each of us. Mine is a tan bear signifying strength. He gazes forward to the horizon looking for adventure and knowledge. It was a touching gesture from a retired major in the Army Rangers."

Nancy trudged on with the handicap of the backpack strap in her hand, through to end of the 10K loop. She was becoming angrier as the short run wore on, using her arm and a bicep muscle to hold the strap on her shoulder. It was an unnatural body position for running, but she had endured the challenge. She writes,

"I was seriously aggravated at the strap, yelped out a few key words, and ran holding up my pack with my hand. When we got back to the start, I threw my pack down and headed over to watch a bunch of penguins just getting out of the water. The penguins calmed me, as they did the whole race, they are just that cute."

When the stage was completed, the competitors and crew boarded the Zodiac boats back to the ship. Scott had heard about Nancy's backpack troubles and showed up to their cabin with a sewing awl. The sharp pointed tool made nice large holes to help thread dental floss through the strap and into the backpack. It was a crude way of sewing the strap back on, but dental floss would have more tensile strength than any thread could ever have. The sewing activity left Nancy's pack crudely but effectively repaired. Scott came through once again, now becoming another honorary member of Team Illinois.

Mary had called a brief meeting in the dining cabin to tell everyone that the ship was heading next to the continent so that the next stage could include a race course across portions of the mainland. It would be welcome news to the group since the race actually claimed it was being held on Antarctica, and they wanted nothing more than a chance to step foot there instead of islands near the continent. It was a discussion of semantics really. The islands all around the continent still qualified as Antarctica. Manhattan is an island too, and you never think of it as not being a part of the United States. In any case, the news of the mainland stage had the group grinning like first graders at recess.

Mary Gadams was describing the stages for the rest of the race because the overall format had been finalized. She had mentioned something about a long-stage, using the phrase "at least 50 miles". This was also the first time Nancy, Joel and Dave had spent this much time with Mary who was always in the background planning the event and taking care of little details. Her humor was starting to show, but Nancy had not picked up on it yet.

As Mary continued to talk about the race stages, one of the Chilean crew mentioned that they might have a chance to go up and see a glacier, perhaps even run a portion of the race there. Before she could respond, another crew member jumped into the conversation to say "I was just up there, and wearing shoes like yours would be very cold and uncomfortable. I don't recommend it at all." Without a flinch or a delay, Mary responded, "Yes we'll definitely go on the glacier."

Nancy began to wonder if this was an anomaly or if Mary was truly the one who enjoyed making the courses impossible. Chuck Walker was strolling around the ship and overheard a conversation between Mary and the course designer for the Antarctica race (Alejo). He was expressing concerns about the temperatures and exposure to the wind and possible snow. Mary responded "Cold? Don't worry about the cold. Believe me they WANT to be cold." Maybe Mary was referring to cold in comparison to the previous three races where everyone complained about the heat. Maybe Mary enjoyed punishing her competitors, no one could be sure. Ian might know the answer to the question, but Ian was not there to comment.

Nancy began to wonder if Ian Adamson was really the one who should have been blamed for the little tortures found at each race. Nancy remembered finding the series of four-story sand dunes at the end of the 50 mile stage at Gobi and wondered now if it was even Ian's idea. Nancy was preparing a huge apology for Ian in the back of her head, just in case she needed to send it after Antarctica.

That night while Dave tried to fall to sleep in his upper bunk, the Dap Mares was doing its level best to induce sea sickness all across ship. The rolling sea was raising and lowering the bow of the ship by nearly 20 feet, rocking everyone to the point of a queasy stomach. Dave had found some extra sea sickness pills and had tried to offer Chuck Walker (in the lower bunk) an extra pill if he needed it. Dave reached down to grab Chuck on his wrist, but forgot about who Chuck was in his former life. Chuck woke instantly and grabbed Dave's arm, then cocked his other fist ready to strike. Dave shouted a series of nonsensical replies, "Stop! Chuck! It's me!" Chuck had decided not to kill Dave for waking him up, and declined the extra medication.

Day Two – Stage Two

The next morning aboard ship, Team Illinois had breakfast while Mary and Alejo negotiated with the Argentine officials who governed the land surrounding their country's research stations there. Antarctica it seemed was a land of settlements owned by other countries. The land in some cases was sovereign territory owned by Russia, or Argentina or just about every other country monitoring weather conditions. Entering any territory required a foreign government's permission. The RacingThePlanet crew would still need authorization to land there and race on the site governed by Argentina.

Sometime after 10:00 a.m. local time, the ship was contacted and permission was granted. Mary shared the news about the landing and then casually mentioned that the second stage would be a distance of 100 miles. Nancy's first reaction was as if she didn't hear Mary correctly. "What? Did she say 100 miles?" In addition to this race being the first multi-stage endurance race in the continent of Antarctica, it was also the first time anyone had run a single stage distance of 100 miles on the mainland. The rubber boats were boarded once again for short bumpy cruise.

The 100 mile stage would wind up spanning two days or more and competitors were required to carry sleeping bags and enough clothing to keep them dry. The race course would have to be restricted to the grounds governed by the Argentinean officials. Multiple loops of different distances and different terrains were marked out where the combination of the mileage, multiplied by the number of laps would eventually total up to 100 miles. The first loop carried a distance of 2.2K up an initial hill then down a gravel road, around a red barn then back up a smaller winding hill covered in penguins, then back to the station's mess hall which served as the race checkpoint. For this race and because of the varying weather conditions, the mess hall doubled as the sleeping shelter and first aid station for the entire 100 mile stage. Sleep was mostly optional.

Team Illinois ran the first loop 10 times and Mary had stopped them all for a mandatory lunch break. Given the temperature and wind, the mandatory break for all competitors was also a way for the race management team to evaluate the health of the competitors.

After the lunch stop, the second loop of the course was opened up to about 3K distance and wound around another part of the Argentina base camp on mostly rocky terrain. The hill climbs were intermittent on this loop but the wind gusts were significant. Depending on where they were on the loop, the wind was pushing at their backs, or hitting them from the left side. Eventually the loop wound around another wooden building and back towards the rookery in front of the mess hall. For Team Illinois this turned out to be about a 25 minute loop of running and walking. The course overall would be made up of firm ground but it was a technical course in its own way. Rather than having to negotiate the energy depleting dune climbs, the rocky terrain required more mental focus as the team avoided potential ankle-twisting obstacles.

A Sister's Marathon

The trail loop included a spectacular view of the harbor from a rocky overhang. Near the tallest rock formation at the edge of the cliff, Christian grave markers and a permanent monument had been built to commemorate those whose lives were lost on expeditions past. Dave had noticed the view and the calmness of the harbor as they passed by it earlier in the day. Dave had called out to Joel to stop without explaining why. "Joel, can you give me a couple of minutes."

Dave wandered over to the rocky overhang and asked Joel to help him retrieve a small bottle out of his backpack. There was a calming silence surrounding Dave except for a slight breeze brushing past his back and out to sea. Dave looked down at the ground at first with a pause and then released the small bottle of ashes. Tamara had run the equivalent of multiple marathons with Dave after all, and Dave had selected a beautiful and calming place for her to rest. The view from the cliff was spectacular, overlooking the calmness of the harbor, the penguin rookeries and a few icebergs floating quietly out to sea.

Joel knew instantly what had just taken place though they had no idea that Dave had been carrying the burden of his sister's death with him in a very real sense. Dave stayed at the overhang looking out into the harbor for a moment, exhaled the breath that he had been holding tentatively, and returned to the trail and his teammates. Nancy turned around and only then realized what had happened. She returned to her team, and hugged Dave hard on top of the cliff. There were no words. There didn't need to be any words. The family of three Illinois siblings who had adopted each other, returned to the trail and started slowly past the harbor and onto another loop to finish the day. A journey had ended for one, while another journey had continued for three.

There would be another mandatory dinner break after the 10 loops were completed and all competitors returned to the safety of the mess hall. The winds had increased to near 40 knots and the weather reports from the ship had indicated a combined wind chill factor of -30 degrees Fahrenheit. When the day had started the winds were manageable and the temperature hovered slightly above zero degrees. The course was becoming dangerous and dark and Mary decided to call the race off after 9:00 p.m. which held up the restart of the race until at least 3:00 a.m. the following morning. There would be time to ingest a non-exciting dinner and potentially grab some sleep on the uncomfortable floor of the mess hall. Joel smiled at the thought of the vast differences in predators they might experience on the floor of their Antarctic cabin. A nocturnal mouse scavenging for crumbs was by far preferred over the scorpions and camel spiders they found near their sleeping bags in the Sahara Desert.

Dave continued to reflect on the memory of Tamara and remained silent that evening, but everyone was quiet and subdued in the mess hall for different reasons. It was a long journey for them all to get there and the realization had also started to kick in that the 100 mile day would be the bulk of the race in Antarctica. Once the stage was complete, it would be a matter of two smaller stages and then a long trip back home. Joel and Dave were already in their sleeping bags and Nancy had positioned herself at the feet of many in the group, trying to avoid the business end of several snorers.

Everyone was awakened around 2:30 a.m. to get ready for the 3:00 a.m. restart. The temperature had dropped again and the winds had increased in speed but they all braved the conditions and headed out for the restart. The pace was very slow because it needed to be. There were obstacles to be avoided and winds to push each competitor in every direction. The mindless loops continued through the morning hours. Nancy was watching the loop times and each was averaging about 30 minutes. She described the events leading up to an encounter with Mary.

"We kept going and I knew that Dave was hurting. Hell, I was hurting too, and I was unmotivated. We kept going and I was counting every loop. I saw Mary at one point, and since all I had to do in my head was calculate loops and mileage, I announced that we had 30 loops to go. Mary said: "Oh, that's not bad at all!" (Mark this down as another reason why we should apologize to Ian). 30 loops is still 90k, or 55 miles."

Team Illinois had hit the halfway point after another two loops, came in for a food break and to attempt to find the feeling in their toes. Some of the other competitors were also in for a break when Mary announced the status of each competitor in the stage and the number of loops remaining in the 100 mile total. Team Illinois had 19 more loops to go until the stage was completed but everyone else seemed to be well ahead of them. Nancy talked about the change in the team's spirit.

"I had no idea where everyone else was. I was amazed that it seemed like everyone was so far ahead of us. I don't know if it was that, or just having our eyes set on a goal, but that moment marked a change in our team. To be honest, with the end in sight, we were able to work a little harder and get it done. We took on a single focus: Get under ten loops before dinner. That was under five hours away, so we knew we needed to be focused. We had been taking a break every five loops, but now, we didn't take rest. We kept moving, kept running, until we made it in, with time to spare. We headed in four minutes early for dinner with nine loops to go."

Joel was running strong the entire race so far and had helped pull them along during some of the monotony of the repeating course loop. What Team Illinois needed was a little motivation and Mary's announcement had done just that. When Team Illinois came to Antarctica, they knew there would be no other team to compete with, but there were other friends and competitors who made it personal at times just to create a competitive tension. It was always friendly at the end of a race, but it was always competitive during the race. Joel heard Mary's race summary and took their ranking in the stage personally.

"Our best (set of loops) came after a two hour mandatory lunch break. Gunnar made a comment to Mary about how far in front of us he was. We took that comment as our motivational device, left the break and went out and ran ten straight loops. We passed Gunnar twice and really worked to pass and stay in front of him."

The rally continued through the day and the loops continued to count down. At one point Dave who had been reclusive during the entire stage, decided to take a break and lay back in full recline on the ground. Joel came over and demanded that he get up telling Dave that the worst thing he could do was stop. Dave argued with him about knowing his body well enough to take the two minute rest, but Joel responded, "I'm the only one here that has run a hundred mile race before and I'm telling you that the worst thing you can do is lay down right now. We have to keep moving!" Dave agreed to get back up and move around to keep the muscles in motion.

Another story was forming during the long day as Kevin Lin struggled to keep up his normal quick pace through the 100 mile stage. The problem would boil down to Kevin's body type and body weight under the conditions in Antarctica. Where Kevin had always been fast and strong through the hot weather desert races, it would be the larger and heavier runners like Scott Smith and Chuck Walker who fared better in the strong wind gusts and blizzard conditions in Antarctica. Dave recalled seeing Kevin up ahead of them on the course, but watching a strong gust nearly pushing Kevin off the trail. During the same stretch of road, Nancy, Joel and Dave had clutched arms together in anticipation of the same gust, but their strength held them firm to the volcanic gravel road.

The End of the 100 Mile Day

Near the end of the long day with only four laps to go, another mandatory stoppage was called around 3:00 a.m. It was a short break and Team Illinois grabbed a nap, woke and headed back out on the course to finish the last few loops. As they rounded two more laps, they could see some of the competitors already gathering and resting inside the mess hall. On the last loop, Team Illinois was hiking in the last few hundred yards past the penguins again and towards the mess hall. Nancy had turned back to Dave and Joel and said, "Lets run it in." Dave replied in pain, "From here?"

They all managed to start the running pace again and finished with hands held together again for the stage completion. It was an anti-climactic completion to the stage with no one to see them and no one to see. The mess hall had become a dormitory and everyone who had finished the stage was already asleep. Team Illinois' time was recorded and they too found a little food before heading back to the warmth of their sleeping bags. It was not like RacingThePlanet participants to shy away from welcoming the rest of their fellow competitors home from the completion of a stage. But the 100 mile distance had crushed everyone. The cold and wind conditions coupled with the monotony of the repeating race loop had taken its toll on the entire group.

A few hours of rest later, Mary woke the group and informed them they had 45 minutes to get ready for departure back to the ship. For some reason, Dave had noticed his jacket lying next to him and the patches that were still holding, with only the corners of some patches coming loose. He looked over at Nancy while he held up a patch and she acknowledged the fact that the fabric glue did work, though the wind had been doing its best to pull them off.

They all waited until the Argentinean base commander arrived, and the entire staff and group of competitors thanked him for allowing them to run on the grounds of Argentina's base camp. After 100 miles and sore body parts, nobody really meant that they were truly grateful for the punishment bestowed upon them. They said "Thank you" anyway. The 100 mile stage idea wasn't the base commander's after all, and it wasn't Ian's idea either.

Heading towards the Zodiac boats, they noticed that the winds had kicked up the waves in the harbor. It would be a challenging ride back to the ship for those who were easily sea sick or had queasy stomachs. Nancy was sure to face herself outwards in case her usual stomach ailment kicked back in.

The Zodiac driver was trying to describe a technique for offloading passengers onto the platform at the bottom of the ladder. In the peaks and valleys of the waves, there was no way to tie up to the ship and let people climb onto the platform while the waves were playing with the height of the boat in relation to the platform. What the driver tried to describe was a method for making a rush towards the platform in timing with the wave, then someone would have to jump onto the platform as the Zodiac bumped into the ship's hull. The Zodiac would be ejecting a passenger onto the platform with each rush towards the hull.

Nancy remembered once again that she was on an adventure and this is what adventurers do. "Risk life by jumping off a small rubber boat, onto the water-level platform of the ship, as the smaller craft rams into the larger ship? No problem." Just be sure to grab onto something when you fly off the Zodiac, and try to keep from falling into the water and freezing to death. "OK, got it."

The group of 15 had been destroyed by their first-ever 100 mile run and energy levels were nowhere near where they needed to be to attempt a maneuver like what the Zodiac driver was proposing. Then again, there was that little topic of motivation again. If they could just get on board the ship, they would have access to a shower, dry clothes and prepared food.

One of the benefits to being in the Antarctic was that you always had your ship. The amenities though few, included warmth, but not too much warmth, hot showers and food that didn't require adding hot water to transform spongy bits into chicken and beans. The utility of freeze dried food is amazing for campers and backpackers, but you don't want to live on it.

As others were boarding the Zodiac boats, Nancy spotted a large shiny purple blob in the water, just off shore. She quickly figured out that it was a jelly fish and decided that it would be a good idea not to run out and touch the thing. The penguins were cuter anyway. Team Illinois and the rest of the competitors started to fill the boats a small group at a time to head to the ship and attempt docking maneuvers.

The boat driver was able to force the nose of the rubber boat into the hull of the ship with the motor still running and hold it there while the water level bobbed up and down. It seemed to provide a better option than bumping into the hull and hoping somebody would make it safely onto the platform. The driver was able to bump and hold the Zodiac relatively steady while the first load of passengers crawled over the nose of the Zodiac and onto the platform. Nancy described her turn to jump.

"The men on the ship were yelling at me to jump and I think I may have closed my eyes because suddenly, I was horizontal and in the air with four pairs of hands helping me upright on the ship. I must have been completely pale and I think I was crying because

Chuck asked me if I was okay and the only thing I could do to reply was to show him my hands shaking."

Joel had a different perspective about the boat ride and the methods used to get the competitors across the harbor and safely back on the ship.

"The ride was wild. The winds were strong and the waves were huge. As we approached the ship, we saw the crew throwing two rope ladders over the side. Chuck and I started laughing. This could be the most exciting part of the trip. Alex, the guide and Zodiac driver, got us on top of a wave and spun us past the boat and around to the other side away from the ladders. When Nan saw the ladders, she put her head down and started to cry. She said, "I'm going to die!!!" between her sobs. After all, we had just completed a 100 mile run and were wearing knee-high rubber boots. Alex told us he was going to pull up to the ship and keep bumping the front end of the Zodiac into the cargo hold. Every time he bumped, someone was supposed to jump into the ship. With the first bump, the first person fell back into the Zodiac. Okay, time to get this together. Every bump, another jump with a catch and toss by the crew of the ship. The crew did a great job and the landings were fun to watch. Kevin from Taiwan was launched like a little toy into the air and landed like a cat in the boat with a huge grin on his face. Scott, who had won the long stage, was the only one who had made it back to the boat immediately after finishing. He was standing on the deck of the ship taking pictures of us as we came in for our rough boarding. He said he had this image of the headline in the next day's USA Today: 'Tragedy at sea! Boat load of Americans lost when their Zodiac capsized in the Antarctic.'"

Fear and drama surrounding the boarding had faded once everyone was on deck while Team Illinois headed back to their shared little cabin area with Chuck. It would be a chance to warm up for real, check for toe and foot frostbite damage, and grab a hot shower. Food would be waiting for them in the galley but most just wanted to hit their bunk and fade off to sleep.

Dave had remained introspective the entire two day, 100 mile distance but he was also working to get past his personal demons and focus on the two people aboard ship who needed him. Nancy and Joel had become his new brother and sister and it was time to rise up and focus on them. He was part of their team after all, and they needed him to be stronger. Dave's grief remained, but he knew that it was time to re-commit to the team. Aside from his struggle with being out of shape, Dave was a strong self-motivator and knew he could rise above the feelings that were holding him back. The third stage would be a chance at a new day, and Dave would have to find a way to focus his energy on the positive things he could still do for the team. In the end, Dave needed Joel and Nancy as much as they needed him.

Stage Three

The ship had started to make the short sail to Deception Island for the next leg of the race which was scheduled for a marathon distance, unless Mary had another surprise in store for them. Nancy was still feeling bad for dumping all the blame for the difficulty of the desert races on Ian Adamson, when the ideas for punishment could just as easily come from Mary. No one knew. The next day of the race could turn out to be final stage and they might have to run the remainder of the mileage in a single day. Nancy shook her head. She was sure Mary wouldn't make them all run a 44 miler after they had just finished their first-ever 100 mile distance. "Right?" The next morning, Nancy woke to painful feet and a wish for the terrain to be easier on Deception Island.

"My foot was very unhappy the next morning, and I was praying for no rocks on the course on Deception Island. Amazingly, there was no wind and the bay the ship anchored in was as calm as glass. The course was much longer than 3k loops, almost 8k I think, so we were told to do I think six loops. The stage started almost as soon as we got to Deception, and I didn't even have time to fill my water bladder, so I carried a full water bottle in my pack. And then, I looked down and realized I had two different shoes on…yes, they were the same brand of shoe but one from a new pair with a new orthotic in it, and a second from the old pair with an old orthotic. That worried me, but I chose not to mention it to the boys, because after all, there was really nothing I could do about it."

Deception Island had an interesting history in that it was a still-active volcano that rested calmly under the sea. The island was crescent-shaped and almost perfectly semi circular. It looked as if the volcano had been scooped out of the island and dumped somewhere out in the ocean. Two centuries ago as they were told, the volcano had exploded and blew the entire top of the mountain into the atmosphere. All that was left was a large crescent island which created one of the best natural harbors in the world. The wind would never have a chance to whip up waves in the harbor, which made for a pleasant and calming trip from the Zodiac boats to the shore. There were also spots on the island to find geo-thermal pools and the word was that in certain parts of what normally be an icy harbor, the water was heated from the still active volcano underneath. There were no takers on swimming the heated harbor. After all, this was no wimpy triathlon stage.

Competitors walked out on the shore slowly, nursing the sore body parts that would not have a chance to fully recover from the 100 mile stage. The soil was nearly perfect for running with smaller rocky terrain and hard packed sand. The volcanic ash and sand were a natural running trail, absorbing a little of the shock as the foot impacted the soil but giving enough support to allow the legs to push ahead. This was Team Illinois' kind of running. The course would be mostly flat and not too technical. There was a good chance to make up some ground on the leaders if Dave could bring himself back into the sport that he had grown to love during the past two years.

Everyone tested the sand on the beach and ran up and down to get a feel for the terrain. The warm up running lasted only a few minutes and Mary was gathering the group back for the start. Dave and Joel had started running strong and pulling Nancy with them slightly away from the rest of the pack. In the early part of the race, Nancy could feel the energy returning to her team. She ran along side with Dave and said, "This is the day. This is your sister's day. Can you tell? She is loaning us her wings". Their speed increased and for the first time in the race, Dave had refocused his attention on two other members of his extended family. Team Illinois was back and running strong again. Joel describes the race format for the third stage and marathon distance.

"We were supposed to run six loops of seven kilometers each. After three loops into the race, the course was changed to a 5.3K course because much of the land we were running on was a protected wildlife area. We ran into a lot of water crossings. Most of them were small enough to jump over or shallow enough to run through without getting too wet. The course was beautiful. There were some hills, but nothing too terrible. The terrain was kind of this crushed volcanic black rock. It was soft enough to run on without sinking, except in one spot where Dave kept sinking to mid-shin depth. The water crossings were all glacier run-offs. When the sun was at its highest peak, we found small waterfalls. As the day went on, the waterfalls got weaker and then stopped running."

In Memory of Tamara

Nancy had summed up the energy they had taken with them during the third stage of the race.

"There really is no other explanation for our performance (in this stage), after a mediocre 100-miler, we were running like we had wings. There are those moments when during a run, everything is going so right, that you wonder just when things would go wrong, but it wasn't going to go wrong that day. The course was shortened to a 5k, which meant one more loop, but it didn't faze us. And despite all the internal worry that each of us must have felt that our legs might not hold up, they did. At the finish, I hugged Dave and thanked him for sharing his sister's strength with us."

The remainder of the stage was calming and uneventful. Team Illinois had continued a maintained pace throughout the day despite the 100 mile distance in the blizzard the previous two days. Their feet continued to move forward easily on the packed volcanic sand, while the rest of the course loop was not so technical as to pull them out of their personal auto-pilot frame of mind. Dave would revisit memories of the previous three races with his new found family, recalling images of Attie and his melted shoe, and the endless dune climbs with Chuck Walker leading the charge. Nancy was wondering again if Ian was the truly the one who chose to punish them all in the hot weather desert challenges. Her thoughts went back to the dune climb punishment at the end of the 50 mile day. The crescent-shaped island made for a perfect marathon loop and most of the group of 15 finished relatively close to each other to close out the day. It was an extended family now, and each of them cheered everyone else on at the finish.

Returning to the ship across the calm waters of the harbor, the competitors all returned to their cabins for another shower and dry clothing. There was an option to head back to shore to explore some of the natural hot springs on the island, but Team Illinois had decided to stay within the comforts of the ship. It was still near zero degrees out there, and a warm bunk was always preferred over frigid air. Some who took the opportunity had returned later with another memory that would last a lifetime, but for Team Illinois it had been a traumatic and yet an uplifting kind of day. Nothing could really top the experience they all shared on a perfect marathon.

Stage Four – The End of an Expedition

Dap Mares had sailed again back to King George Island for the final loop of the 150 mile challenge. It was difficult to compare the way each competitor felt at this stage of a cold weather race, to how they felt after the long-day of a hot weather desert. Bodies take the same sort of impact punishment as the feet pound out the same overall distance, but how would the deserts compare? It was easier by far to run a distance race without the hindrance of added clothing, and it seemed that cold weather conditions were more difficult to protect against during the run.

In either case it was clear that all competitors were managing the same health issues leading to the last day of the desert challenge. Regardless of the race or the continent, preparation for the final stage of any race meant managing blisters and skin loss, favoring an injury to a calf or a knee, and managing food and water so that the body could keep it down. Though Nancy experienced fewer sour stomach episodes in Antarctica compared to the hot weather races, her stomach was still tied up in knots and unable to consume much food at all. Everyone was safe and in relatively good health which is of course, the only thing that really mattered. Scott Smith's Talisman gifts were doing well to protect the 15 who had ventured there from the other side of the world.

Before departing for the last stage, Mary Gadams reviewed race finish times through the last stage of the race. Everyone knew where they stood in the rankings and Team Illinois had made up significant time on marathon day. Just before departure, most of the group stayed together and came to the realization that this might be the last time they would see each other in competition. There was nervous tension in the air because of that, but the stories from the previous desert races had started to pour into the room. Laughter is the best cure for tension, in almost every situation. The group of 15 competitors who had conquered three other continents and the world's most extreme deserts, were reliving the memories of bad food and massive blisters and Ian's course designs. Nancy reminded herself to send Ian an apology letter for all the things she had said in the past, when it could have been Mary's fault in the end. The memory of any desert challenge would be diminished however if the course was easy. Mary and Ian already knew that, but Nancy would learn.

The banter continued for more than an hour until it was time to head off to shore for the final stage. Zodiac boats were boarded and the group headed off to shore on King George Island. After waiting a few final minutes, Mary started the race and Team Illinois embarked on their last stage of their last endurance race together.

The course started easy which allowed Nancy's stomach a chance to settle down and the pain in her feet to subside. She always felt more comfortable a half hour into a run than at the start. The blood starts pumping and the circulation to those body parts needing oxygen starts to get the supply. Nancy's engine was warming up. Joel and Dave likewise were getting loose and they all could tell that the final stage would be a good race day for Team Illinois. This was always their best day.

Just as their body-engines were ramping up to full capacity the course took a sweeping turn up to the top of the glacier that Alejo had promised to include on the course. Feeling more like wet packed snow than ice, the surface of the glacier was not as bad to run on as they feared. No one really had any "glacier running" experience to fall back on. It was pretty safe to assume that few if any of the competitors had actually run on a similar surface.

Completing the first loop of the course, Team Illinois had passed Mary who was stationed back at the starting point near the beach. Nancy had asked how much more, and Mary replied "One more loop". Team Illinois had completed the first nine mile loop in ninety minutes and Nancy knew they could get the second loop done in the same time period. As they turned back onto the glacier, the Team Illinois engine had started to slow down. For all of Dave's focus and energy spent on the marathon day, Dave was now hitting the wall. Nancy had started to take the lead and fly ahead, her stomach still in knots but not holding her back. Joel had to call out to her, "Nancy, you're not paying attention. Dave is hurting. Get it together and stick with us."

The team clustered back together to finish the race now only a few miles away. Autopilots had kicked in and all three were just pounding out the pace around the back side of the island loop, towards the shoreline and the awaiting crew. Nancy describes the finish line.

"We got to the point where we could see the finish. I think I got a little too excited and my stomach started acting up, you know, the dry heaves. Maybe it was from exhaustion, maybe excitement, but I let it do its cramping, looked at the guys and said, "Let's fly". And we did, right to the finish. I was happy and sad and I wanted to cry, because it meant so much to be done. When I did cry, it was not because I felt like I had done the impossible (like the first race in Atacama), but because it was over and it was one of the most meaningful journeys in my life. At that moment, I was grieving for the adventure that had ended. Don't get me wrong, I'm happy to try new challenges, but this experience and this goal was two years in the making, and there were many, many sacrifices along the way, and now, with the goal accomplished comes so many questions: What next? Who am I now? Can we ever relive what Team Illinois accomplished? And so, with a background of icebergs, Team Illinois accepted our finisher medals, sipped champagne and hugged Mary, Cathy and Mike. We then went back inside Alejo's home who lived right on King George Island and sat with the other competitors. Even though we laughed, when I look back, I think we all must have shared that same feeling of sadness to be done."

In the end, 15 elite endurance racers had completed a monumental series of four desert challenges on four continents, each 150 miles or more in distance. Antarctica was by far the most difficult challenge, requiring heavy clothing for protection, limited visibility during freak blizzard white-out conditions, but with just as many hills to overcome. Scott Smith emerged as champion of Antarctica, with Chuck Walker finishing second and Kevin Lin finishing third. Lisanne Dorion took women's championship honors and all others finished well to round out the field.

There were only 15 that qualified for The Last Desert, and they had all proved their versatility and their strength of will in overcoming this historic and most unique challenge. The elite 15 had proved their strength in the previous three hot weather desert races, finishing the Atacama Crossing, the Gobi March, and the Sahara Race challenges when so many others had failed. Congratulations to all.

Antarctic Competitor	Country	Age
Satoru Otsuka	Japan	65
Masashi Hayakawa	Japan	62
Alasdair Morrison	Scotland	57
Brent Weigner	United States	56
Gunnar Nilsson	Sweden	50
Scott P. Smith	United States	50
Vincent Carroll	Ireland	46
Lisanne C. Dorion	United States	40
Charles Walker	United States	39
Nancy Fudacz-Burrows	United States	39
Derek Kwik	Hong Kong	37
Dave Kuhnau	United States	36
Joel Burrows	United States	31
Kevin Lin	Taiwan	28
Matthew Chapman	Australia	29

Pictures from the "Last Desert" 2006

Photo provided by Dave Kuhnau (above). Before the Last Desert race, Nancy finally admits to the 4 Deserts series being 'her idea' while Joel and Dave remained innocent bystanders in the process.

Photo provided by Michael A. Shoaf (right) Nancy's enthusiasm was infectious before the race, as the select group of international competitors waited outside their hotel for a bus to the airport.

Photo provided by Michael A. Shoaf (above). Dave Kuhnau runs with the memory of his sister lost recently to cancer. Her picture remained with him the entire race.

Photo provided by Michael A. Shoaf (below) Another dog befriended the competitors before the start of the race. He took position to watch over the group in front of the hotel and their gear. The similarity to another canine guardian angel met in the Atacama Desert was uncanny.

The Power Of Team

Photo provided by Dave Kuhnau (above). Thank you to our sponsors. Dave Kuhnau shows the patches from multiple sponsors who helped them reach the dream of racing in Antarctica.

Photo provided by Michael A. Shoaf (below) Country flags and competitors pose for a group picture once arriving on the islands of Antarctica.

Photo provided by Michael A. Shoaf (above). The exploration ship Dap Mares rests quietly in the harbor as Zodiac boats shuttle competitors to and from shore.

Photo provided by Scott Smith (below) A former whaling station, the islands around Antarctica are littered with whale bones. Scott Smith grabs one vertebra near a whaler's signpost.

The Power Of Team

Photo provided by Scott Smith (above). The Zodiac boat meets rough waters on its way to the shore of the Argentinean military base called Esperanza.

Photo provided by Michael A. Shoaf (below) Local Antarctica resident, adventurer and race course designer Alejo, rides the Zodiac like a tethered surfboard on his way to shore.

Peter Wortham

Photo provided by Michael A. Shoaf (left). Mary Gadams, Founder of **RacingThePlanet** and the **4 Deserts** series of endurance races takes a rare break from the madness of organizing an international event.

Photo provided by RacingThePlanet (right) Photographer and videographers Cathy Cole and Michael A. Shoaf are on the receiving end of a photograph this time.

The Power Of Team

Photo provided by Michael A. Shoaf (above). Team Illinois approaches a monument remembering those lost on expeditions in the past.

Photo provided by Michael A. Shoaf (below) Penguins routinely attempted to join the race, but were by far more graceful in the water.

Photo provided by Michael A. Shoaf (above). The paradox of a blizzard in Antarctica means plenty of snow but no accumulation. High winds take the dry powder out to sea.

Photo provided by Michael A. Shoaf (below) Dave Kuhnau takes a break between distance loops near the end of the 100 mile race stage. Team Illinois completed the 100 miles in just over 25 hours.

The Power Of Team

Photo provided by Michael A. Shoaf (left). Dap Mares crew struggle getting a Zodiac boat off shore in the high winds and blizzard conditions.

Photo provided by Michael A. Shoaf (below) Steam bubbles up from the ground on the active volcano known as Deception Island.

Photo provided by Michael A. Shoaf (above). In lock step over a hill with a glacier in the distance, Team Illinois continues to pound out the miles on Antarctica.

Photo provided by Michael A. Shoaf (below) Glacier fed stream crossings were common and cold as teams were forced to run through them along the course.

The Power Of Team

Photo provided by Michael A. Shoaf (above). Team Illinois continues its trek along the shore with more ruins of a whaling station off in the distance.

Photo provided by Michael A. Shoaf (left) Running across the actual glacier, teams had to navigate cracks and holes in the surface as well as deep streams formed from the mid-day ice melt.

Photo provided by Michael A. Shoaf (above). Joel carries mixed emotions at the end of the race, happy to have completed the Antarctica race, yet sad that the 2 year journey was over.

Photo provided by Michael A. Shoaf (below) The crew started to gather up the equipment after the race was over, while icebergs took up residence in the harbor.

The Power Of Team

Photo provided by Michael A. Shoaf (left). Flags served as course markers along the race trail but the local residents didn't seem to mind. All materials were removed after the race was complete. RacingThePlanet competitors left only footprints behind.

Photo provided by Michael A. Shoaf (below). Nancy and Dave shared the emotions that seemed to flood everyone after the 4 Deserts series was complete.

Chapter 10 - Ending the Journey

The Day After Antarctica   February 1, 2006

Alejo, the local King George Island resident and course designer for the Antarctica race had let his facial hair grow to the point where he had started to take on the look of a mountain man familiar with the extremes of the South Pole. It was another subtle indicator that all RacingThePlanet course designers seemed to be the kind of people who took pleasure in imposing extremes of the environment on visitors. Alejo had been a great stand-in for Ian, and Mary seemed to appreciate the way Alejo had designed the difficult stages in Antarctica. Of course the news would leak out about who actually decided on the 100 mile stage, and Mary wouldn't have anyone else to blame that idea on.

Team Illinois had won the team division by default. It would have been good to race against at least one other team in Antarctica but motivation was found in forms other than head to head team competition. For any person attempting a significant challenge like Antarctica, the real sense of pride and accomplishment comes with the simple completion of the challenge.

Without the benefit of a competing team to run along side them, Team Illinois would have to find support from their friends who ran with them. When the goal was only to finish the race, Team

Illinois' performance would not have been stellar. It was indeed an accomplishment to complete the journey, but Team Illinois had already gained experience in finishing well, not just finishing. With a little motivation from some comments by Gunnar, or when they were passed on the course by Chuck or others, Team Illinois found inspiration to keep them moving. The strength of the team is what separated them from the rest of the team in any race. Joel summarized his thoughts on winning as a team.

"As individuals, we are strong and confident, but as a team, we can accomplish anything. When we chose Atacama as our first race, we wanted to race as a team because we believed in a philosophy of 'strength in numbers'. As the races progressed, we watched other teams fall apart. Strong trios became three individuals; egos became stronger than the 'group', a lack of understanding and communication lead to bad decision making. We can take pride in being the first team to: complete all four deserts, win three desert races and stay together as a single group for all four events."

The competitors were wandering around the shores near Alejo's home, still offering personal congratulations to each other at the end of a very long two year journey. Congratulations and thanks were also offered to Alejo for being the perfect host and helping to show them some of the beauty of Antarctica.

The collective group eventually returned to the gravel landing strip and the awaiting plane back to Punta Arenas, Chile. It would be a chance for everyone to recuperate further after the 155-mile challenge in the cold. The hotel would provide for larger beds and a bigger shower and of course, room service. The accommodations on board the ship Dap Mares were glamorous when compared to the tent camps of Sahara, Gobi or Atacama. Who wouldn't after all, prefer a padded bunk and a real shower on board a ship between race stages, but having the option of dialing '6' for room service back on shore sounded so much more civilized.

The Power Of Team

After arriving back in Punta Arenas, Mary Gadams asked the group if they wanted to say goodbye right there or if the gang want to get together one more time for dinner. No one was eager to end the journey given the accomplishment they had all just shared. Nancy was the first to jump in and say that she needed to have dinner with everyone "one last time" and the group broke up to head back to their individual rooms and get ready for a later dinner. Nancy, Joel and Dave had decided to change their plane tickets and take a later departure to accommodate dinner, and still allow some discovery time in Uruguay before flying back to the U.S. Tickets were changed, clothes were changed, and their perspectives on many things were beginning to change as well.

Somehow the cohesive little three-person working unit known as Team Illinois had grown to include so many more members now. The group could have been labeled with many names given the specific desert challenge or the stage. So many individual competitors had shared stages, shared motivation and shared hands at the finish line with Team Illinois. Sometimes it was "Team Chuck" helping lead the charge up the dunes, or "Team Nielsen" as Jacob helped to set their pace for several stages in two of the races. In Antarctica, Scott participated as everyone's teammate providing symbols of protection as they all embarked on unfamiliar terrain and race conditions. Everyone there in Punta Arenas for that matter, was a member of a very recently formed but close knit family. It was hard to say goodbye. Nancy remembered the last dinner with her extended family.

"Everyone looked clean, relaxed and happy. Mary ordered Pisco Sours for everyone, the wine flowed freely, and I had steak and fries and laughed and told everyone how great they were. There was a moment though that stands out. Dave brought a beautiful book 'Antarctica' with him and asked everyone to sign it. It was what Alasdair Morrison (Scotland) wrote that still brings me to tears. He wrote: 'Team Illinois, the heart and soul of RacingThePlanet.' Oh, I know it's not true, but I love the feeling that our experience made everyone else's experience a little richer too, and that it would have been a totally different ride without us."

The Staggered Path back Home

Dave, Joel and Nancy did break away from the group after all the goodbyes had been exchanged and promises to reunite had been made. There was some talk of getting the same group back together a year later to race somewhere in the Himalayan Mountains. No one was sure if that was a joke or not, but the idea was tossed out for further consideration.

Team Illinois had first flown into Buenos Aires, Argentina as a jumping off point back to the U.S., but then took an immediate detour via a long ferry ride to Uruguay for some more sight seeing. Upon arrival, they found transportation in the form of gas powered scooters which may or may not have been a good idea based on Nancy's history with bikes. Despite the risk, all three "scootered" their way around town to buy trinkets and some local artwork. It was a way to remember each competition with locally made artwork, and it would adorn shelves and mantles next to their medals and trophies. Shopping for local art was also a nice way to relax from the stress of the competition.

They all became reflective in Uruguay, and started to comment about what the Antarctica race meant to them, or what the whole desert series meant. There was a new theme developing as they talked about how they all grew together as a team and how the tools they had used to motivate themselves and help each other excel, were also helping each of them in their personal and professional lives.

Team Illinois had become successful as a competitive trio because of the chemistry, the mutual bond between them, and their commitment to work together no matter the hardship. What Team Illinois didn't make the connection to (until then), was that the same core attributes used to describe why they had become

The Power Of Team

successful together, were the same core attributes that Nancy, Joel and Dave were unconsciously applying to their own personal lives.

The conversations continued back and forth all day, in between stops at local art galleries and in search for ice cream. At one small parking area, Dave and Joel had turned into what was a big enough spot for all three scooters in front of a side walk. Nancy was following the boys but failed to apply her brake as she approached the sidewalk. She had jumped the curb and headed towards the back brick wall. Without braking, she crashed into the wall and dumped the scooter down on its side. Nancy escaped with nothing more than a sore thumb and a bruise. The scooter lay on its side, wheels still spinning, with no more than a new scratch or two in damage. All that time near sheer cliffs, on top of mountains, crossing fast moving canyon rivers, and avoiding deep cracks on a glacier, Nancy had her brush with death on a Uruguayan scooter.

Shopping and relaxing on their excursion had come to an end and it was time to head back home. Returning to Buenos Aires, Team Illinois had finished up with one more early dinner, and then took a cab back to the airport and the first of multiple connections.

When the events of a two week desert challenge come to a close, no one expects to be met with continuing challenges once the race is over. Yet at the airport, the medallions and trophies earned by Team Illinois had suddenly become suspicious weapons discovered in their carry-on luggage. "These are heavy and could injure someone", the security agent tried to tell them in his best broken English. Dave's street artwork suddenly became a treasured "national artifact" that he was apparently trying to smuggle out of the country. It was interesting that at this part of the story, after all that had happened to Nancy, Joel and Dave the past two years, after completing all four desert challenges, they might be detained in Argentina as terrorists and smugglers.

Nancy played the "chick card" as Joel had described it, and she started to cry in the security line. Dave was frantically looking for the receipts that proved he bought his "national artifacts" from an art store. A female security agent approached the scene and began asking about the situation from the men conducting the luggage search. Joel did his best to help explain the situation.

"I told her in Spanish, 'nosotros un equipo do corriando de los Estados Unidos. Corrimos en Antarctica por dos ciento cincuento kilometros-y ciento sesenta kilometros en Esperanza (the Argentinian Base).' Their eyes opened wide with amazement and they let us through."

Joel had remembered that Esperanza was the Argentinean base on Antarctica and suddenly everything was "OK" for the American team and their lethal medals. The woman security guard had also told Joel that his wife had "cried at the right moment", even Dave's artwork was passed through and the three happily boarded the plane. Nancy took pride in her performance. Joel thought it was worthy of the Academy's consideration. Nancy was taking notes about her whole experience at Antarctica and the final leg of the four desert challenges. She writes:

"I still cannot explain what this adventure meant to me. I'm not a different person because of it, I'm just more me, and better. I am so grateful for the opportunity to have raced with amazing individuals from all over the world, to have shared stories and laughed with so many of you about the most profound things to the most crass and inane. I pray that our paths will meet again. I am honored to have been a part of their adventure. For the fifteen individuals who shared this journey, you are all people I strive to become. Thanks for sharing yourselves and your dreams with me."

Chapter 11 - In Nancy's Words

The question I get asked most often after the obligatory "Why?" is, "Are you done yet?" I began to hear this question from many people after our first Ironman, then emphatically after I returned from an attempt at Ironman Brazil with a broken collarbone after a spill on the bike. For the most part, I never asked those same questions of myself, until I met the Atacama Crossing. The 2004 Atacama Crossing will always be the high-bar measure of "hell" that every other race will be compared to. I am not exaggerating by saying that every day, in fact almost every moment in Atacama, I questioned why I was there and vowed never to race again. I dreamed about catching up on the latest movies, organizing our gear-cluttered home, going back to school and starting a family. I wanted to move away from the suffering and insanity. I dreamed about who I would become, more social, a better performer at work, perhaps a mother.

I had moments like this in each and every race. During the long day at Gobi, I dreamed that I would leave this crazy world behind and build my new home back in Chicago. I dreamed of holidays with my kids and learning how to cook more than a frozen pizza, and a beautiful, clean home that we could entertain in. Every time we would return from a race, the question would resurface: "Are you done yet?" And I would reply, "Yep, just one more and we're retiring."

It didn't take long for us to sign up for the Sahara Race after Gobi, and I set my eyes on the big prize: Antarctica. Of course Antarctica would push my homemaker fantasy back another year, and I started to get more questions like, "When will you be done with this quest? What do you have to prove now? Don't you want children? Aren't you hurting your body?" These questions plagued me and I did my best to avoid not only the people who would ask them, but even thinking about them myself. When pushed, I could always say, "After Antarctica".

Antarctica came and went. After each race, there was a natural letdown. All the excitement of a huge effort would now be complete and we would return to the banality of life, but after Antarctica, I felt really lost. Not only did I have to come down from the high of completing a race of Antarctica's magnitude, but I had to refocus on who I was, and what I wanted. It had been over two years of qualifying in other desert races, then getting ready for Antarctica. Really, from December 2003 until January 2006, life for me was sharply focused on the RacingThePlanet series. After we finished with Atacama (which we began preparations for six months in advance), we had signed up for Gobi. Once we committed to Gobi, there was no doubt in my mind that we would finish all four desert races. This all-consuming race life is filled with super highs and super lows, and it is never boring. I think now that it's all over, I'd even take back the super lows just to feel those fleeting moments of pure elation when arriving at the finish line.

I know I'm not alone in this. After Antarctica, Dave had to refocus on work and everything else he had responsibility for, and we rarely saw him. Joel began to refocus on new goals: getting his black belt in Tae Kwon Do, thinking of new career options, and being social again.

I questioned what I was doing every day and about two months after returning from Antarctica, I found myself in the Human Resources Director's office at East Bank Club, tearfully telling him how much I hated my job. In retrospect this was probably not the best career move for me, but he seemed surprisingly supportive. I told him I wanted to coach others at the club, and drop most of my other managerial responsibilities. I wanted the freedom to race and coach and just find myself. I took a pay cut to do what I wanted, and with some new freedom, momentarily found some relief from my fears that I would never feel as great as I did during these races. I took some time away from work, signed up for a 100-mile run and tried to move on.

Runners sometimes ask other runners whether they are "running to" or "running from" something. I guess I fall into both categories. Running from fear that I'm not good enough, that I won't live up to some people's expectations, that I am getting too old, don't pay my bills on time, etc. I seem to also be running towards that feeling of belonging and pride in being involved with something bigger than myself. I get that same feeling of pride and belonging in a big marathon, watching thousands of runners ahead and behind me, all of us moving to something better and bigger than ourselves. I also got that feeling in the Four Deserts. Running is my time to think, push, ache, cry, laugh at myself and mostly, just be - me - moving forward. I have run away from both awful times in my life, and run to celebrate. It was not long after I signed up for a 100-mile race when Mary Gadams called to ask if we would help with the 2006 Atacama Crossing as race volunteers.

When I was little my mom woke me up early one summer day and told me that she was going to take me to a local amusement park Great America. I remember how I could feel the excitement rising in my body - I suppose everyone responds differently to great news, or anticipation of something great, but I get warm, and start twitching or tapping my foot. I feel my stomach move a little closer to my throat and my lips turning upward to a smile that I can't contain. That's how I felt when I talked to Mary. I wanted so badly to relive where we had been, and I wanted to share that feeling with others. I quickly agreed to take all my vacation time (and more) and agreed to go to Chile. It didn't appear that Dave could go at first, but he managed to change his plans and Team Illinois was one again, but as volunteers.

Of course, not everything was roses. Joel and I decided that even after agreeing to help with the course in Chile that we would use the 100-miler we signed up for as a "training run" for the event. Now, I know you're thinking, "What moron uses a 100-mile challenge as a "training run"?" I agree, it was stupid but I wanted so badly to go to Chile on an upswing. I wanted that feeling of accomplishment fresh in my mind so that I could look at each competitor during their suffering and know in my heart what they were going through and know that they could do it.

I couldn't do it. At mile 55, my mind became filled with the same doubts I had in the Atacama Desert. I was terrified by who I was, a psycho runner who at age 39 was denying children for her husband and family. I was a bad homemaker, a bad employee, a bad friend, and now, even a bad runner. I couldn't even do the thing I was compelled to do. I started sobbing. These weren't sobs of pain, but deep, deep sobs of total self-doubt and hatred. I was a loser. How could I look any competitor in the face in Chile and tell them they were strong? How could I justify finishing any of the Four Desert races? I finished only because I had a great team. It had nothing to do with me. Nothing. I was a loser, a total loser. It goes without saying that at mile 62, while Joel was leading in the men's race, he dropped out with me. I was so ashamed. We drove back to Seattle the next day, and I tried to tell myself it wasn't important, it was just a bad day, but I couldn't.

You can't really underestimate the feelings that arise in a very long endurance event. I think what happens is that with each mile, all our effort goes into moving forward, and we have no more energy to bottle up things that are lurking within us. There's no protection from sadness or elation. The fatigue makes each emotion raw and strong, so the lows are gut wrenching and the highs unbelievable. That's just the way it is at mile 60, or 5 days into a 150-mile race. The worst personal hell becomes complete elation at the finish line.

Two weeks after "DNF'ing" our 100-miler, we headed to Chile. I found it amazingly comforting to see the RacingThePlanet staff, especially Jan Richardson. I pushed back the memories of the failed 100-miler, and got to work with Joel on the course.

Ii is nearly impossible to create a race in a foreign place where you've got to create campsites and plan dinners, gear checks, and oh yeah, a 150-mile course. That being said, I wasn't mentally prepared for the chaos that naturally ensues in such an undertaking. I had also forgotten something very, very important. Every competitor hates the course team during the race. As an athlete, you are exhausted, aggravated, and sometimes lost, and guess who you blame? The people who set and mark the course. And, yes, we were hated. At the end of the long stage, I was stationed with Pierre, the course director at a dry waterfall. Our goal was to help everyone safely down. As fewer and fewer competitors were coming in, I backtracked along the route to cheer the athletes in. I ran toward a team who were now near completion of their race. I yelled out, "Great job, you're almost done!" Their response was to scowl and tell me that the course wasn't marked properly, that the course was much too difficult and that it was "ridiculous". I tried to appease them, and then walked them to Pierre who would take the brunt of their anger, but their words hurt me. I had hoped for an adventure where I felt like I was sharing my experience with other athletes, and it wasn't that at all. That team tongue-lashing darkened the race volunteer experience for me. I left Chile empty.

Our volunteer activities in Chile left me empty in other ways too. I dropped ten pounds in the Atacama, and came back lighter and stronger for all that time on my feet. Unsure of what to do next, I did the one thing that always seemed to keep me sane. I ran. I ran a lot, and surprisingly well. I found myself right on my best running times. At nearly 40, I was running as well as I had years before. At our track workouts, a few guys asked what I had been doing to "turn it up". I couldn't answer them with the truth, that just filling the competitive void made me push a little more, and left me a little hungrier. We came back in the thick of triathlon and marathon coaching responsibilities in Chicago and fortunately for me, I couldn't focus too much on being sad, but rather focused on what I really wanted to do in Chile, cheer on our students and watch them succeed as athletes. Their success kept pushing me to run more, but I knew I was running away from all the questions that plagued me. What did I want? Did I want a child? Did I want to keep racing? Am I anything without racing?

I was turning 40 and I still didn't know who I was, aside from the simple definition of being the only child of a Polish immigrant father and Cuban-American mother. My family's working roots were middle class with my dad a warehouse foreman and my Mom a flight attendant. My parents were married, divorced, remarried and divorced again. During the first divorce in what I can describe as a sort of "hippie" phase in our lives, my Mom and I lived in a yoga ashram. Yes, strange as it seems, I went from Catholic school during the day to yoga ashram at night with my fondly called "Swami Mommy". I guess you could perhaps call this the perfect blend of learning environments for a later 150-mile race in a far away place. I had learned the concept of hard-working discipline from my father, balanced with the love for exploration from my mother.

Though daily life as a kid was a little more interesting for me than most, I grew up not really belonging to anything. I was too different in grade school and I didn't have many friends, and that feeling always kept me always an arm's length from the rest of my family and friends. I identified more closely with the "outcasts" in high school and college, and made my friends among them, but once my time in school ended, so did my friendships. It's not that I don't make friends, I do, but I have a tendency to be mistrustful of people who haven't seen me at my best and worst. It goes without saying that Joel and Dave have been there, and in many ways, they have become the siblings that I never had. When you see yourself as an outsider, the one thing you want more than anything is to belong somewhere. That is where my fantasies came from in the desert - that deep desire to be connected with someone and something. Dave and Joel gave me something to belong to. I was a part of Team Illinois - and for one of the very few times in my life I felt like I mattered. Giving that up at the end of Antarctica was more painful than I could imagine.

Joel had suggested we do a race for my 40th birthday. Of course, I couldn't just settle for one race, and one grew to two, which grew to three, and then five. Without answering the questions plaguing me, I designed an insane "Gauntlet" of 5 races in 5 weeks including an Ironman, 2 marathons, and 2 ultra marathons. I tried to get Dave to join us but he would have no part of it. I somehow convinced Joel to do these races in honor of my 40th birthday, but now the questions from other friends were unavoidable. As soon as I signed up for the first of five races, a dear friend of mine dropped a letter off for me. The letter said she was worried about me - that I had nothing to prove - that I might hurt myself - and that I had to finally address why I was doing all this. I didn't run for a week after I got that letter. My friend was seeing me realize my worst fear. I had become a psycho, compulsive runner. I felt like I was nothing without racing.

I thought long and hard about that letter. It's funny how memories serve you when you least expect it. I was walking into the local Starbucks thinking about Cathy's letter when I looked over at a table I had been sitting at a year before with a friend. My friend Kaye and I were talking about racing, and need for it. I told her "I love it. It is the one place where I feel like I am where I am supposed to be." The 4 Deserts races magnified that. Every day of each race, I would finish hand in hand with my teammates, knowing I belonged. There was nowhere else in the world I was supposed to be but besides these two wonderful people. And, I mattered. It couldn't have been without Dave or Joel, and they couldn't have done it without me. Kaye told me, "You are nuts, but I admire it. Rather than hide it, you need to embrace that part of yourself." She was right. For me, the universe is right for me when I am running as hard as I can and see Joel waiting for me at the finish. The universe is right when I see Dave at a track workout, and we joke about the wind or the cold, or just about anything else.

I am at my best in these races - raw, dirty, scared, and elated. But the amazing thing about them is that they are real. There is nothing more awful than the self-doubt that arises when your legs just simply won't move anymore, and your stomach will just not take any more food or water. But, it's real - as is the unbelievable effort it takes to keep putting one foot in front of the other when all your senses tell you not to. There is truly nothing more amazing than hearing a drum in the dark in the distance that signifies the end of a 60-mile day. The feeling of accomplishment is something I strive for every day, and I doubt I can live without it. It's creating those accomplishments in every day living that continues to be my own personal challenge.

If you're wondering, we completed the Gauntlet with the JFK 50 miler where Joel and I ran through the finish hand-in-hand in a 50-mile personal best for both of us. The "Gauntlet" culminated with Joel throwing me a surprise party for my 40th birthday. You know the old joke that you wouldn't want to be a part of any club that would have you? I looked around that night at my friends from near and far (Racing the Planet competitors Scott Smith and Chuck Walker came), and realized that I should thank my lucky stars that these wonderful people could like me with all my idiosyncrasies. I am a runner. I am a competitor, I am a teammate and I am a champion. I love it. I love being there at the end of the day, with men, wondering how a woman could keep up. I love chasing someone down in a run and getting the pass, or having my competitor push into a different gear just because I am there. I love feeling like my legs will fall off and then somehow finding the strength to go on. I can't give it up, ever.

I miss Team Illinois more than anyone could imagine. Although I see Joel daily, I miss Dave's daily presence in our lives. I found so much meaning for myself in our team and what we accomplished. Now, I am left trying to figure out how to find that meaning in my daily life. It's been a struggle for me. I've struggled personally, professionally and as an athlete. I don't know what's in store for me - perhaps I will end up in my little fantasy world with kids and my beautiful house, or maybe I'll be where I am - running and coaching athletes and loving it. In the meantime, I'll keep running. After all, the 5th RacingThePlanet challenge will begin in Vietnam on November 25, 2007, which also happens to be my birthday. Guess what I'm asking for.

Chapter 12 - In Joel's Words

There are many things that make us individuals. Where we were raised and live, people we meet, things we do, experiences we have. I have been lucky in that I have been many places and met many people in my lifetime. With all of the racing we have done, there tends to be one question people ask. "Why?" The response to this question is not an easy one, but I think I know how to start to explain the answer.

Many years ago when I was in high school, I identified myself as an athlete first and a scholar second. As I matured and began to travel the world, I found the "athlete" to be a very integral part of who I am, while I have tried to hide the "academic."

The high school years were tough for me especially because I identified myself "first" as an athlete. Even after a nine inch growth spurt and fifty pound weight gain, I was only 5'9" and 150 pounds. It was not exactly the most physically gifted body for a bright athletic future, but I loved being an athlete. Nothing could replace the feel of stepping on a field and knowing you had prepared yourself to compete against others. I believed in my heart that I was a competitive athlete. My coaches unfortunately, did not always feel the same way. I met with some success during those years, but nothing that set me apart from the millions of other kids my age playing high school sports. Rather than letting these experiences limit me, I decided to continue pursuing my athletic dreams once I got into college.

I spent four years as a member of the Miami of Ohio gymnastics team. During college, gymnastics consumed me. I practiced and competed for most of each school year. Being on the team not only meant finding my best friends in college, it allowed me to travel all over the country with them to compete. Although I spent the majority of my time landing on either my head or my butt, I enjoyed participating in the sport. I was never a talented gymnast, but I liked the camaraderie of my teammates and the thrill of competition. During those years, I realized sports was a way for me to build self-reliance, strength and character. All aspects I can appreciate now as an adult. In my last year in college, I was lucky enough to get an internship with Dan Dalrymple, the head strength and conditioning coach for all varsity athletics at Miami. I spent the entire year working with him, learning the aspects of program design, sport specific needs, working with athletes and coaches, and writing my daily journal for my advisor. It was by far the most important academic time I spent in college because it opened my eyes to a profession I had been unaware of up to that point.

Once I graduated, I was in a state of flux. I had spent four years of college as an athlete in a sport that held no future for me. I had no idea what to do with myself. I was questioning my identity. Not long after this, I met Nancy. I'd like to say the rest is history, but our story is still being written, so I know that is not the case. Nancy and I began as friends or better put, running partners. She was looking for someone to run with, I was looking for a new athletic direction to head in. She introduced me to running with the idea of completing a marathon. I didn't even know what that was at the time, but I signed on the dotted line and committed myself to the event. Thousands of miles later, we have now been married since 2000. In that time we have raced on every continent but Australia, raced in deserts, at altitude, in heat, in cold, trained, untrained, prepared, unprepared, you name it and there is a good chance we have raced it, attempted it, or looked into doing it.

These years have taught me many things. There have been times when introspection led me to question my motivation and desire to keep on pushing beyond my limits. I've had to struggle with those demons as well as fighting the urge to simply quit. Surprisingly, I have found out what I am. Despite all of the athletic accomplishments, I am human. I realize people look at the events we have competed in and think we are superhuman, but that is just not the case. We pride ourselves on our ability to push the envelope, to continue pushing forward even though our bodies may not want to, constantly challenging our own limits and breaking through barriers. Doing this makes us feel alive in a way most can not understand. This brings me back to my initial question. "Why?"

There are many different ways to answer this question. I believe some people are born to move, and then there is everyone else who hasn't learned yet how to overcome. Truthfully though, the answer for us is more likely, "because we can". I have found that there is more to life than just "work and go home", I've learned that my world is larger and more accessible than the world of my parents. At the end of the day, the definition of "greatness", my "greatness", is defined solely by me.

I am driven partially by phrases I've heard in my youth: "You are small but mighty." "I had big hopes for you, but you didn't achieve them." We have all heard statements like these in the past. What we do with the feelings these statements generate, can lead to defining moments in our lives.

This begs the obvious question. "What was my moment?" I really had no great epiphany. There wasn't a flash of lightning that made me sit upright and say, "I need to travel and race to define myself". What did happen was love. Nancy and I use racing as an important part of our relationship. Yes it is part of our identity as a couple, and yet it is not the sole thing that defines us. So many people who race give their lives over to the event. By doing this, they miss all the wonderful things that lie on the side of the road. Many of our best friends are people we have met along the way, people whom we keep in touch with because they are kindred spirits. Some events are about the experience as much as they are about the medals or the championship. By racing, Nancy and I are able to set goals, create a realistic path to follow, and momentarily dwell on a successful plan before setting our sights on the next challenge. Along the way, we have met with failure, tasted defeat, tempted fate, smiled, laughed, won, and at times, achieved momentary greatness. All of these things drive us to continue. All of these things we have done together.

So, I am human. I work, eat, train, race, sleep (occasionally), and repeat. The daily cycle of life can become so routine. Maybe there is something else inside of me that drives me to go out and conquer, to vanquish those inner voices that tell me I can't. It could be that the voice that says "I can't" drives me to find a challenge that seems unrealistic to the uninitiated. I think it is a combination of all those things. It is an uplifting feeling to prove a nonbeliever wrong. It's empowering to set your mind to a goal and accomplish it. I think I secretly like squashing the limitations someone places on me into little pieces.

I used to believe that I was not an academic, at least not in the true sense of the word but racing has provided me with moments of solitude in which I have been able to self-explore. I know this may sound counterintuitive. After all, racing should be about working at your maximum potential from the start of the event until you finish, not over thinking the event at hand. The training and racing, however, give me time to "self-medicate." I can step away from the hectic day-to-day things and work on myself. I have thought of business ideas, workout plans, goals, etc. all while pounding out mile after mile. No, this is not academic in the sense that I am not necessarily learning from a textbook or professor, I am, though, learning about myself. It is amazing how little we know about our capabilities, strengths, and weaknesses until we are faced with a situation demanding our immediate attention.

Typically, I am not a patient man. For some reason, I believe I function at a high level when things are swirling around me at break-neck speeds. The training, racing, teamwork aspects of my life have taught me to react and respond to situations, environments, the highs and lows of life. More importantly, racing has taught me to be patient with myself. I know that even when my body is failing, my mind is still working and it is only a matter of time before my brain brings my body back around. Like everyone, my life has ebbs and tides. I try to balance those moments out to the best of my abilities. I tend to be an intrinsic person and feel I do some of my best work by myself. It gives me a chance to problem-solve, think, rethink (sometimes even rethink the think-and-rethink). The solitary moments of activity provide me with a physical outlet to work off energy. They also allow me to work through issues that weigh on my mind.

How deeply do we usually delve into our own psyches? Can we actually trust in the hope that we can accomplish things we never thought possible? It is a challenge to learn to believe in yourself. It took me years to be able to ignore the negative energy of others in order to put myself in a position for maximum success. That does not mean that everything I touch is golden, it does mean that I have to believe in my convictions and work to achieve my goals. Solitary moments out on the pavement, in the pool, in the weight room all allow me to visualize the endpoint of a particular journey. All of these journeys have become a part of my history. I know I want my life story to be interesting, insightful, possibly inspiring to others. I mean come on, I am a five foot nine inch, 150 pound Jewish kid from the suburbs of Chicago. What could I possibly know about being athletic!

I realize how much of this must sound. Youthful disappointments on the athletic field have stuck with me through everything else I have accomplished. People must think I need serious couch time, so I suppose I must clarify. The successes, failures, achievements, and relationships I experienced as a young man did not jade me. On the contrary, they helped make me who I am today.

I can remember two coaches in particular who affected me at 18 as much as they do now at 31. The manner in which they dealt with me as an athlete, student, person and the way in which they pushed me to strive for a form of perfection, and showed me how to look at problems and see multiple ways to solve them are extremely integral parts of who I am. I can hear my high school swim coach Tim Caldwell, hollering at me from the deck every time I am in the pool. The knowledge he imparted on me has stood the test of time. I am able to hear his voice when I run and train, pushing me to stay on cadence and reach for that elusive next level. I can feel Dennis Fink, my soccer coach's hand on my shoulder as he gives me advice and direction on what he wants and needs me to do on the field. I learned to be a team player during those times. I found ways to reach into myself, into that dark area where potential hides, and grab a piece of inner strength when I need it. Looking back at my past and those experienced has allowed me to create my future. Many of the accomplishments and accolades I have received as an adult have come as a result of my development as an athlete in my earlier years.

Another key point I have learned is that my ability as an athlete came from years of hard work. What may appear to others as "natural ability" actually took me as much time mentally as physically to develop. My work ethic began as a kid playing sports with my dad, my skills blossomed during my teenage years, and my body awareness and strength have continued to improve with each year. If I am able to view myself as an athlete and create my own athletic path to follow, there can be no limitations, only bumps in the road. The challenges and the way in which we attack and survive them often make better tales than the event itself.

The RacingThePlanet series has provided me with a most interesting and rewarding experience. As a member of Team

Illinois, I realized we were only as strong as the weakest person on any given day. The three of us all had our fair share of the good and the bad. I watched Nancy repeatedly go through what we called the "puke and rally", a time in which she would get sick and then rally to finish the day. She was able to find strength from somewhere deep inside that she had been unaware of, but leant to our team daily. She is the strongest female competitor I have ever had the privilege to be around. I watched Dave mourn the loss of his sister in stoic silence as he slowly pulled away from us only to realize he had us to lean on at any time. He possesses an iron will that does not know the meaning of the word quit. In his darkest moments, he was able to find a rallying strength to lead him back to conquer the task in front of him. He embodies each event and emboldens those around him to work at a higher level than they may have thought possible. I pride myself on being a far stronger person than I may outwardly appear. I found myself physically losing it during a stage and I fought with despair as my mental faculties began to fade. I remember digging deep, urging myself to keep fighting, to never give up. Sometimes, it is the inner mental strength that leads to physical strength in order to maximize potential.

Through it all, we always had each other. It was amazing to watch other teams self-destruct. They would eliminate themselves because they were unable to do something for each other that came naturally to us, "care" about each other. We knew early on that our team needed to gel. Dave, at the start, was an unknown quantity. We had never raced with him and we were unsure how he would function with us. In our first race, we came together. We took care of each other. Over the course of the Four Deserts, Dave became less of a teammate and more of a brother. The three of us share a bond in experience, in caring, in creating a family that most teams never achieve. Through the highs and the lows, and there were a lot of both, we have always stood by each other with unwavering support. We believe in ourselves, in our team, in our goals. That is what made us complete the races. It is also what made us champions.

As with any team, we had our share of troubles. We had to learn to communicate with each other in regards to training, racing, resting, etc. Truthfulness is often difficult, but we knew there were no shortcuts if the goal was to win. I think we all were able to feel the old statement: "There is no 'I' in Team." Somewhere along the way, we added this: "but there is in win." With the support of the team, each individual found ways to improve their own performance. Believe me, Team Illinois likes to win.

It is often hard to tell others what they need to hear hear. On a small team, it becomes apparent when someone is not pulling their weight and dealing with their responsibilities. We had team meetings, usually over a meal, and aired our dirty laundry. By keeping the dialogue open and direct we were able to avoid conflicts during the races. I think Dave and I only had one disagreement over the course of the Four Deserts (a miracle since I like conflict). We were able to talk through it and move on without damaging our relationship or more importantly, the team. To this day, we all keep the communication open, direct, and frequent. Not too many days go by without checking in with each other.

So what else have I learned? Since completing the Four Deserts races, our lives have gotten increasingly busy. We have all returned to the grind of daily work, leaving less time for us to spend together as a team. Dave has been working and traveling and Nancy and I have been traveling and racing. The roads have not all lead to the same place at this point. I know we miss the time we spent training and racing and are looking forward to our next adventure together, rebuilding Team Illinois into the entity we lived through for two years. Alone we work to make it through the weeks, together we are strong enough to race against the world.

Chapter 13 - In Dave's Words

Every journey taken in life has a beginning and an end. The four desert challenges have been a wonderful journey that took me and two of my closest friends to new highs, and also created new definitions of the word "pain", from both mental and physical perspectives. This journey also redefined my personal definition for the words "commitment" and "believe".

During the last two and a half years of this journey, many people have asked me the same questions, "How did you get started with desert racing?" or "How did you get here?" The question is usually quickly followed up with a statement that goes something like, "That's crazy…I don't even drive 150 miles let alone run it." The question is difficult to answer because I don't really know what it was that started me down the road to be right here, right now. I could blame my crazy, funny, loveable teammate Nancy, but she is just going to blame the desert racing idea on a burrito and a magazine article anyway. Joel always blames Nancy for anything crazy that we end up being involved with, so I can't really blame him. Instead, I have come to the conclusion that it has more to do with who we are and what we believe. I think that because we in fact "believed" in ourselves and each other, our lives and our decisions were influenced by that shared belief. In short, what we believe, became the fuel for our own reality.

I have often wondered where I would be today if for some reason I would have said "no" to Nancy when she first asked me to do this "fun desert race". I think of the countless experiences and people I have met from all over the world who have also participated in these races. I think of my new friends from Hong Kong, Korea, London, Singapore, Ireland, Japan and China, and many more from here in the United States. These experiences and friendships have lined the path that led me to where I am today. It has been a long road with many hours of training, planning, racing and even more training. It would have been easy to quit many times during this two year journey but for a number of reasons I didn't, and our team didn't either.

I have my two teammates to thank for helping to get me here. Joel and Nancy have been a brother and sister to me throughout this entire adventure. They are my family, my friends, my teammates, my biggest critics and the people who have seen me at my highest high and my absolute low. They are a key reason to how I ended up here, and for that I blame them and thank them in the same breath.

What I've Learned

Besides all the experiences, people, places or the memories that will last forever, I think the biggest lesson I've learned from this two and a half year journey can be summed up by the following statement. "Believe in yourself. Believe in those who surround you in life. Believe in a purpose for your life, and believe that your life is what you make it." This little mantra continues to prove to be worthwhile and influences my life everyday.

The message I would hope that each person understands after reading this book is simple. "Believe". Believe that you can be a better person physically, mentally, emotionally, spiritually and holistically. Believe that what you do each day matters to more people around you than you realize. Believe that most things in life are possible. Simply wanting something is not enough. Truly believing that you can obtain your goal is the key to success. Believe with conviction and passion.

During the last seven years of competitive running and through other business ventures, I have met many people at the very beginning of an event where they had already determined they might not win or complete the challenge. They had already convinced themselves that failure is highly probable. This has always left me wondering what the purpose was for them attempting the challenge if they had already convinced themselves that they had no chance of beating the odds, winning the race or even finishing what was started. What is the purpose of training or educating yourself if you believe that you do not stand a chance against your competition in the competition or in the business world? Just as believing that you cannot do something is a very self-fulfilling prophecy, believing that "you can" is even more powerful.

My first five professional years were spent working in a large global consulting organization where I found a repeated piece of advice from my managers that showed up on each annual performance review. The area of improvement always seemed to suggest a common "flaw" in my work approach. It would typically say something to the effect of "Dave is an ambitious and hard working individual, but is far too optimistic in his goal setting and expectations for performance. He would be better positioned for future responsibilities and stable growth if he would make more realistic goals which would be easier to accomplish and then exceed those goals should the opportunities become available to do so."

What? Are you serious? This philosophy promotes the idea that aiming for something you know you can achieve is preferable to setting higher goals and believing you can accomplish them. Aspiring to mediocrity just leads to mediocrity. Granted that seven years ago I would have struggled to believe I could finish a marathon, let alone a 150 mile foot race. But every step of the way over the last seven years, I believed I could do more and find new competitive levels within myself. It became an evolution where I would constantly set higher goals and affirmed within myself that I was capable of accomplishing them.

My favorite quote is by Marianne Williamson and is written on a picture that hangs in my home office. It is a picture of the "yellow train", Nancy, Joel and me running in tight formation across the rocky floor of the Gobi Desert. Marianne's quote is all about aspiring to goals that make us reach beyond safe ground, regardless of the fact that others may try to hold us back.

To this day I still set ambitious, optimistic and sometimes lofty goals for myself in my racing, personal growth and my business, despite the potential disagreement from my consulting managers. I believe each of these goals are possible and that I can accomplish many, if not all of them. I may fail in reaching a goal, just as we did in the "Atacama Crossing", but the lessons learned from believing you can do it are far more valuable than aiming low and hitting that mark every time. Believing in yourself is one of the best things that you can do for yourself. Believing in someone else is one of the highest compliments you can give to that person.

My sister Tamara believed she could beat the cancer that had taken over her body. She didn't believe she could do it alone, but instead believed that with holistic medicine, her faith in God, healthy living and regular exercise that she could win the battle with her cancer. For five years she won that battle everyday. Even though her choices might not have been my choices, I had learned to respect her decisions and observe how vehemently she believed in her own path. Even in her final days, a part of me believed she could beat this cancer, simply because she believed so strongly she could.

So what lies beyond this desert racing journey? I honestly hope that there are many more adventures to come, even some that my mind has yet to dream of or those that Nancy can con me into. (Right Nancy?). In all honesty, I cannot thank Nancy and Joel enough for thinking of me and asking me that day. If I had said "no" to them that day, who knows where that path would have led me, or where I would be today without those experiences.

As I think of what lies ahead I remember a race from September of 2004. Joel, Nancy and I had signed up to compete in Ironman Wisconsin just seven weeks after the first Atacama Crossing race. I was excited about the competition because this race would be the first full distance triathlon that my immediate and extended family would be able watch and experience. Prior to the start of the race my Mother asked me when she should expect me to finish that day. My response to her was "Mom, I am shooting for a 12:45 finish so look for me around that time on the finishing clock."

After a long, hot, grueling day I started to calculate my remaining distance on the run and decided I was possibly going to be short and not finish under 12:45 as I had told my Mother. I knew she and the rest of my family would be waiting on the right hand side of the welcoming gallery just before the finishing line. Despite how horrible my legs and stomach felt, I pushed on harder to finish in my "promised time". As I neared the Capital building and finish line I could see I was going to have to sprint the last quarter mile if I was going to finish near my target time. I streaked down the finish corral towards the finish line and picked my family out of the crowd screaming encouragements to me. The clock above said 12:44:37 and there was still ground to cover before the finish line. As I finally crossed I looked up to see the clock reading 12:44:58. I had finished 2 seconds ahead of my goal and my family was there to meet me.

Shortly after my finish, the effects of the final hard sprint started to affect my stomach, and I felt sick. In "Nancy Burrows" fashion I found the nearest tree to bend over and threw up whatever remained in my stomach. My father was there to make sure I was still alright, trying to do as much as a parent could given the circumstances. He had always worried that I was going to hurt myself in one of these races. I kept reassuring him that this is par for the course and that puking sometimes comes with pushing the limits. He leaned over and said "Dave I don't know about this pushing yourself like this, what are you going to do when you are 60?" Laughing and trying to hold back my last gag reflex I said "Dad…hopefully I am winning my age category in the race."

For the last seven years my Father had heard stories about my distant races from the four corners of the earth, but only seeing the more local races I've participated in. During those years I had asked him if he would be interested in doing a marathon with me. My father has been in a wheelchair since a job related accident in 1981. Still, I offered repeatedly to come along with me and let me push him in a sports chair while competing in a marathon. Every year he politely declined and said he "didn't believe he could do it". Jokingly I always replied, "But I'm going to be doing all the work". Still, his answer would be "no".

In my sister's final days she told me how she had a dream that the three of us, my Dad, my sister and I, were running a marathon together. She asked if I would help train her once she had beaten the cancer, so we could all run a marathon together. This fall her dream will come true. My father finally agreed to do a fall marathon with me. This October 7th, 2007 my father and I will carry some of my sister's ashes with us at the Lakefront Marathon in Milwaukee Wisconsin. The three of us will run the race that she dreamed of. It is great to see my Father's excitement and know that he now believes we can do this together. It is just the next step, the next adventure and the next challenge for both of us.

What started on that chilly morning in May 2004 where 3 teammates crossed their first finish line hand-in-hand in that first pre-Atacama training marathon, has now come to a close. Just like our first race we crossed the final finish line in Antarctica hand in hand as well. The "Power of Team", the life experiences shared with my friends and partners has transformed my life and the journey has been a precious and rewarding experience. I look forward to the next adventure with my teammates.

Remember, your life is what you make it.

Chapter 14 - The Power of "You"

Both Nancy and Joel had said it. There was something more to be learned from the series of desert challenges than just how to put together a good team.

Back in Dave's Brownstone in early February, the three of them had an extended conversation about how they each had fundamentally changed. They spoke about how much more they appreciated the little things in life and how precious "time" was. There was also an air of assuredness in everything they said. It wasn't necessarily the tone in their voices, or any arrogance in the way they spoke of their victories, but a new form of confidence was surrounding them all.

Dave talked about the mind being the hardest muscle to train because it "wants to give up so easily". Nancy followed that perspective with a reminder about her uneasy stomach that would never settle down, on any stage in any race. The body seemed to work so hard to convince the mind that it needed to stop, it needed to sit, it needed to lay down out in the open sun. Looking back on what they had learned, Nancy added, "The body lies".

What Team Illinois proved to themselves and to the world, was that the human mind and body can most always be driven beyond the boundaries it sets for itself. Nancy proved that her body could finish the race at Atacama after needing an intravenous drip to keep her system functioning. Joel could pick himself up and lead the team in the Sahara Desert when his other two teammates wanted out of the race. Dave could find the mental strength to finish the last challenge in Antarctica, when the death of his sister had taken away his desire to train or compete.

No, Not Me

Many people react to stories of "personal challenges overcome" by assuming that there was something inherently special about the person or team being outlined in the story. The easiest way to talk yourself out of attempting something difficult or challenging is to convince yourself with, "I can't do it" or "that other person was stronger, I could never accomplish the same thing".

Forget physical endurance for a moment, the "No, not me" excuse is also used for most scenarios when people start looking towards a difficult challenge. Traveling to a strange country, learning a new difficult process at work, attempting a new art project or almost anything that might be a "stretch" of mental or physical ability and many people will simply back away. "No, not me. I can't do that. I'm too old to learn. I can't travel there, I don't speak the language. I can't perform that new process, it's too hard."

Dave Kuhnau weighed 270 pounds in 1997. Minor aches and pains became more common from the weight of his body on his back and knees and feet, and his energy level seemed to drop more each year. At some point Dave had decided that he had enough of being heavy, decided that some sort of change in his life was needed and running would be a way to help drive that change. He started walking and running short distances and had gradually increased the distance into miles.

Alasdair Morrison, a RacingThePlanet veteran, is 57 years old and lives and works in Hong Kong. Alasdair is still climbing mountains and running desert races and competing with people half his age. Alasdair learned very early on that obstacles and challenges are just little things to be overcome. Mount Fuji and Mount Kilimanjaro were two little obstacles that Alasdair also stepped over.

Satoru Otsuka from Japan is 65 years old. A retired manufacturing worker, Satoru is still an active marathoner and Alpine skier and managed to cross all four desert challenges as well. Satoru managed to beat other competitors one-third his age out in the desert sands of the 4 Deserts series.

Brent Weigner is a 56 year old seventh grade teacher from the U.S. Brent, a three-time cancer survivor, is still showing himself and his students that the human mind and body can overcome anything. Brent was one of the elite competitors who had finished all other desert challenges and qualified for the Last Desert in Antarctica.

In a way there is something special about the people highlighted in this story and it isn't because they were able to accomplish the milestone, cross the desert or climb the mountain. What made them special, was their personal commitment to try. They took the initiative to say "yes, I am going to start running", or "yes, I am going to take on that next challenge". From that perspective you have the same opportunity to achieve things you never thought possible, by simply making the same commitment.

The good people in our story also learned that when their selected challenge started to become difficult, all they really needed was a little extra focus and drive to get them to their goal. These people were special because they had figured out what was needed to push the mind and the body beyond the point of giving up.

For anyone to be a positive contributor to a team, they must first become a believer in their own ability to succeed in the face of adversity. Again, this does not mean that they necessarily need to have special skills or be at the peak of physical condition. A successful team contributor is simply someone who can get past "No, not me", and change their perspective to "Yes, I believe down to my soul that I can."

Stepping Stones

Once someone agrees to get past the expectation of "No, not me", aside from the limitations of a mental or physical condition, everyone has the ability to accomplish things that they believe to be difficult or impossible. The path to success then, depends on the individual's ability to see themselves accomplishing the goal. Often when the goal represents a substantial change to someone's current ability, the only way to get there is to work their way up to that final challenge. When Dave began running at 270 pounds, his first thoughts were not about running a marathon or winning a desert endurance race. Finishing a single mile was a tough enough milestone for Dave.

Joel, Nancy and Dave all needed to learn "how" to succeed before selecting difficult challenges like marathons or triathlons. For each of them it was a matter of setting small goals and making sure they reached them without ever giving up on that original target. The path to their success in the desert was dependent on taking small steps, each a little more difficult to achieve than the last. Eventually they worked themselves up to the ability and the confidence needed to complete the 150 mile distance in the desert.

Dave's first goal in 1997 was running a single mile, then two, then five. Each distance was picked by Dave because it sounded like the goal was out of reach. Dave had learned that he could get to that next goal by sticking to the work and then focusing on the target without giving up. Dave increased the goals a little at a time like stepping stones to the next significant challenge. Nancy never started out her physical training and athletic lifestyle by thinking, "I'm going to compete and finish a triathlon." She had to learn how to accomplish smaller goals before reaching for the lofty one.

Individuality

Individual success or failure should never be the focus of a team effort. The team either succeeds together or fails together as one cohesive unit. They stick together as a group no matter the hardship, working together until the daily goal is met or the final objective is reached. Still, within every team structure there are specialty skills brought by each individual team member that help to enrich the fabric of the group.

Before Nancy or Joel or Dave could have ever been a contributor within a team structure, they needed to figure out for themselves that they could overcome difficult obstacles and could succeed on their own. What made each of them unique also made them a great contributor to the group. Dave's overall body strength and his internal motivational demons helped him to lead Team Illinois at Gobi. Joel's martial arts training and other forms of cross training had prepared him to be the strong leader in Sahara, and Nancy's intestinal fortitude (sorry for the pun Nancy) during her near collapse in Atacama helped all three towards a strong finish in the Chilean desert.

Each member of Team Illinois had already learned to be an individual competitor before coming together as a team. They had learned how to train and in the event of a loss, how to pick themselves up after that setback. What makes them unique and makes other kinds of specialty teams unique too, is their ability to celebrate the individual strengths of their team members and also to extract a binding contract or commitment from each of them for the benefit of the team.

What About Me?

So here's the 64 thousand dollar question. What makes any of the people mentioned in the pages of this book different from you? In every example provided, the people who have learned to overcome their first stepping-stone challenge or the ones who have accomplished their first major milestone did so because they simply wanted to. These remarkable people became successful at achieving their goals first as individuals then together as a team because they stuck to their plan until the goal was achieved. After learning that a little extra effort allowed them to reach that goal, it became easier the next time around to achieve the next goal. They all wanted to be successful first, and then they learned about the effort it took to get there.

The successful individuals outlined in this book are just people after all, people just like you. Some were out of shape and overweight, but still could turn themselves into highly motivated and highly competitive human machines. Some were older and retired, but still found the desire to reach for the next near-impossible goal.

We all have the capability to do great things as individuals. We all have the ability to work hard to reach for what we previously thought was unattainable. It just takes the ***want*** to get started. Success begins when you identify your first small goal and take the steps necessary to get there without ever giving up on that original target. Learn how to be successful in making that small step, then plan for next larger goal. In time, you may be running your first marathon. You may be organizing for first charity function. You may be heading up your first business project team. You may be building your first house. Whatever the goal, the members of Team Illinois had figured out that all they needed to do is want it bad enough. The same applies to you.

Parallels to Other Types of Groups

For business groups or charity committees or sports teams, success or failure of the team is measured by whether or not project dates are met, key milestones are achieved or fundraising targets were realized. In most cases the corporate definition of team is a temporary one, where the key team contributors are dispersed after meeting the goal or surpassing the milestone. The interesting paradox here is that the most productive and close knit teams are typically the ones punished for doing what they were asked to do. "Thanks for all your hard work and supreme effort, but we're going to break up the group and move you all to other departments." The project team disbands, the committee members move on to other committees, the sports team trades its players at the end of the season. Project teams or committees as an example are by definition a temporary entity much like Team Illinois' two-year RacingThePlanet project.

For Team Illinois, the personalities and skill sets to be mixed together in their team formula could have been volatile. Put three strong over achievers with strong personalities in the same room and they could have just as easily torn each other to shreds. For that matter, put a husband and wife together under an extreme set of circumstances and someone is likely to get trampled. Usually it's the husband, but that's another book altogether.

Each member of Team Illinois had a firm understanding about what their role would be in relation to the others. Differences in personality and individual strengths were celebrated, never coddled or belittled. There was cooperation between all members and a willingness to support another teammate when one of their weaknesses was encountered. There was constant humor, dedication and compassion available within the group. Most importantly, Team Illinois never quit on the common goal.

This blend of complimentary skills and personality traits with the mutual willingness to make a strong commitment to the team, were the building blocks of Team Illinois' success. The same characteristics that made their team successful, are the same basic characteristics that should apply to all teams.

Lessons from Atacama

It's straightforward enough to look at the preparation, the execution and the results from Team Illinois in their first desert race at Atacama and draw parallels to any multiple-member team or special group. Whether it is a business project team, a committee assigned to manage a charitable event, or a sports team built for the beginning of a new season, they all share the same preparation for the event.

There is one stated goal.

There is a sponsor for each project, organized sporting season or special event.

Budgets are set, and expenses are managed.

Team members are selected with special skills or for specific roles. Experience is key to success.

The timeline is defined for each event, project or season and it reaches a conclusion.

Preparation is required for each group before and during the event, project or schedule.

Adjustments are made. Members may change, goals are refined, equipment may change.

Unknowns require contingency planning.

There is consensus on what "success" actually means.

Team Illinois started the "project" of the Atacama Desert with the correct approach. Simply put, they expected to win the race. Despite not having ever attempted that sort of challenge, there was some evidence to suggest that they could actually achieve that goal. Nancy was the first one to make the comparison between finish times posted in the Runner's World article and her own past performance in marathons. Once the team was built and Dave was added to the husband and wife duo, all three had agreed that it was a lofty goal but totally achievable with the right preparation and training.

Each member of Team Illinois could run 26.2 miles in just over 3 hours. For an amateur runner these are more than just respectable finish times. Combined as a team at just over 3 hours, Nancy, Joel and Dave would be an international force to be reckoned with. This was the basis for their confidence in stating the original goal.

Nancy became the official sponsor and cheerleader. After becoming excited about the possibility of a new challenge, she managed to easily convince her husband then quickly recruit Dave to round out the team. Hers was a slightly different role when compared to other types of organizations. Nancy's sponsorship was not financial, but it was key to the formation of the group and the definition of the team's goal.

Parallel to planning for a fund raising event, Team Illinois had a budget and a training regimen that they estimated for the achievement of the goal. Travel expenses were estimated, specialized equipment was identified and suppliers were compared for best price, while the training activities were mapped out on a calendar leading to their departure date for Chile. Team Illinois did their best to estimate monetary expenses and work load associated with training for the Atacama event, but they did not have any direct experience budgeting or training for that type of desert challenge.

While training for their trip to Chile, some adjustments had to be made to the equipment they had already purchased. New packs from GoLite distributed weight better and proved to be less of a strain on shoulders and spine than their previous backpack equipment. The training regimen also changed, and Team Illinois was spending more time off road on longer runs to hopefully prepare them for the rugged terrain of Atacama. Adjustments for Team Illinois or any group for that matter, are typically unplanned overhead. Team Illinois learned early in preparation for Atacama, that they would be faced with unexpected variables that forced changes to equipment and training.

Taking a business perspective in preparing for a significant physical challenge like Atacama, there are events that can only be described as "known unknowns". A backpack you planned on using proves to be sub-standard once tested under competitive conditions, or a shoe placed near a fire might be affected by that fire. For these examples, you can still plan on incorporating a contingency budget or resource plan to accommodate these potential, logical unknowns. Atacama would teach Team Illinois to plan for those little contingencies in the next desert challenge.

Lessons from Gobi

To begin a discussion about what Team Illinois learned from the Gobi challenge, let's use an example from the sports world. Take your favorite home town team where there was a known disharmony in the clubhouse. It could be for any reason. Someone doesn't believe in the goal, or half the players didn't trust one of their teammates or a star player is resented for the money he might make. It could be any real issue or perceived issue that forces a division within the team structure. How did your team do that season? Take a slightly less talented group of people where the chemistry between them is binding, where they are mutually invested in each other's success, where they all believe in each other and the common goal, and we have a winner.

At Gobi, Team Illinois was much better prepared for the physical rigors of desert endurance racing than they were at Atacama. They had learned from Atacama which training regimens worked well, and which training activities needed to be changed. Where Team Illinois had been originally built on speed, it would require stamina and strength rather than speed to conquer a desert race at RacingThePlanet. Training for the Gobi Desert included more stair climbing and running hilly terrain with weighted backpacks. Nancy, Joel and Dave would still be a fast team, but they were better prepared for the dune climbs and mountain ridges of Gobi and the Turpan Basin.

Team Illinois would learn the benefit of physical preparation and improvement of research into their own body chemistry under stress. Improving the equipment slightly over what they all carried at Atacama made a small weight reduction in their backpacks and the overall comfort of their running gear was improved. An ounce saved was an ounce that didn't need to be carried 150 miles across the sand. Electrolyte supplements were also changed as each member of Team Illinois adjusted personal blends based on their own unique body chemistry. It would be a significant change that would benefit them all throughout the Gobi March.

Finally, it was motivation that drove Dave and Team Illinois through the tough spots in China although it would be a blend of positive and negative motivational factors at play. At times, the team was driven by their desire to win the race for which they had painstakingly prepared. At other times when their pace was slipping, Dave returned to the specific memory of a friend belittling the team's effort from Chile, and it alone would be enough to fuel the engine on Dave's ship. In other instances, motivation came from a fellow competitor who had passed them between checkpoints or had challenged them along the way. Without the constant presence of motivation, Team Illinois may not have won the desert race at Gobi.

Lessons from Sahara

First, the concept of team should never include the abandoning of a teammate under any circumstances. What some teams decided to do not only took them out of the team competition, but also put the separated teammates at potential medical risk. As discussed in the Sahara chapter above, if those teams had stayed together under the guidelines of the competition, they would have finished with a better chance at team trophies. The European team along with Team Illinois had set an original pace so punishing that combined; they had knocked out the three other teams from the competition by the second day. All the other teams needed to do, much like the American team from Illinois, was simply finish the race as a cohesive working unit.

Based on the success of Team Illinois through three desert races, all other teams would have to ask the following questions before even thinking about assembling a competitive desert endurance racing team:

Would each member be viewed as an integral part of the group?

Is there a common and agreed upon goal?

Were everyone's strengths and weaknesses accommodated or even taken advantage of?

Was the commitment to each teammate as important as their commitment to the team goal?

Is everyone committed to the leadership within the team, whether singular or shared?

The second difficult lesson learned during Sahara, was related to the negative impact of having the team's goal and the competitive game plan wiped out on day three of a seven day race. Team Illinois struggled both physically and mentally in trying to keep up any sort of pace once they knew all other teams were out of the competition. Of course those accolades would be premature if Team Illinois never finished the remaining stages. Once the competitive goal was removed, so was Team Illinois' motivation to keep running strong.

Team Illinois would learn to change their strategy mid-stream, picking intermediate checkpoint completion times and smaller targets to get them to the next checkpoint or to the end of the stage. They would start to include little rewards like more rest time at a particular checkpoint if they could complete a certain distance by a specified elapsed time. It was a challenge to find the motivation to push the pace when there was nothing to be gained from a shorter overall finish time.

Lessons from Antarctica

Many of the same challenges that faced Team Illinois after the third stage at Sahara would be in place for all of Antarctica. Entering as the only team to qualify for the race, their motivation would have to found somewhere other than competing side by side with another team. Motivation would come in the form of target times and stage finishes rather that heads-up competition.

Preparation for the race was completely different as well. Previous experience from the three other hot-weather climates would not help them when it came to assembling equipment and clothing for the below freezing temperatures and high winds of the Antarctic continent. Similar to the preparation for Atacama, Team Illinois would have to go back to research and advice from those who might have experience racing in that sort of climate. Full jackets and running pants would not make the 150 mile crossing any easier, and guessing at combinations of equipment would have Team Illinois over-spending in preparation for an environment in which they had no experience. The same is true for any team entering completely unknown territory, the preparation is often best-guess and the budget goes higher as contingencies are planned for unknowns. Team Illinois wouldn't know how best to pack and dress for the conditions until they had arrived on the continent. Adjustments would have to be made upon arrival, but Team Illinois had prepared for those contingencies. That last sentence translates into: "Nancy made sure they all packed enough extra types of clothing".

Personal tragedy can affect the human body in multiple ways as well. The burden that Dave carried prevented him from training properly for the demands of Antarctica and he was not physically prepared for the race. Mentally, Dave would have a difficult time motivating himself. He had made a promise to his teammates however, and a teammate honors their commitment. Nancy and Joel were there to help pick him up throughout the race, challenging him to keep moving. In the end, Dave had learned that he could still focus on the team's goal and get through the challenge.

The final lesson from Antarctica was that "glory is fleeting". Team Illinois would celebrate their completion of The Last Desert and remember the three other races that helped to get them there. The jubilation associated with completing the series of the 4 Deserts was leaving them almost as quickly as the money that had left their accounts to pay for the race. It was an expensive but life-altering journey that had come to an end. Team Illinois would also find that the journey was more rewarding than completion of the actual challenge. It had been two years of preparation and training, two years of anticipation and rewards, and two years to bring three people as close together as humanly possible. With the final goodbyes being said round the dinner table, many things that had previously influenced their lives would now change. Each of the 15 competitors who had made the trek to Antarctica had all completed the four-desert journey. Many were already beyond the excitement of the 4 Deserts challenge and asking the question, "What next?"

Picking Team Members

Successful teams don't just come together accidentally; they need to be built with purpose. Nancy and Joel would require a third team member to run The Atacama Crossing with them. Selection of this teammate would turn out to be a more important decision than either of them could imagine. Although both Nancy and Joel were looking for someone who was in good enough physical shape to handle the rigors of the race, they also looked for a personality that could blend in well with their own. The new addition would need to share the same energy and commitment to the event, and understand that leadership would be shared. Welcome, Mr. Kuhnau.

The same is true for any type of group, permanent or temporary. Member selection is critical to the success of any team, but not everyone on the team needs to carry the same attributes. Some of the best teams including Team Illinois carry their own skill diversity. On any given day of any desert race, a different team member would take the leadership position while the other two followed and supported the lead.

The one thing Team Illinois did right at the start, without ever really knowing about the importance of the decision, was to build a specialty team where each member had complimentary personalities and value systems. Each remained a unique individual to be sure, but Nancy, Joel and Dave carried similar core personality attributes. Each carried a positive mental attitude where each goal was viewed as achievable. Each maintained a sense of humor when the stress of the day became overwhelming. Each truly cared about the mental and physical well being of the other and took a personal stake in the other's success. Perhaps most importantly, knowing at the start that their other teammates had made the same personal commitment to the goal, each member would not let the other fail. When one had a bad day or a tough race, the other two were there to pull them along no matter the circumstance. Finding those traits in a potential team member might be viewed as a difficult task, but the dividends are endless. Don't just look at skill sets when building a team, look at the person and the personality if at all possible.

For other types of teams and groups, the importance of chemistry, shared focus, and energy also depends on the stress level expected for the project. The higher the expected stress level, the more important it is to build a team that is resistant to stress. This is where collaboration, focus on a common goal, diversity of strengths, and energy become critical to success. For teams or committees with more reasonable goals, flexible schedules and lower stress, the importance of these team characteristics is reduced to some degree only because there is flexibility in the schedule and room for issue correction.

Removing Team Members

When under high stress with a short timeline goal, the chemistry of the team members working towards that goal becomes critical. In remote cases where one team member becomes disillusioned with the project and its goals, becomes destructive or cannot function at any level with the rest of the team, it may be time to remove them from the group. It's also best to recognize that a particular team member may not be a good fit as early in the project as possible. This minimizes the emotional impact to both the individual and the team when one that person is removed from the group.

Under conditions where a team member is merely struggling with the workload but remains committed to the goal, it is the team's responsibility to pick them up and work together as one cohesive unit. Assuming that effort was made to select the correct people for the team and there was a common goal when the team originally formed, more damage might be done to the whole team if that struggling teammate is removed. The message to the rest of the group would be "Pull your weight or you're kicked off the team." There are better ways to increase the productivity of the group without resorting to that sort of negative reinforcement.

For Team Illinois, it would have been difficult to remove any one of the three members once the first race at Atacama had begun. It would have been best to recognize that there was a conflict of personality or goals early in the pre-race training schedule. Changes to the team could have been made in time for the trip to Chile. Once the race began, Team Illinois was committed to the common goal regardless of any conflict that might have risen during the event.

Team Illinois was successful in Chile for many reasons, but the most important reason ties back to the chemistry and commitment between Dave, Nancy and Joel. Regardless of adversity or shortness of temper while on the course, they had made a commitment to work through the challenges and remain a cohesive unit. The same commitment should exist for all team members on any project, or any initiative.

Physical Collocation

If Dave had lived in New York, Nancy in Chicago and Joel in San Francisco, it is unlikely that they would have been as effective as a team during their first race in Chile. The six months of hard training they all shared was a bonding experience for them. They shared a common vision and a common goal at Atacama, but they would not have been able to adjust to personality traits and quirks, or learn how to compliment each other's skills had they trained or competed separately.

So too does a project team, a sports team, or a community group need to work together in close physical proximity to get to a productive state. Every team needs to bond, and take a personal interest in the other team member's success. A team of individuals is no team at all.

Better interpersonal communication is easier to achieve with physically collocated teams but more importantly, team members will take a personal stake in each other. Pictures of family members on desks, awards and recognition certificates, after work bonding activities all provide a direct path for learning about your new teammates. The only way to "care about" or become mutually invested in someone new, is to learn more about them, discover parallels in activities and interests, to invest in them. There is a better chance of understanding everyone's personality and skill set differences, strengths and weaknesses, and a better chance to bond as a group when they all are in close physical proximity.

Today's technology allows for physically dispersed teams, web based meetings, and shared enterprise architecture resources across the globe. For large companies with dispersed divisions or departments, these technologies allow for a cost effective way to share information and conduct informal near face to face meetings. Productive hands-on work under the same conditions? Not even with the very best of technology.

For smaller specialty teams who are tasked with a very specific or highly complex chunk of work, or who are mutually dependent on each other to get that work done, they must exist together in the same physical space. Adapting the RacingThePlanet team rule; Teams must not be visually separated from each other while executing the task, or working towards the goal. Anything other than physical collocation under these circumstances means greatly reduced productivity. Take any example where you need an answer to a question immediately to keep a process moving forward. If you have to call another city to get your answer, in another time zone, worse yet where the time zone is plus or minus 10 hours, and you've lost an entire work day. Go ahead and calculate the number of internal and consulting resources you paid while waiting for an answer, and then double the total to include opportunity cost. Yikes. It might be cheaper to build a new office space and pay relocation expense to bring them all together.

Celebrating Diversity

People on a team are like fishing lures in a tackle box. Each one serves a different purpose under different conditions, but all have proven to be successful at one point or another. Some people need to process information visually, others prefer to process it verbally. Some will be non-stop performers while others will need a hand now and again. Some may be self-starters and leaders, while others require some guidance and verbal support. The key, or more accurately stated the art of putting together a successful team depends heavily on the blend of skill sets and personality types selected.

For a smaller team like Nancy, Joel and Dave, it becomes more important for the personalities and skill sets to blend well. It's almost a mathematical conclusion. If one of the three team members was a bad fit with the other two, refuses to collaborate or won't make the effort, 33% of that team is ineffective. On a team of 10 people with varying skills and personalities, one poor performer only impacts the team effectiveness by 10%. There is a better chance of team success in the second example, because the rest of the team can pick up the 10% slack.

Team building really isn't about mathematics at all, but more about feel. Regardless of the backgrounds or ages of those being considered for the team, the most important factor to consider is each member's willingness to collaborate with the strengths and weaknesses of others on the team. They must all be committed to the goal, and hopefully all of them have experience with project or goal success somewhere in their recent past. A friendly, collaborative team full of "No, not me" or "I can't do it" people, is also doomed to failure.

Temporary Teams but Permanent Collaborators

Teams by definition most times, are temporary entities. The two-year collaboration for Team Illinois and the RacingThePlanet series of the 4 Deserts is a great example of that. It is clear once you meet Nancy, Joel and Dave however, that their collective experience is the very glue that will bind them together forever. They shared in the adversity, the heavy lifting and the accolades equally. They overcame mental and physical limitations to keep moving forward towards their goal.

For any team structure that creates this productive and personal bond between teammates, they will find success and maintain those productive relationships once the project or event is complete. It would be wonderful if the productivity and positive energy from those team members could be kept flowing indefinitely, but that is not the nature of some team structures. The benefit of belonging to a successful team is that the learned concepts of shared trust and collaboration and the creation of positive energy will live on well beyond the bounds of the project. Those people are the ones you'll want to target for the next project, season or event. Good friends and good coworkers stay connected. Good team members like Joel, Nancy and Dave are hard to find and good to hold on to.

The Power of Team and You

Any of the three from Team Illinois could easily have been considered an individual competitor first. Each had excelled in their professional career as well as in the amateur sports world. They each had learned that nearly anything can be accomplished, and they based that perspective on personal experience. They had learned early in life that big goals can be attained through smaller steps towards that larger goal. Success was somehow "assured" if they just worked hard enough to get there. That success oriented attitude as individuals also made them a valuable teammate to any group.

Understanding the path that Team Illinois took to become international champions, and that they all started out as nice, regular, unique but average human beings, you now have the opportunity to begin your own quest in exactly the same way. Once meeting Nancy, Joel and Dave, you would not consider them to be extremely tall or extremely short. They deal with money issues every month and pay bills or make decisions on which things they can or can't afford. They wash their own clothes, take care of their own cars, spend as much time with family as they can, and struggle to maintain relationships when work makes larger demands for their time. They have good days and bad days, wake up with headaches and sore backs, grumble when they pay taxes, and enjoy the simple things in life.

All three grew up with fears and doubts while wondering if they would ever be successful at what they chose to do. As children and young adults, all three of them met influential people who inspired them and also people who did their best to drag them down. Individual stories of growing up as an insecure teenager, is much the same as for any of us. We all tried to figure out back then what things we might be good at, and we looked for some positive energy to help guide us. Somewhere along the way however, they each found a love for athletic challenges, received that positive feedback and inspiration. Their skills grew from there.

Should you have the opportunity to meet them now, Nancy Joel and Dave would appear to be confident and self assured, with a pragmatic view into life and how life's challenges should be dealt with. They all have grown personally and professionally, and have learned how to be successful in just about everything they attempt. They only started out as average people. You might not consider them to be average now. Dave's cooking skills? Now that begs for the use of the term average. Apologies, Dave.

Their story and the reason they wanted to share it, had more to do with inspiring other people to take on their own personal challenges a small step at a time (whatever that might be), and less to do with convincing people to immediately start running marathons and desert races. The lessons learned by Nancy, Joel and Dave were that they each had to start with very small goals first and work their way to loftier challenges over the years. Finding something you are passionate about is the first big step. After that, success is determined by the level of effort you make to reach your goals. You can do it. Nancy, Joel and Dave know you can. You know you can.

One step at a time.

Epilogue

As Nancy, Joel and Dave headed back to their work lives after the RacingThePlanet 4 Deserts series, knowledge of being able to overcome just about any obstacle went with them. They accomplished so much as a team, but they also became stronger individuals as a result of the team experience. Now as they returned to their normal lives back in Chicago, each carried with them the personal knowledge that they could truly accomplish anything they set their minds to.

Nancy returned to the East Bank Club and found more joy in coaching other people and encouraging them to reach their own personal goals than she did with the administrative responsibilities of running exercise programs and scheduling employees. Her career shift allowed her more time to work with others, and more time for the personal joy of running.

Joel continued personal training and coaching activities as well, and accompanied Nancy on her recent Birthday quest of five separate endurance events spread across the country. Joel is also working with Dave on at least one start-up business venture, while they both are in the process of coordinating an advanced training program for those interested in participating in a RacingThePlanet event.

Dave returned home and diverted much of is energy into building two small businesses. He had reduced his own running activities down to 25 miles per week but is ramping up for his fourth triathlon in Idaho, June 2007. Dave is also planning a unique marathon challenge which would include his father who is now wheel chair bound. Promising to run a marathon with his father, Dave and his dad will carry the memory of Tamara with them, while Dave pushes a modified racing wheelchair the 26.2 mile distance this October. Special thanks to Kristine Hinrichs and the Lakefront Marathon race staff for making this possible.

Mary Gadams and RacingThePlanet have since expanded the desert racing series to include what some of the previous 4 Deserts competitors have called "The Roaming Race". The inaugural race location was announced to be Vietnam in 2007, while other future race locations may include Iceland, Bolivia, Kazakhstan, Socotra, Peru and Siberia. It will be a departure from desert climate racing, but one that will include other challenging terrains. Nancy, Joel and Dave will be racing once again as Team Illinois for the inaugural roaming race in Vietnam.

Since returning to port and dropping off her load of 15 competitors and RacingThePlanet crew, the good ship Dap Mares sank seven months later in the Straights of Magellan on September 22, 2006. The picture of its maybe-not-so-final resting place can be found on a few Antarctic message boards. Dap Mares rests not quite fully submerged, and listing 40 degrees to port. The only picture available of the incident suggested that it could be rescued for repairs.

Charlie Engle (USA), Ray Zahab (Canada), and Kevin Lin (Taiwan) have recently started another quest to cross the entire expanse of the Sahara desert. See their amazing story on the National Geographic website.

Chuck Walker decided to pay Nancy a surprise visit during her recent 40th birthday party. Armed with only a web-based set of directions, Chuck exited the Chicago O'Hare Airport, put on his backpack and ran the 15.3 miles to Joel and Nancy's home in time for her surprise. Why take a cab when you can dodge them in traffic. You're a good man, Chuck.

Attie was never seen or heard from again. RacingThePlanet had returned to the Atacama Desert region again in 2006, but Attie did not reappear. The competitors from Atacama 2004 wish to thank Attie for watching over them and keeping them safe while visiting the Chilean desert.

About the Author

Peter Wortham has been a technical writer, a recurring national user conference speaker and an executive advisor in the software industry, consulting with numerous Fortune 500 companies in the formation of highly specialized and highly productive teams. Peter graduated from Oakland University in Rochester, Michigan in 1986 with a Bachelors degree in Management Information Systems, and holds Project Management certification from George Washington University. At Oakland University, he was an active member of the university newspaper staff as a photographer and amateur feature writer. Employed later by PeopleSoft and Oracle corporations, Peter offered formal executive presentations and enterprise implementation strategy documents to a variety of global customers. His creative writing endeavors continued in tandem with his corporate travel, as Peter has authored numerous short stories and two novels within the last 5 years.

Peter was born and raised in Detroit during the 60's and uses the memory of those working class neighborhoods as a foundation for characters in his other fictional novels. Wortham's first book titled: Bondage, Gunshots and Mergers, takes a humorous look at the life of a traveling software consultant, and the trials and tribulations that come with the job. Blue Wednesday is fictional work about a serial killer and the FBI's futile attempts to catch him. These works are available online through Authorhouse, Amazon, Borders, and Barnes&Noble online booksellers. Learn more about Peter or his books at: http://www.peterwortham.com